BEST OF
ENEMIES

BEST OF
ENEMIES

THE LAST GREAT SPY STORY
OF THE COLD WAR

—◇—

GUS RUSSO *and*
ERIC DEZENHALL

TWELVE

NEW YORK   BOSTON

Twelve
Hachette Book Group
1290 Avenue of the Americas, New York, NY 10104
twelvebooks.com
twitter.com/twelvebooks

First Trade Paperback Edition: October 2019

Twelve is an imprint of Grand Central Publishing. The Twelve name and logo are
trademarks of Hachette Book Group, Inc.

The publisher is not responsible for websites (or their content) that are not
owned by the publisher.

The Hachette Speakers Bureau provides a wide range of authors for speaking events. To
find out more, go to www.hachettespeakersbureau.com or call (866) 376-6591.

Library of Congress Cataloging-in-Publication Data

Names: Russo, Gus, author. | Dezenhall, Eric, author.
Title: Best of enemies : the last great spy story of the
Cold War / Gus Russo and Eric Dezenhall.
Description: New York : Twelve, [2018] | Includes index.
Identifiers: LCCN 2017056747| ISBN 9781538761311
(hardcover) | ISBN 9781538761328 (ebook)
Subjects: LCSH: Platt, Jack, 1936–2017. | Vasilenko, Gennady, 1941– |
Spies—United States—Biography. | Spies—Soviet Union—Biography. |
Spies—Russia (Federation)—Biography. | United States. Central
Intelligence Agency—Officials and employees—Biography. | Soviet Union.
Komitet gosudarstvennoĭ bezopasnosti—Officials and employees—Biography. |
Espionage—United States—History. | Espionage—Soviet
Union—History. | Male friendship.
Classification: LCC UB271.U5 R87 2018 | DDC 327.1247073092/2—dc23
LC record available at https://lccn.loc.gov/2017056747

ISBNs: 978-1-5387-6133-5 (trade paperback), 978-1-5387-6132-8 (ebook)

LSC-C

10 9 8 7 6 5 4 3 2 1

CONTENTS

*This book is dedicated to the memory of Jack Platt
and to the men and women who serve in obscurity
for the purpose of intelligence gathering.*

Recruitment is almost like a first love—a fateful, tragic love, whose price is sometimes paid in freedom, if not life itself. Danger, fear, the sense of uniqueness, bind the agent and his control so strongly that in many cases they develop an addiction to each other.

—Major Yuri Shvets, KGB officer 1980–1990

Dramatis Personae

Americans

Aldrich "Rick" Ames (b. 1941)—In 1962, Ames joined the CIA, where he began working in the SE (Soviet/East Europe) Division with Jack Platt in 1972. He started spying for the Soviets in 1985 (earning $4.6 million). Like Robert Hanssen, he sold out many CIA assets who were friends of Gennady Vasilenko. One major asset destroyed was Dmitri Polyakov (TOP HAT), who had been supervised by Sandy Grimes, who then led the team that was successful in rolling up Ames, with the help of AVENGER (Colonel Aleksandr Zaporozhsky). Arrested in 1994, Ames is now serving a life sentence in the Federal Correctional Institution in Terre Haute, Indiana.

Milt Bearden (b. 1940)—Born in Oklahoma and raised in Washington State, Bearden was recruited by the CIA in 1964 while studying Chinese at the University of Texas, Austin. Bearden was a CIA station chief and covert officer in numerous overseas postings, including Bonn, Sudan, Lagos, Hong Kong, Pakistan, and Afghanistan, before becoming chief of the SE Division in 1985. After retirement in 1994, he became an author and often consults with Hollywood filmmakers, most notably Robert De Niro, on spy films. He is a recipient of the CIA's Distinguished Intelligence Medal.

W. Lane Crocker (1943–2000)—Crocker was assistant director in charge of the FBI Washington Field Office (WFO) in the 1970s and 1980s. He coordinated the FBI-CIA joint KGB Squad activities with the CIA's Haviland Smith and Jack Platt. He retired in 1996.

Robert Anthony De Niro (b. 1943)—The iconic New York–born actor is a seven-time Academy Award nominee (two-time winner), a six-time British Academy Film Award (BAFTA) nominee, and an eight-time Golden Globe Award nominee. In 2009, he was among the five recipients of the Kennedy Center Honors, presented by his friend President Barack Obama. He was given the Cecil B. DeMille Award in 2010. He also produced, directed, and co-starred in the film *The Good Shepherd*, a history of the early CIA. In the mid-1990s, while researching that project, he came to know and befriend Milt Bearden, Jack Platt, and Gennady Vasilenko.

John Denton (b. 1941)—aka "Mad Dog." A New Jersey native, Denton joined the FBI in 1969 and was assigned to a crime division in North Carolina. In the late 1970s, he transferred to counterintelligence at the Washington Field Office, where he befriended Dion Rankin and Jack Platt. He retired in 1999, after a thirty-year career, and is an honorary "Musketeer."

Ron Fino (b. 1946)—A former official of the mobbed-up Buffalo, New York, Laborers' Union (Local 210), Fino is the son of a mafia boss. For years, he secretly worked as an undercover consultant for the FBI and the CIA, helping put scores of major mafia figures in prison. He became an importer of vodka and used his Russian contacts to try to free Gennady Vasilenko from Russian prisons.

Burton Gerber (b. 1933)—Gerber, a career CIA officer, was the SE Division chief from 1984 to 1989. Prior to that, he had been Chief of Station in Sofia, Belgrade, and Moscow, in addition to operational postings in Germany and Iran. He retired in 1995, after thirty-nine years of service.

Sandra "Sandy" Grimes (b. 1945)—Raised in Colorado, Grimes joined the CIA in 1967 with a degree in Russian. On her first day, she reported to the CIA's ironically named Ames Building; she became a key "mole hunter" who helped catch turncoat Aldrich Ames. She was an analyst in the CIA's Clandestine Service for twenty-six years.

Robert Hanssen (b. 1944)—An FBI agent assigned to Soviet and computer sections, Hanssen spied for the Soviets for twenty-two years of his twenty-six-year FBI career. His disclosures led to the executions of numerous CIA assets by the Soviets, including a number of Gennady's friends. He is considered the most damaging spy in US history. One of the documents he transmitted to the Soviets led to Gennady's first imprisonment in 1988. Hanssen is serving fifteen life sentences at ADX Florence, in Colorado, a "supermax" prison.

Edward Lee Howard (1951–2002)—After a short stint in the CIA, from 1981 to 1983, Howard was fired, and he subsequently sold out a number of the Agency's Moscow assets to the KGB. One of those compromised, Adolf Tolkachev, was executed in 1986. Howard was a former student of Jack Platt in his Internal Operations Course (IOC), and he used what he had learned there to evade capture and escape to the Soviet Union in 1985.

Dan Moldea (b. 1950)—Investigative reporter and best-selling nonfiction author, Moldea was Jack Platt's friend and played an important role in helping Gennady Vasilenko when he was wrongly imprisoned in Russia in 2005.

Leon Panetta (b. 1938)—Panetta has served in high office positions, including secretary of defense, White House chief of staff, and director of the Office of Management and Budget. In 2010, he was serving as President Obama's CIA Director when he oversaw the spy swap that brought Gennady Vasilenko to the US permanently.

Ronald Pelton (b. 1941)—In 1979, after spending fourteen years at the National Security Agency (NSA), a financially strained Pelton sold out a number of technical spying operations, including Operation Ivy Bells, to the Soviet *rezidentura*, or station, in Washington, where he was handled by Gennady Vasilenko. KGB turncoat Vitaly Yurchenko outed him to the FBI in 1985. Although sentenced to three consecutive life sentences, he was released in 2015.

John "Jack" Cheney Platt III, aka Cowboy, aka Chris Llorenz, aka Charles Kneller (1936–2017)—A twenty-five-year veteran CIA case officer, Platt is best known for his tenure in the Agency's SE Division and for his revamping of its Internal Operations Course (IOC). After his 1987 retirement, he volunteered to help the FBI identify the traitors who were destroying assets and twenty years' worth of technical intelligence.

Molly Marr "Polly" Platt (1939–2011)—Jack Platt's sister, Polly Platt was an esteemed Oscar-nominated motion picture production designer and executive. She designed such films as *The Last Picture Show* and *Terms of Endearment*, and produced *Broadcast News* and *Say Anything.* Polly Platt was the first woman inducted into the Art Directors Guild.

George Powstenko (1926–1990)—A Ukrainian-born radio engineer who immigrated to the US in 1949, Powstenko became a leader in the Washington, DC, Ukrainian community. As a manager of a championship amateur volleyball team, he became very close to Gennady Vasilenko, often serving as his "cutout" liaison to Jack Platt and Dion Rankin.

R. Dion Rankin, aka Tracker, aka Donald Williams (b. 1946)—Rankin was an FBI agent who specialized in interrogation, tracking, and polygraphy. Assigned to the WFO in 1976, he became a close friend of Jack Platt and Gennady Vasilenko. In the '90s, he worked on the team that ultimately identified Robert Hanssen as an FBI traitor. He is the third "Musketeer."

Paul Redmond (b. 1941)—Redmond served in the Clandestine Service of the CIA as an operations officer for thirty-three years, from 1965 to 1998, working in Europe, Eastern Europe, and East Asia. He became the Agency's first associate deputy director for operations for Counterintelligence and supervised the team that identified CIA employee Aldrich Ames as a KGB spy.

Mike Rochford (b. 1955)—Rochford joined the FBI in 1979 after studying Russian at the Defense Language Institute in Monterey,

California. When he was assigned to the WFO's CI-4 Squad, he investigated Russian spies and played a key role in obtaining the KGB's file on their prized asset Robert Hanssen.

Haviland Smith (b. 1929)—A twenty-five-year CIA veteran, "Hav" served as Chief of Station in posts that included Prague, Berlin, Langley, Beirut, and Tehran. He pioneered many countersurveillance techniques and other field tradecraft, and became chief of the counterintelligence staff, where he mentored Jack Platt in the late '70s. Smith retired in 1980.

Michael J. Sulick (b. 1948)—Sulick joined the CIA in 1980, with postings in Eastern Europe, Asia, Latin America, Poland, and Russia. He served as Moscow Chief of Station from 1994 to 1996, chief of Central Eurasia Division from 1999 to 2002, and director of the National Clandestine Service (formerly called deputy director of operations), and he helped place Gennady on the 2010 spy-swap list, after which he retired.

Jeanne Ruth Vertefeuille (1932–2012)—Vertefeuille joined the CIA as a typist in 1954, then obtained postings in Ethiopia, Finland, and The Hague. She learned Russian and became an expert on Soviet spies. In October 1986, she was asked to lead the task force investigating the disappearances of the CIA's Russian assets. Eight years later, she, along with Grimes and others, identified Aldrich Ames as a double agent.

Russians

Victor Cherkashin (b. 1932)—Cherkashin achieved the rank of colonel after four decades with the KGB's Foreign Intelligence Service (now the SVR). Following postings in West Germany, India, Austria, and Lebanon, he became the counterintelligence chief at the *rezidentura* in Washington, DC, where he supervised, among others, Gennady Vasilenko. He retired from the KGB in 1995 in order to focus on his family and his international security consulting business, Alpha-Puma.

Mikhail Yefimovich Fradkov (b. 1950)—A politician and statesman, Fradkov was the prime minister of Russia from March 2004 to September 2007. He also was the head of the SVR from 2007 to 2016 and negotiated the 2010 spy swap with his CIA counterpart, Leon Panetta.

Vladimir Kryuchkov (1924–2007)—From 1974 until 1988, Kryuchkov headed the foreign intelligence branch of the KGB, the First Chief Directorate, which oversaw covert intelligence gathering. From 1988 until 1991, he served as chairman of the KGB and was the leader of the abortive August 1991 coup.

Sergei Lavrov (b. 1950)—Diplomat Lavrov was the Russian representative to the United Nations from 1994 to 2004. He is currently the foreign minister of Russia, in office since 2004. He negotiated a "reset" with the US that facilitated the spy swap in 2010.

Valery Martynov (1946?–1987)—In the early 1980s, Martynov was a Line X (scientific espionage) KGB agent based in Washington, DC, where he was a colleague of Gennady Vasilenko. He was flipped by the FBI in 1982 and given the code name PIMENTA, before he was betrayed by Hanssen and Ames in 1985 and executed by the USSR in 1987.

Sergei Motorin (1946?–1987)—In the 1980s, Motorin was a Line PR (military intelligence) KGB agent and, like Martynov, worked out of the Washington, DC, *rezidentura*, where he became a good friend of Gennady Vasilenko. He was flipped by the FBI's CI-4 Squad in 1980 and given the code name MEGAS. Also, like Martynov, he was sold out by both Ames and Hanssen. He was executed in 1987.

Vladimir Piguzov (d. 1987)—Piguzov was a KGB agent and CIA asset code-named JOGGER, recruited in Indonesia in the 1970s. After he was reassigned to the KGB school in Moscow, he furnished the Agency with background intel on KGB trainees, including Gennady Vasilenko. Although it is widely believed that he was betrayed by Ames, Jack Platt contended that Edward Lee Howard had identified him to the Russians.

***Dmitri Polyakov (1921–1988)*—**Polyakov was a member of the GRU (Soviet military intelligence). His FBI code name was TOP HAT. Handled by Sandy Grimes at the CIA, Polyakov provided the US with valuable military information for decades. He was betrayed by Ames and Hanssen, and executed in 1988.

Aleksandr Nikolayevich Poteyev (b. 1952)—Poteyev was an SVR officer assigned to Department S (coordinating foreign spies). In the 1990s, he was posted to New York, where he was recruited by the CIA. In 2001, he sold out Russia's "Illegals," their unregistered agents who had been living in the US under phony "legends" for many years. They were not arrested right away because US authorities wanted to keep an eye on them. Weeks before the Illegals were arrested in 2010, Poteyev disappeared in the US with his estimated $2 to $5 million bounty. According to one Russian news service, Poteyev passed away in July 2016 carrying out an assignment.

"Anatoly Stepanov" (b. circa 1948) (pseudonym)—KGB counterintelligence (LINE KR) officer who worked with Gennady both at the Yasenevo HQ and the DC *rezidentura* in the seventies. In the eighties, he obtained a high-ranking position in Department S (Illegals). Before leaving the KGB after the fall of the USSR, Stepanov made off with the KGB's file on their prized US double agent (Robert Hanssen) and later sold it to the FBI for a reported $7 million. He lives in the US under a new identity.

***Gennady "Genya" Semyovich Vasilenko, aka ILYA, joint CIA and FBI code names MONOLITE and later GT/GLAZING (b. 1941)*—**Vasilenko was a volleyball champion and KGB Line KR (counterintelligence) officer assigned to the DC *rezidentura* in the late 1970s. Twice arrested and imprisoned by the KGB/FSB, he was falsely accused of being a CIA asset. He was a close friend of Jack Platt.

***Dmitri Yakushkin (1923–1994)*—**After attaining a degree in economic science, Yakushkin joined the KGB, rising to the rank of major general. In 1975, he was assigned to be *rezident* (similar to the

CIA's Chief of Station) at the Washington, DC, Soviet Embassy. That posting made him the most powerful KGB officer outside the Soviet Union. In Washington, he supervised the activities of hundreds of spies, such as Gennady Vasilenko, Sergei Motorin, Valery Martynov, and Anatoly Stepanov.

Vitaly Sergeyevich Yurchenko (b. 1936)—KGB officer Yurchenko was in charge of North America operations at the KGB's Yasenevo headquarters, where he was a colleague of Gennady Vasilenko. After twenty-five years of service, he defected to the CIA in Rome. He was flown to Washington and debriefed, ironically, by Aldrich Ames. Some in the CIA believe he was actually a "dangle," pretending to defect to the US; although he outed minor American turncoats Edward Lee Howard and Ronald Pelton as US traitors, he re-defected back to the USSR without giving up Russia's most prized moles, Ames and Hanssen. Years later, he was awarded the Order of the Red Star by the Soviet government for the successful "infiltration operation."

Aleksandr Zaporozhsky, possibly AVENGER (b. 1951)—Zaporozhsky was convicted in Russia of having been paid $1 million *each* by the FBI and the CIA in 1993 for the information that may have led to the arrest of Aldrich Ames. Gennady Vasilenko had known Zaporozhsky since the '70s, when both worked in the Africa and Asia division at KGB headquarters in Yasenevo. Zaporozhsky was arrested by the KGB in 2001 and sentenced to eighteen years in prison. Released in the 2010 spy swap, he flew back to the US with Gennady. Today he lives in the eastern US.

Aleksandr "Sasha" Zhomov, aka PROLOGUE, aka PHANTOM (b. 1954)—Zhomov was a KGB officer in the Second Chief Directorate (internal counterintelligence) who offered to sell information to the CIA in Moscow in 1987. Over Grimes's and Vertefeuille's objections, the SE Division accepted Zhomov, who was, in fact, a "dangle," sent to protect the USSR's valuable assets Ames and Hanssen. Zhomov dropped his overture to the CIA in July 1990 after receiving a substantial payment from them. Obsessed with avenging the later losses of Ames and Hanssen, Zhomov became the KGB's mole hunter, overseeing the arrests and torture of Gennady Vasilenko and Aleksandr Zaporozhsky.

Organizations

CIA (1947–present)—Established by the National Security Act of 1947, the Central Intelligence Agency is the United States' civilian foreign intelligence service, obtaining information primarily through the use of human intelligence (HUMINT). The CIA, headquartered on 258 acres in the Langley community of McLean, Virginia, has no law enforcement function, and is mainly focused on overseas intelligence gathering with only limited domestic intelligence collection.

FBI (1908–present)—The Federal Bureau of Investigation is the United States' domestic intelligence and security service, focused on counterterrorism, counterintelligence, and criminal investigation. It operates under the jurisdiction of the Department of Justice, reporting to both the attorney general and the director of National Intelligence. Primarily a domestic agency, the Bureau maintains fifty-six field offices in major cities throughout the United States and sixty legal attaché (LEGAT) offices in US embassies and consulates across the globe.

FSB (1995–present)—The Russian Federal Security Service (Federal'naya Sluzhba Bezopasnosti) is the principal security agency of Russia and the main successor agency to the USSR's Committee of State Security (KGB). Analogous to the United States' FBI, its main responsibilities are within Russia and include counterintelligence, internal and border security, counterterrorism, and surveillance, as well as crime and federal law violation investigation. It is housed in the KGB's old headquarters building in Moscow's Lubyanka Square (formerly Dzerzhinsky Square).

GRU (1810–present)—Formally known as the Main Intelligence Directorate, the GRU is the foreign military intelligence agency of the general staff of the armed forces of the Russian Federation. It is Russia's largest foreign intelligence agency, deploying over six times as many agents in foreign countries as the SVR, the successor of the KGB's foreign operations directorate (PGU KGB). It commands more than twenty-five thousand Spetsnaz troops.

KGB (1954–1991)—Headquartered in Moscow's Lubyanka building, the KGB was a military organization. The Soviet Committee for State Security (Komitet Gosudarstvennoy Bezopasnosti) was the successor to the Cheka, OGPU, NKVD, etc. The KGB's main functions were foreign intelligence, counterintelligence, and domestic operative-investigatory activities. After 1991, KGB operations were divided between the FSB (domestic) and the SVR (foreign).

MVD (1802–present)—Formally known as the Ministry of Internal Affairs of the Russian Federation, the MVD (Ministerstvo Vnutrennikh Del) is the interior ministry of Russia. It oversees police, traffic, drug control, and economic crime investigations. The ministry is headquartered in Moscow.

Spetsnaz (1950–present)—Translated as "special purpose," Spetsnaz are elite tactical special-forces units controlled by the FSB, MVD, or GRU. They carry out anti-terrorist and anti-sabotage operations but are often deployed against Russian counterrevolutionaries, dissidents, and other undesirables. The idea for the units was envisioned decades earlier by military theorist Mikhail Svechnikov in order to overcome disadvantages faced by conventional forces in the field.

SVR (1991–present)—The Foreign Intelligence Service of the Russian Federation, the SVR (Sluzhba Vneshney Razvedki), is Russia's external intelligence agency and the successor of the First Chief Directorate of the KGB. It is tasked with intelligence and espionage activities outside the Russian Federation and with negotiating anti-terrorist and intelligence-sharing arrangements with foreign intelligence agencies. The SVR consists of at least eight known directorates: PR (political intelligence); S (illegal overseas agents);

X (scientific and technical intelligence); KR (external counterintelligence); OT (operational and technical support); R (operational planning and analysis); I (computer service—information and dissemination); and E (economic intelligence). Its headquarters is in the Yasenevo district of Moscow.

1

APPRENTICE SPIES

Forced recruitment almost never works because you've got somebody against their will and they resent it.

—Jack "Cowboy" Platt, CIA case officer

August 27, 2005,* Great Falls, VA

Oh no, not again, *Cowboy thought. Hanging up the phone, sixty-nine-year-old retired CIA case officer Jack "Cowboy" Platt recalled something F. Scott Fitzgerald had written about "the dark night of the soul," and now he knew exactly what it meant. Sitting in his darkened den in Northern Virginia, Platt stared at a photo of himself together with the subject of the call, his Russian "younger brother" and former KGB man Gennady "Genya" Vasilenko. The framed memento had been taken during a recent Shenandoah Valley hunting trip. Better times, for sure. Tonight's communication had changed everything and tempted Jack to drive to a location he hadn't visited in twenty-five years: the ABC Liquor Store just down the road from CIA headquarters in McLean. The bottle had come closer to killing him than the Soviets ever did.*

Platt looked at his left hand, mangled by a grenade that had malfunctioned during his stint in the Marines, and thought, Jesus Christ, Gennady was

---

* Most of the dates and specific locations (such as prisons) referenced in this book are based upon the personal recollections of Jack Platt and Gennady Vasilenko. CIA officers and KGB agents are not permitted to remove files and notes upon retirement; therefore the authors worked with the book's principals to portray relevant dates as accurately as possible.

probably cursing me out as they tortured him. *The thought was intolerable, because it was Jack's fault. It was his scheme that had brought them to this. Tipped off by Gennady's son on the phone call from Russia, Jack then read the sickening details on the Internet. His "best laid plan," which had quietly succeeded in rolling up one of the United States' most damaging traitors ever, had blown up in the worst way: Gennady, coincidentally known to his peers as "Russian Cowboy," had been rounded up and imprisoned in Moscow for the second time. And it was Jack's fault—again.*

In a notorious Moscow hellhole of a prison, confused and terrified, sixty-three-year-old Gennady also recalled his hunting trips with Cowboy. Two days earlier, on the first day of hunting season in the woods surrounding Moscow, he had been at his rural dacha with his mother; his girlfriend, Masha; and their young children, his second family. As the country celebrated its annual Moscow Days, Gennady was in the front yard "playing with the kids" when he caught sight of ten or so black-clad Spetsnaz encircling his property. I am about to become the first victim of hunting season, *Gennady thought. As he reached out to shake hands with the sheriff, an acquaintance, the commandos pounced, beating the pulp out of him and breaking his knee in front of his hysterical mother, girlfriend, and children. "If you step one inch in any direction, we'll shoot you in front of them," one guard snarled. Then they hauled him off to hell.*

Hell for Gennady came in many waves. First he was taken to the local police station, where he was told that illegal explosives had been found at his apartment. All the residences of his immediate family had been ransacked. The troops had "found" more explosives in Gennady's homes and cars. In fact, the evidence had been planted to frame up the arrest. They even had been secretly coating his car with invisible explosive particles so he would have residue on his fingers. For the icing on the cake, the FSB had planted World War II–era explosives in Gennady's garage so they could charge him with terrorism.

Finding him at the police station, his oldest son, thirty-five-year-old Ilya, brought him a change of clothes from home, but the only jacket Gennady had at the dacha was the one Cowboy's FBI friend Dion Rankin had given him years before, the blue one emblazoned with FBI ACADEMY. Just perfect, *thought*

Gennady. They already think I'm with the Americans. *He was so anxious to take off his bloodstained T-shirt that he put the FBI sweatshirt on anyway.* "Fuck 'em," *he said, uttering Cowboy's favorite curse, which Gennady had appropriated years earlier.*

When FSB thugs came into the room to soften him up with continued beatings, Gennady knew this was not about old gunpowder or boxes of hunting bullets. It was about vengeance. Concussed, he began vomiting and bleeding on his FBI sweatshirt. Drifting in and out of consciousness, lying in a pool of his own blood, he realized that today was his daughter Julia's birthday.

Assuming their captive was now sufficiently pliable to an admission, the goons got around to the real reason for the brutality: they wanted Gennady to confess to helping the US ferret out an American traitor four years earlier— perhaps the Russians' most valuable double agent ever. The Russian bureaucracy was in damage-control mode since the asset's exposure, and they couldn't just allow those who they thought facilitated the hard-won spy's arrest to get away unscathed. They had to send a message, and Gennady was that message.

The beatings and mental torture were unending. Throughout it, the police, and later the FSB, had one question: "How did your American boyfriend turn you into a traitor?" *And the answer was always the same.*

"Yebat' sebya! Ya ne predatel'!" *yelled Gennady.* Go fuck yourself! I'm not a traitor!

March 1979, Washington, DC

> *When you're up to your ass in alligators, it's very difficult to remember that the initial objective was to drain the swamp.*
>
> —A sign on Cowboy Jack Platt's desk at CIA headquarters

Jack remembered racing down Washington's Capital Beltway in an alcoholic fury to meet the "target" for the first time at a Harlem Globetrotters game, having likely already pounded down his typical twelve to fourteen beers for the day. Appropriate, he figured, because this possible recruit he was going to meet was a hard-partying Russian and the best lead the CIA's domestic station had had in a while.

Thirty-seven-year-old Gennady Vasilenko was the new KGB man in town, the son-in-law of one of the godfathers of the Soviet hydrogen bomb, Vladimir Goncharov, and the game these days was all about nuclear war: preventing it in the best case, starting it first if need be, and finding ways to survive it. Both sides believed it was going to happen, too, to the point where Soviet agents were assigned to drive around Washington at night to see if and when an inordinate number of lights appeared to be on in the White House and the Pentagon, in theory betraying an uptick in activity and perhaps indicating an imminent attack. Jack's mission—his actual job description at the CIA—was to "turn" Soviet agents stationed in the US, to get them to betray their country by giving the Americans military and political intelligence, especially as it related to nuclear secrets. Jack had been at this assignment for about a year and hadn't flipped anybody.

"In almost sixty-five percent of the cases, the prime motivation [to turn] was revenge," Jack would reflect in retirement. His conclusion was drawn from a study of fifty traitors he had undertaken for the Agency. "Revenge for a true wrong or a perception in his or her head that something terrible had been done to him or her by that system and 'I'll make 'em pay.'" Other methods, of course, included the tried-and-true blackmail over a target's weaknesses, the big three being sex, gambling, and booze. However, in the thirty years of the CIA's existence, the Americans had almost no success in turning KGB agents in Washington, despite having much to offer. The Soviets met with similar frustration. Former KGB agent Yuri Shvets estimated that for every two thousand approaches, only one was successful.

"Failure is the norm," Jack said, and what he lacked in number of recruits, he made up for in quality throughout his career. "Not one of the people I recruited ever got caught." Jack never resorted to the blackmail technique; it wasn't his style. "Forced recruitment almost never works, because you've got someone against their will, and they resent it. You have to re-recruit them every time. Besides, with a forced recruitment, there's a damned good chance that the target just goes back to his boss and tells him what happened." (Nonetheless, Jack and his CIA recruitment team had already created a generic list of vulnerabilities using the acronym MECMAFO: Money hungry, Ego, Criminal acts, Midlife crisis, Addiction, Family trouble, and Outcast loners.)

The few notorious blackmail operations that actually succeeded got blown out of proportion in spy folklore, Jack explained. "Everybody knows the story of the British foreign service officer who liked little boys," referring to the trope that most spying is rooted in blackmail. "Okay, fine. That's one case when the KGB got somebody that way, but everybody goes back to that one case! It's not the norm." Jack added that violent persuasions to turn a source are equally fanciful. "In twenty-six years in the CIA I never carried a gun."

A native of San Antonio, Texas, John "Jack" Cheney Platt III was born on February 18, 1936, at Nix Hospital. Jack inherited not only his family's devotion to military service but also their gene for alcoholism, experiencing frequent blackouts until a successful rehab stint in his forties. "My grandfather was an alcoholic, my father was an alcoholic, his brother, and my mother had three nervous breakdowns," Jack recalled. "They had cocktails every night before dinner. My sister, Polly, and I snuck sips in the kitchen when we were kids. She died an alcoholic. I

didn't stand a chance. I was a beer-aholic. A twelve-pack a day guy, minimum."

Jack's only sibling, younger sister (by three years) Mary Marr "Polly" Platt, grew up to be an Oscar-nominated art director and production executive. Married for a time to director Peter Bogdanovich, she also became the first woman inducted into the Art Directors Guild.* Despite their divergent politics—Jack a growling Texas conservative and Polly a show-business liberal—the siblings adored each other and were best friends. Their relationship was reminiscent of that between *To Kill a Mockingbird*'s tomboy, Scout, and her brother, Jem, each child protecting the other from neighborhood predators. In her unpublished memoir, Polly recalled smashing a local boy in the shins with a shovel when he caught Jack off guard in a street scuffle. Even as aging parents and grandparents, they were known to reenact creative renditions of their childhood, making spectacles of themselves. Jack's daughter Leigh tells how they would go to restaurants and start whining like small children, banging utensils: "Weeeeee're huuunnngrryyyyy!"

The sibling bond had a darker side as well. Polly's and Jack's children all recall watching in horror as the two got rip-roaring, falling-down drunk together in Paris. "They fell into a hedge of rose bushes and came out bleeding profusely," remembers Polly's daughter Antonia Bogdanovich. "The bloody mess only made them laugh harder."

Their parents were New Yorker John Cheney Platt II, a career army officer, and Vivian Hildreth Marr, of Newburyport, Massachusetts. During World War I, Platt Sr. left his undergraduate studies at MIT, where he had been a champion boxer and a brilliant student, to enlist in the army. Early in his military stint, Platt Sr. was dispatched to Mexico, where he engaged José Doroteo Arango Arámbula, aka

---

* Credits include *The Last Picture Show*, *Paper Moon*, *What's Up, Doc?*, *The Bad News Bears*, and *Terms of Endearment* (as production designer); *Pretty Baby* (as screenwriter); and *Broadcast News*, *The War of the Roses*, and *Bottle Rocket* (as producer). The 1984 movie *Irreconcilable Differences* is loosely based on the story of Polly's marriage to Bogdanovich in the 1960s.

Pancho Villa. For the next three decades, Colonel Platt and his family were posted to places like New Jersey, California, Illinois, and Texas as Platt gained a reputation as a noted court-martial judge. After World War II, Platt was sent to Bremerhaven, Germany, during the occupation, where he was in charge of two thousand German POWs, many from Erwin Rommel's Afrika Korps. He returned to Germany for another tour from 1949 to 1951, during which he was a judge in the Dachau trials. He was also a judge in the famous Hesse crown jewels heist, in which a US colonel stole items valued at $2.5 million ($30 million today).

Young Jack was well aware of his father's service and what, to Jack, was a noble battle for justice against a monstrous enemy. Sometimes there really were battles between good and evil, and there was no doubt in Jack's mind that his father's—and the United States'—work to bring down tyranny was such a battle.

"I actually believed what President Kennedy meant when he said 'Ask not what your country can do for you,'" Jack explained, adding that his early experiences overseas also had a profound effect. "I'm a proud, unreconstructed patriot who knows it's a privilege to be an American citizen."

Vivian Platt suffered from acute mental illness for much of her life and spent serious time in mental health institutions, having the first of her nervous breakdowns when the family was stationed in Germany. "Polly judged her mother harshly and blamed her for being weak," according to an article in *Premiere*. "I realize now," Polly told the magazine, "that perhaps my mother had not fulfilled her own promise, her own gifts—and she was living in a world where that was not even considered." Still, Polly described life with her mother as excruciating; the Platt children never knew when their mother would erupt and begin torturing their father over some triviality, such as the way he carved roast beef. Even worse, according to Polly's daughter Sashy Bogdanovich, Vivian once willfully drove off a bridge—with young Polly in the car. Not only a likely suicide attempt but also one without regard for her child. The children of alcoholics and wildly unstable parents are known for seeking to control all possible variables in a world they come to see as capricious and treacherous. With Platt Sr., who died of cirrhosis and emphysema, and Vivian, who experienced a grotesque death of alcoholism, Jack and Polly got a double dose and managed the aftershocks for the rest of their lives.

Polly had vivid memories of postwar Germany, a place filled with the smoldering ruins of conflict. Their father took young Jack and Polly on a tour of the Dachau concentration camp "so we'd never forget what happened there," Jack said. Seeing such landscapes, Polly said, "I started fantasizing that I had these incredible powers, that I could rebuild all the broken buildings." Both Jack and Polly, in their future careers, would be known as caring, team players. "There's a tradition in the Platt family for bringing home the wounded," Jack said. Platt Sr. lived long enough to see Neil Armstrong's shoes find their rightful American footing on the moon in 1969—an expressed goal—and died soon afterward in Polly's guest house in California, she having made good on a promise to never put him in an assisted-living facility.

In the early 1950s, the Platt family relocated to Hingham, Massachusetts, where Jack's father, by now known as a gifted man with a drinking problem, worked for the city of Boston as a consultant on the civil defense staff, making contingency plans for dealing with fallout from a first-strike nuclear attack. Jack went to Phillips Academy in Andover in 1953 and, from there, to Williams College (in Williamstown) on a full scholarship, the alma mater of a number of CIA vets, later including Director Richard Helms. In the '50s and '60s, Williams was still an all-male "Little Ivy" school, consistently ranked

JOHN CHENEY PLATT, III
Home Address: 4 Home Meadows Lane, Aingham, Massachusetts. Fraternity: Phi Gamma Delta. House Secretary. Major: History. Prepared at Phillips Andover Academy. Dean's List.

Jack in his 1958 Williams College yearbook.
(Courtesy Carl Vogt)

among the top five colleges in the country. Ninety percent of the students were pledged to a fraternity, a system that was abolished in the late '60s. The drinking age in Massachusetts was twenty-one, so weekend road trips across the nearby state lines into New York and Vermont, where eighteen was the rule, were a regularity, and Jack was often the wheelman. When beer wasn't the quest, girls were, with Jack leading "panty raids" on Bennington and Sarah Lawrence colleges.

Simultaneously, Jack began to inhabit his cowboy persona. He was a student who, according to one friend, "could drink more than any of us." Classmate David Grossman described the school as having 250 students in each grade, but Jack stood out. He majored in history, with an emphasis on Russian studies, and consistently made the dean's list. "I didn't even know him, but I knew *of* him," Grossman says. "Jack was known as a hot ticket, a rough rider, and a tough guy. But at the same time, everybody seemed to like him." Classmate Joe Albright refers to him as "the wild one at school." Albright remembers one typical "Jack story": during a pledge-week party, an inebriated Jack Platt drove his motorcycle into his frat house, the infamous Phi Gamma Delta, up the stairs to the second floor, most assuredly to grab another six-pack. Classmates began referring to the boot-wearing San Antonio native as "Cowboy."

Phi Gamma Delta's president and Jack's lifelong friend Carl Vogt (who later became Williams's president) remembers Jack as being the anonymous architect behind some of the greatest pranks in Williams's history, covert ops that presaged his career as the CIA's master of surveillance avoidance—only Carl and one other friend ever knew who had pulled off the stunts. At the time, students were allowed only three unexcused class absences, and the school maintained the precious "cut list" in a binder kept in a secure room in the Hopkins Hall administration building. According to Carl, Jack obtained the blueprints for the underground steam pipe system that ran between all the campus buildings, and late one night, he managed to squeeze into the pipeline and traverse it into Hopkins Hall, where he made off with the cut list for all one thousand undergrads. Jack then drove the binder to his favorite New York bar, where he burned the pages in the parking lot.

Then there was the time when the iconic First Congregational Church in the center of town had its seven-story steeple vandalized. A mysterious person (Jack Platt) had climbed up to the large clock on the steeple and removed all the large gold numerals except for the randy 6 and 9. Or the time when a vintage 1925 fire truck in Bennington was pushed down Route 7 from behind by someone's car (Jack's) all the way to the Phi Gamma Delta frat house thirteen miles away. The FBI, called in due to the interstate nature of the crime, was not amused. Jack, then a junior, was fined thirty-five dollars by local authorities. It was one of the only bits of mischief in which Jack was identified.

Although Jack possessed an impish sense of humor, he was so laid-back that he attained the nickname "The Rock." He was also known as the smartest guy in the class; he took meticulous—and illustrated—notes, which he lent out to his lucky pals. He was generous not only with his notes but also with his compassion: as pledge chairman, he supported Carl's move to open the pledging to black students.

While at Williams, Jack studied with Robert G. Waite, a pioneering teacher who had a great influence on Jack and his classmates. Waite, a psycho-historian specializing in Adolf Hitler, caused intense controversy with his *The Psychopathic God: Adolf Hitler* (1977) because he attempted to suspend his moral judgment whenever possible, even if the topic demanded otherwise. Later in life, Jack applied Waite's method when working with spies from the hated Red Menace, the USSR. He already knew he would enter the Marines after graduation, having spent two summers in the Platoon Leaders Class (PLC) cadet program, where he consistently ranked number one among his forty-four fellow cadets.

Jack missed his 1958 Williams graduation ceremony because he got into a serious car accident while chauffeuring three fraternity brothers on a road trip to Saratoga Springs, New York. He was most likely visiting his sister Polly, a student at Skidmore College who regularly arranged dates for his friends. To avoid an oncoming car, Jack swerved and hit a tree on Route 9. Three of the four men were hospitalized, Jack included. The car was totaled.

In June 1959, Cowboy married Paige Gordon, a cousin of a cousin, whom he met at a party at about the same time he received a commission as a second lieutenant in the United States Marine Corps. "I thought he was okay," Paige says with characteristic wryness, but she really started liking Cowboy when she saw how others in their circle responded to his impish sense of humor. Today, slender with short dark hair, Paige looks much younger than a woman in her late seventies.

She conveys precisely where she stands with either a clear expression or an economy of words that complemented Cowboy's rowdiness. From a young age, the Platt girls referred to their parents as "Lady and the Tramp." Paige was raised by her mother and stepfather in Armonk, New York, on a farm that her family eventually sold to IBM to build its headquarters. Her biological father, Arthur Gordon, was an author and ghostwriter for the legendary motivational figure Norman  Vincent Peale. Her mother was very kind when she wasn't drinking, Paige remembers, but died of alcoholism—a fate that would later prove to be pivotal in how Paige managed her life with her husband.

Jack was assigned to the Marine corps base at Camp Lejeune, North Carolina, as an intelligence officer in 3rd Battalion, Kilo Company. According to Jack's lifelong friend Major General Matt

"Matty" Caulfield, this was an amphibious task force that often conducted exercises in the Mediterranean Sea. Jack's key responsibility was prepping and commanding a beachhead assault team. His
meticulous field reports saw him promoted in early 1962 to recon
leader of Alpha Company, 2nd Recon Battalion. "Jack and I hit it off
instantly," says Caulfield. "I never met a man like him before. He was
terrific in the field, never got lost. Jack had a great relationship with
the troops. They took to him in a way I've never seen before." Once
during cold-weather training in Pisgah National Forest in North
Carolina, Jack rescued an entire company from a blizzard. A quarter
of them got frostbite, but they all survived. Caulfield says Jack should
have gotten an award for this rescue.

At Camp Lejeune in 1961, three years into Jack's four-year career
in the Marines, a flare grenade exploded in his hand, costing Jack
his left middle finger to the first knuckle (later, as a spy, he often
wore one black glove to hide this obvious identifying characteristic
from the enemy, a habit that conjures up images of Peter Sellers's
Dr. Strangelove, a fictional player in the nuclear game). Caulfield
adds some color to the incident, explaining that Jack was such a committed instructor he kept his own unused inflammatory devices for
improvisational use during training. These "pyros" he felt were necessary to train his students properly. He had ripped them off and
kept them in a hidden locker, buried somewhere unknown to anybody else. A flare grenade went off accidentally one day when he
was retrieving his stash. Early in their relationship, Jack told Gennady that he got the injury in a showdown with Carlos the Jackal.
Gennady didn't believe him and could tell that Jack didn't believe it
either when it came out of his own mouth.

In October 1962, one year after Jack's first child, daughter Leigh, was
born, the Cuban missile crisis almost incinerated everything Jack held
dear. During the nuclear brinksmanship, Jack was a first lieutenant

in a Marine reconnaissance battalion off the Cuban coast, ready to scream ashore if and when President Kennedy gave the order. His job was to provide the broader US military with the intelligence needed to pulverize the Cuban—or Russian—military into submission five thousand yards from the beach inland. He fully expected he would be engaged in combat in Cuba when the missiles started flying.

Before he embarked from Camp Lejeune for Cuban waters, young Jack had told Paige that nuclear war was a strong likelihood. He added that, given what he knew about nuclear war, it wasn't worth worrying about too much because it would be over faster than the human mind could process. The war he would face in Cuba, however, was a different story. That would be a conventional engagement, and those could be long and bloody.

Caulfield had a different take on what would have happened in a shooting war based on what he later learned. He says Jack's battalion was excited about the possibility of a firefight on Cuban shores. What they didn't know was that there were twenty thousand Soviet soldiers and *tactical* nukes on the island. Jack's platoon would have been annihilated.

While they were training for the big Cuban engagement on Vieques Island, Jack defied orders and surreptitiously made off with better weapons than those he had been ordered to take. Jack and Caulfield were recalled to Camp Lejeune for disciplinary action just as everybody else was heading south during the missile crisis. However, once the general was given the full picture, he chewed out the officer who had moronically ordered them to use inferior weapons in the first place. Jack and Caulfield turned around and headed south to Florida just as the crisis receded.

After the Cuban missile crisis, Jack returned to Camp Lejeune, and to Paige and baby Leigh, to decompress and contemplate his post-Marines career. He soon had a life-changing conversation with his favorite uncle, Dick Platt Jr., also a former Marine, as well as a member of Yale's Skull and Bones, a secret society known for its links to the American intelligence community. During a Christmas 1962 exchange, Dick mentioned that because of the empathy Jack demonstrated for his Marine trainees, he might not be capable of invoking the extreme discipline needed in the field and therefore would likely not see advancements in a military career. Dick Platt then suggested a relatively new organization, the Central Intelligence Agency, where Jack might thrive, especially with his having lived overseas and his language skills: German and, to lesser degree, Russian. At the time, Jack wasn't quite sure what the CIA was. Nevertheless, in 1964, Jack applied and was accepted as a case officer recruit at the CIA.

2

ALL ROADS LEAD TO WASHINGTON

Have you ever killed anybody?

After completing his operational training at the secret "Farm" facility, located near Williamsburg, Virginia, Jack spent two years at the CIA's new Langley headquarters, a period that proved instrumental to his great successes down the road. This was due in large part to his being assigned to work with the man who taught him the real tricks of the trade, counterintelligence whiz Haviland Smith, who was referred to as "an illusionist" because he consulted magicians in order to learn about deception and misdirection. Smith soon gained Jack's friendship and, more importantly, his respect. In addition to being an expert in field surveillance detection and deception, Smith had the confidence of the suits in the Agency's seventh-floor executive suites. "He knew where all the bodies were buried," Jack recalled.

A Russian studies graduate of the University of London and former Chief of Station (COS) in Prague, Hav Smith achieved legendary status among US spies for his innovative methods of combating the enemies' aggressive surveillance, especially behind the Iron Curtain. In Prague, where Smith's field officers were subject to crushing, lockstep scrutiny, the COS was forced to become inventive in order to carry out the mission. Thus were born techniques such as "moving through the gap," the "brush pass," and the "moving car delivery."

A field officer learned to create a momentary gap in surveillance by lulling the enemy into complacency with a repeated pattern of mundane errands done day after day at precise times (going for a coffee, getting a haircut, returning the babysitter, etc.). When the opponent relaxed for a few seconds, certain that the CIA officer was just getting his daily newspaper, a gap in surveillance might be created. And only a few seconds were needed in order to progress to the next Smith contrivance, the brush pass, wherein the officer walks past his asset and, without acknowledging him in any way, makes the handoff. A gap could likewise be created between two cars as the first car turned a corner, with brake lights disabled, allowing the driver to make an exchange or a dead drop through a window before the trailing car made the same turn and spotted it.

These and other breakthroughs were embraced by Cowboy Jack, and he added to them his Marine-inspired toughness, eventually passing the lessons on to the next generation of CIA officers, the rookies who would be inserted behind the Iron Curtain.

It wasn't easy, though. Both Hav's and Jack's unorthodox new techniques were constantly met with disapproval from the suits above, who were risk averse in the extreme. Between the Agency bureaucracy and Cowboy, a man who had no interest in careerism and only sought to complete a mission, a tension grew, which only increased over the course of his career. Caulfield says, "The big problem Jack had was with phonies." It didn't help that Jack broke the Agency's dress code on a daily basis with his uniform of a Stetson hat, Lucchese "shit-kicker" boots, tattered blue jeans, and L.L.Bean hunting vest. The nickname "Cowboy," Paige explains, described more than her husband's attire and "wasn't meant as a compliment" coming from his CIA compatriots. The feeling was mutual: "Neckties cut off blood flow to the brain," Cowboy was fond of saying. "That explains the mentality on the seventh floor." Even without Cowboy Jack's sartorial choices, his purposeful gait through Langley's hallways made him stand out. "Jack moved at warp speed," one colleague recalls. "I think it was an upshot of his years evading surveillance in the field. I always used to ask him, 'Where the fuck are you racing to?' He'd just smile as he disappeared down the hall."

Jack's locker-room language, peppered with his favorite four-letter word, the "f-bomb," only added to the friction. CIA officer Burton Gerber, who would later become Jack's boss in the SE (Soviet/East Europe) Division, recalls how he and Jack had to have heart-to-hearts about Jack's foul language: "I tried to encourage him to tone it down, but Jack never seemed to take the input. He wasn't confrontational; he just was unaware of how he spoke." Fellow SE officer Jack Lee explains that "Jack alone was given a lot of slack because he was so good."

As to just what set Jack apart skill-wise, his oldest daughter, Leigh, describes it this way: "His whole demeanor is that of a person relaxed and without a care in the world. This face of tranquility and mellowness is deceptive. He doesn't miss a thing." Fellow officer Brant Bassett says succinctly, "Cowboy embodied the best of what we were—total dedication to the mission, a hard worker who only cared about helping his country. He was the opposite of the careerists he had to answer to. And a genuine iconoclast." Jack's confidant John "Mad Dog" Denton of the FBI says, "When things got crazy, Jack got calm."

Claiming that one is motivated by patriotism and not career advancement is a familiar refrain, but Jack made his aversion to bureaucratic upward mobility into high art. "You're either a headquarters asshole or a street guy like me," Jack told newsman Dan Rather years later. For Jack, it was all about being posted to wherever the threat to the American "fragile experiment" seemed most acute.

As Leigh wrote, "For my father, [headquarters] was akin to an assignment in 'hell.' CIA headquarters was a stuffy, bureaucratic place filled with power struggles, political turmoil, and overall poor judgment." Jack often described CIA chiefs as having an old OSS "parachute mentality," meaning that if someone could parachute into

Europe during the war, they were considered qualified to work at the CIA. "For the next year, he worked at Langley and kept his eyes and ears tuned for other assignments."

In 1965, relief from the cubicle tedium came in the form of a coveted posting in Vienna, Austria. The Platt family now numbered five, with twin daughters Michelle and Diana born the previous year. "Paige knew what I did," Jack readily admitted. "It's up to each overseas case officer whether to tell his wife. In fact, Paige became my reports officer." Reports officers edited CIA operatives' memoranda and sent them back to headquarters for review. "She also helped when it came to entertaining. At a party, I'd say, 'That's the target. Put on your best bra.' She gave me a .357 Smith & Wesson Magnum for my thirtieth birthday. I also have a Marlin 336 and a .30-30 Winchester, model 1854. But Gennady was much more proficient with guns than me."

Paige describes attending an endless procession of "smile parties" in Austria where everyone drank and the wives just smiled until their faces hurt. Wives often served as their husbands' eyes and ears. "Everybody drank too much," Paige says, admitting she was not a good drinker and was mindful of her mother's all-consuming alcoholism.

On returning to the US a few years later, the Platts bought a two-story red brick house on Myer Terrace in Rockville, Maryland, but it was to be mostly rented out, as Jack would continue to solicit and accept overseas postings—anything to get away from headquarters. He hoped he wouldn't be posted to *the* hot spot, Vietnam, where he wouldn't be allowed to take his family. That wouldn't work for Jack—he knew how many Agency families had been fractured by the absence of fathers.

Through the intercession of friends in the CIA hierarchy, Jack was assigned to the Laos operations desk, where he worked to save the lives and families of Laotian assets/friends and see them resettled in the USA—this in preparation for Jack's being posted in the Asian country. He enrolled in the Agency's language school, where he studied French for the better part of a year in advance of joining the Soviet operations team at the station in Vientiane, Laos, family in tow. The country had been a French protectorate for the first half of the twentieth century, and although rural areas still spoke Lao, a good number of the citizens in the capital of Vientiane spoke French.

In Laos, from 1972 to 1974, Jack coordinated closely with a cabal of "Black Thai" Laotian spies known as the Kangaroos, whose job it was to keep the CIA apprised of the visits of foreigners, especially Russians. Jack also frequented a popular local bar called The Purple Porpoise, which was owned by a lovable magician named Montague "Monty" Banks. The bar was an Asian version of Rick's Café Américain from the movie *Casablanca*, rife with spies and conmen from a dozen countries. While Monty regaled Jack's kids with card tricks, their dad was off in a corner plying a Kangaroo asset. The kids were engulfed in the spook world, and when popular movie prints arrived at the US commissary, Jack brought home his favorites. Leigh especially remembers watching the James Bond thriller *Live and Let Die* when Jack brought it home for her birthday. "I believe we watched it at least twenty times in three days," Leigh recalls. Similar movies were brought into the home at least once a month during their time in Vientiane.*

Entertainment got even more real for Leigh, whom Jack used as cover while he took photos of Chinese Communist operatives enveloping the country. He routinely claimed that he was just an American dad on vacation with his young daughter. The ruse worked until Laos was falling to the Communists and a Chinese military officer confiscated his camera.

When the Platts' tour was up, Jack became so concerned that all the accumulated furnishings would fall into enemy hands on the day they left that he staged a robbery of his own house. He alerted his

---

* Leigh authored a wonderful memoir of her family's adventurous overseas tours entitled *Sticky Situations: Stories of Childhood Adventures Abroad* (Infinity, 2003).

many Laotian friends that the night before his departure he would be out for a few hours with the family, so they were welcome to help themselves to everything except their luggage. He asked only that they share the spoils with their poorest neighbors. Dozens of Laotians saw the family off the next day.

By far the most important takeaway from the Laos years was the added tradecraft tutelage by his coworkers Brian O'Connor and George Kenning Jr. These men, like Hav Smith, had developed successful field detection and evasion techniques that became part of Jack's own arsenal.

Laos was also a critical juncture in the Platts' marriage, because it was in that political and climatological cauldron that Paige realized Jack had a serious drinking problem. "Alcoholism is insidious, slow in coming," Paige says, haunted as she recalls military pilots drinking and *then flying* at Camp Lejeune. "Alcohol flowed like water wherever we were stationed." The "goodbye parties" for intelligence personnel in Laos would literally last three or four days, Paige remembers, and it got more intense as Laos and Vietnam collapsed politically. Given her mother's fate, she held out little hope that any alcoholic had the capacity to abandon the bottle. She knew she was headed for a showdown with Jack, but there were serious challenges to consider: Children. Finances. Getting a lawyer. These were the days before communication between spouses vaulted into the zeitgeist as a cure-all. Besides, Jack was a spy. *Communicate?* No, spies kept their mouths shut.

Before Jack's two-year Laotian stint wound down, he had complained to his family about a likely, dreaded recall to hell—i.e., Langley—but out of the blue, he learned of a vacant Agency position in Paris. He grabbed it before anyone else had a chance. By coincidence, his friends and colleagues from Laos, O'Connor and Kenning, also transferred to the City of Light. So the stage was set for a good experience all around.

The entire Platt family was excited about the Paris relocation—finally a Western country with good schools for the girls. Their Rockville home again would be occupied more regularly by strangers than by the actual mortgage holders. One drawback to the new posting was that the Platts, accustomed to 100-degree Laotian living, were virtually "freezing" all day long for the first few months in France. The advantage for Jack was to be working with some of the finer senior case officers in the CIA.

A Paris assignment that was especially close to Jack's heart was the continued liaison with Kenning and O'Connor in efforts to save their Laotian assets, many of whom had become like family. Working with fellow Paris Station officer Larry Riddick, Jack accelerated the paperwork that allowed hundreds of Laotians to resettle in the US, and he maintained contact with many of them for the rest of his life.

Jack quickly gained a reputation as the Paris Station prankster; often at formal embassy receptions he executed hyperbolic pratfalls ("Plattfalls") just to see the honor guards' reactions. His serious Paris Station responsibilities included assisting in the training and preparation of a Russian scientist (working for the US) to return to Moscow. He also dealt with forty-two leaked CIA names, published by the French newspaper *Libération* in 1976 as CIA officers working under cover of the US Embassy in Paris. Jack was one of them. Disgruntled CIA officer Philip Agee had orchestrated the treason, and Jack wanted badly to get his hands on him.

Within days of the *Libération* disclosure, French classmates asked Leigh if her dad was CIA. She had always thought he was employed by the "economics section" of the State Department, assigned to various embassies. She assumed he kept getting transferred because of his coarse language or, worse, that he was some kind of criminal. Did they move around so much because he was afraid of getting nicked on an unsavory scheme? Leigh thought this way because she had been in the midst of devouring the Hardy Boys and Nancy Drew mystery books. Her curiosity had also been piqued when her parents forbade her to go on a school trip to the Soviet Union though they had let her go on an earlier trip to Spain.

After overhearing her parents discuss their tapped phones during the *Libération* scandal, Leigh demanded the truth. Jack admitted he was with the CIA, actually saying, "I'm a spy." He conceded that he hadn't let her go on the trip to the Soviet Union for fear that the KGB might learn of her identity, kidnap her, and hold her as a pawn. The high schooler was both thrilled ("Totally cool!") and relieved, telling her dad, regarding their constant relocations, "I thought it was because you couldn't keep a job."

Weeks after their initial showdown, Leigh approached her father again and asked him a question that had been plaguing her: "Have you ever killed anybody?"

After a beat, Jack answered, "I never pulled the trigger."

Michelle Platt remembers finding out about her father's career a little differently. One day, while Aunt Polly ("Hollywood Polly") was visiting them in Paris, Polly let loose about Jack's being a spy. Michelle was stunned. She had been under the impression that her father was a Foreign Service officer, which made sense because the family was always moving around the world. "It's impossible to keep secrets in a family forever," Michelle says. Jack was not pleased about sister Polly's loose lips and told her so. "Not everybody wants their name in lights!"

Diana knew something was different about her father and his friends when she was instructed on how to interact with her "uncles" should she run into them publicly. Jack told her, "If you see Uncle Larry in public, you walk up to him like you don't know him and ask him what time it is. If he gives you a big hug, acknowledge him and hug him back. If he just tells you the time like he doesn't know you, scram."

Paige briefly worked for the CIA, but Agency work was not a

great gig for women in the Cold War era. Nevertheless, she helped Jack in some of his exercises. "My mom always worked," Michelle says. Paige had taught English as a second language in Laos and worked for a temp agency, *Forbes* magazine, and a computer company. Even when he encountered Paige's colleagues, Jack kept his cover by using the name Mr. Gordon, taking Paige's maiden name. Paige had the business sense in the marriage, recalls Michelle, acknowledging, "My father was not a great businessman."

Despite many warm family memories of globetrotting and ski trips in Austria, the Platts weren't exactly the Brady Bunch. "We were latchkey kids," Michelle says. Marital tension brewed beneath the surface, as Paige was tiring of Jack's alcoholism and was perpetually contemplating leaving him, which partly explained her self-reliance.

In the Platt family dynamic, Paige was the disciplinarian, Jack the troublemaker—despite Paige's futile efforts to exploit her husband's fabled Marine fearsomeness. Leigh recalls her mother being annoyed with her when she was young and admonishing, "Wait until your father gets home." When Jack got home, he would sternly agree that he would deal with the delinquent Leigh. He would then proceed to take her into the bathroom and tickle her until tears gushed from her eyes. Once he was satisfied that her tears were sufficient, he would tell Leigh to go and tell her mother that she was crying because of how strict he had been with her. Eventually, Jack's un-scariness on the domestic front became common knowledge to the Platt girls' friends. "Everybody wanted our dad to be their dad," says Diana. One of Jack's future business partners said, "Paige's eyes must ache from all the rolling."

Jack's battle with the bottle may have created personal turmoil, but none of his colleagues would say it affected his work. In fact, by this point, he had received a number of Agency performance citations for his success in the field. When asked to explain the accolades, he said, "When I was overseas I had a successful recruiting in every posting."

A critical assignment for him came in 1975 when he toured CIA stations around the world with one of the USSR's most damaging defectors, ex-KGB officer Yuri Nosenko. It was Nosenko who had informed the Warren Commission that, among other things, while the Soviets were aware of presidential assassin Lee Harvey Oswald, they thought he was a kook and would never have mobilized him to take violent action against a US president. Jack's mission was to facilitate Nosenko's secret briefings of CIA officers of critical intelligence, including how the KGB had infiltrated US embassies and bugged the embassy in Moscow. Jack was proud to have such an important asset in his care. He also took note of how Nosenko's instinctive fondness for American life animated his cooperation with the CIA—this despite having been kept in solitary confinement for three years by Jack's suspicious predecessors in the SE Division. It was a lesson that would apply to another KGB officer with American tastes who would soon enter his life.

In 1978, the Platts left Paris and settled again in the US, and Cowboy Jack returned to the Agency's dreaded Langley headquarters, where he joined three hundred other SE officers. The SE was known to be the most elite, secretive, and cliquish division at the CIA, but Cowboy had little need for in-crowd mentality; he was all about the mission. By far the most fulfilling of Cowboy's new tasks was continuing to assist in the resettlement of refugees from the war-torn regions of Laos, Vietnam, and Cambodia. However, most of Jack's time was spent in the counterintelligence world, and that was another story altogether.

At this time, the Agency was helmed by Jimmy Carter appointee Admiral Stansfield Turner, and like Jack's numerous other executive nemeses, Turner was set in his ways, reflexively refusing to explore creative methods for conducting espionage. Thus, always looking to get away from the CIA's bean counters and careerists, Jack succeeded, after six months at SE, in having himself assigned to one of the newly established domestic stations: the DC branch, where he managed "Soviet recruitment operations." The secret facility, located in Bethesda, Maryland, was housed in the recently built (1972) thirteen-story Air Rights Center at 7315 Wisconsin Avenue—just thirteen miles (but a universe) away from the suits on Langley's seventh floor. The station operated in four small rented offices under the commercial cover of a consulting firm. In the lower right-hand corner of Jack's desk was a fully stocked cooler for beers, but the best part for Jack was being reunited with his friend and mentor Hav Smith, who was the new outpost's Chief of Station. (Jack's ultimate boss was SE Division chief Dick Stolz, former COS in Moscow and one of the Agency's most respected officers.)

Although it is widely perceived that the CIA has a strictly foreign mandate, this is not the case. Its Domestic Operations Division (later the National Resources Division) was formed in the early 1960s, with the sole mission of targeting and recruiting foreign nationals of interest living in the US. However, once a target was identified, the Agency had to coordinate with the FBI, which, per regulation, would take the lead on the joint operation. Of course, as has been extensively documented, this interagency arrangement, rife with career rivalries, did not always operate as smoothly as would be hoped.

The aim of the CIA's new DC Station was to target—and turn—KGB officers working out of the Soviet Embassy. "I was doing what we called 'residency analysis' of the Soviet compound," Jack recalled. "By our count, they employed over one hundred spies in Washington, either KGB or GRU [military intelligence]." The effort, which was coordinated with the FBI's W. Lane Crocker, had failed for forty years to turn a local KGB man, although the Russian-speaking Crocker had a legendary reputation for unmasking KGB agents in the US. The fifteen FBI assignees to Crocker's so-called KGB Squad, or CI-4,* held to their mantra: "Identify, penetrate, neutralize." Like

---

* "CI" stood for counterintelligence, while the number denoted a specific target. In this case, "4" represented Soviet counterintelligence, or Line KR.

the SE Division at the CIA, it was often described as the best squad in the Bureau.

Now, with the specter of nuclear annihilation ever on their shoulders, it was hoped that in combination with the skills of the CIA's best, the FBI could end that losing streak. For Jack, the joint operation also meant new friendships with G-men, as well as a burgeoning respect for their bureaucracy, which seemed to move with more energy and efficiency than his own CIA's.

Jack had long ago concluded that a doomed strategy for turning an asset was the "cold pitch"—cornering a target by surprise and proposing a spy arrangement. To illustrate his point, Jack told the story of a CIA deputy of his named Nick, who was tailed by the KGB to a menacing monastery in Kiev called Pechersk Lavra, or Monastery of the Caves. Pechersk Lavra was known for its ominous and narrow corridors, where many prominent Orthodox Christians had been buried over the centuries. In a ham-handed cold pitch, a KGB agent, who had met Nick in the Sudan, followed him into the catacombs and proposed that he spy for the Soviets. "In the movies," Jack said, "the target surrenders, fearing for his life." In reality, the op had all the power of a wet fart. Nick told the sinister agent, "You gotta be shitting me." Nick simply walked out of the caves, called Jack, and said, "You're not going to believe what the Russians just tried." Not only did the KGB fail to turn Nick; the CIA removed him from his post at the State Department just to be on the safe side, thereby ensuring he could never be of any value to them, and alerted the US intelligence community of what the Soviets were up to.

In Laos, one of Jack's best recruits had been a high-ranking Laotian official known as the "Lenin of Laos." "Lenin's" primary value was to keep the CIA informed about political movements in the Laotian hierarchy. Special emphasis was placed on advance warning of any coup attempts.

In Paris, there had been Jacques Rossi, a Polish-French educator.

A one-time aide to Leon Trotsky and an interpreter for Stalin, from 1936 to 1953 (Stalin's death) Rossi had labored in the Soviet gulag system. Rossi had provided Jack with extensive intelligence on the gulag, and Jack had recognized that exposure of the gulag system presented a powerful propaganda tool. He encouraged Rossi to write about it. Eventually, Rossi published *The Gulag Handbook: An Encyclopedia Dictionary of Soviet Penitentiary Institutions and Terms Related to the Forced Labor Camps*, which painted a devastating portrait of the dark side of the workers' paradise.

In Washington, DC, the FBI-CIA joint operation was initially headquartered on the eleventh floor of the Washington Field Office (WFO), which, since 1951, was located in the Old Post Office at 1100 Pennsylvania Avenue NW (now the Trump International Hotel).* In addition to the fifteen members of the CI-4 Squad, more than seven hundred Bureau employees worked in the building—an edifice that was universally considered to be in decrepit condition, with faulty electrical wiring and broken water pipes. Agents covered their desks with tarps at the end of each day in order to catch plaster falling from the ceiling. "It was a dump, concrete falling all around us," recalls Dion Rankin, a member of the Squad. The FBI agent in charge of the field office called it "the worst space in government."† The ghost of Chief Crazy Horse was said to live in the basement, where he had been briefly imprisoned. The building, which had been slated for demolition a number of times, was home to rats, bats, and roaches. "There was no ventilation, so we left windows open. As a consequence, pigeons flew over our heads in the office. But we loved it.

---

* An offshoot of the joint operation, called Operation Courtship, would soon be based in Springfield, Virginia. The name was said to have had a double meaning: "court" for FBI director *Judge* William Webster, and "ship" for CIA Director *Admiral* Stansfield Turner.
† A year after the building opened, an accident there took the life of DC postmaster James P. Willett. On September 30, 1899, Willett fell ninety feet (twenty-seven meters) down an open elevator shaft. Nothing more than a flimsy wooden barrier had prevented access to the shaft. Willett died a day later.

It was hysterical." Another fellow agent remembers the only nod to modernity: "We at least had a high-tech secure line to Langley. We called it our 'Cone of Silence.'"

CI-4 and the rest of the field office would soon be moved into the top two floors of a new WFO facility in the Harkins Building (1900 Half Street SW), situated in Buzzard Point on the Anacostia River, across from Bolling Air Force Base. For the next seventeen years, the WFO would remain in this area named after turkey buzzards, which are known for picking clean the bones of dead animals, and it is situated on the lowest lying area of the swamp that Washington, DC, was built upon. Buzzard Point was the definition of a "lateral move," with many agents preferring to stay at the centrally located old firetrap.

Two or three days a week, Hav Smith's officers from Bethesda, like Jack Platt, would trek down to "the Point" to strategize with men like Rankin, who would, per regulation, take the lead on any recruitment operations. FBI man Harry Gossett notes that a recruitment pitch often occurred just before a KGB officer was preparing to be rotated out. The Bureau had recruited an army of informants working inside convenience stores favored by the Russians—preferences detected through surveillance. "The sources helped us with the triple T, the 'toilet tissue trigger,'" Gossett says. "When we learned that the Russians were buying huge amounts of toilet paper, we knew they were headed back to Russia, where the toilet paper is infamous for having the feel of fine sandpaper. You'd know if you ever went there."

Often after work the staff repaired to what the locals referred to as the "Bilge Bar" on the first floor of the Gangplank Restaurant, a double-decker restaurant-bar at the nearby, newly opened (1977) 360-slip Gangplank Marina, a buoyant trailer park situated on the Washington Channel, which runs beside the Potomac. Washington's only floating restaurant (which cheekily advertised itself as "The Capital's Finest Floating Restaurant") was the current hot spot for partying spies, lobbyists, politicians, and even the occasional astronaut. For FBI and CIA personnel, it was a good place to release the tension that naturally went with preventing a nuclear war on a daily basis.

(Courtesy Linda Herdering)

For the first year or so at the WFO, there was little progress. Assets were as hard as ever to recruit. "Mostly we just harassed KGB guys incessantly," Rankin recalls, "by taking their parking places, blocking their parked cars, and, if they tried to lose us on the road, boxing them in on the highway, slow-speed, so they couldn't take the exit they wanted. We once forced Gennady's fellow KGB officer Alexander Kukhar to drive thirty miles outside Washington when he was trying to get to his apartment in Alexandria. He was a hothead, anyway, always trying to outrun us, which is never done. But after depositing him somewhere south of Quantico, Virginia, he never tried to lose us again. If we couldn't recruit them, then we just wanted them to give up recruiting us and go home."

But in late 1978, a glimmer of hope came over Jack's transom. One day first-year undercover case officer Patrick Matthews (a pseudonym) came to Jack with a lead. "We got a goddamned winner," Matthews said. "I was at the Young Diplomats Club with a Russian madman. It was a snowstorm, and this character, who claims to be a Soviet diplomat, took me there. I met him at a volleyball game—apparently he's been here over a year. He hangs out at volleyball courts near the Pentagon, the Department of the Interior, the Mall—everywhere there are government jocks on their lunch hour and after work. I played volleyball and tennis with him last fall. Anyway, he said he'd pick me up because he'd been to the club before. We get in the car and there were ten or twelve unpaid parking tickets on the floor. He floors it and spins around, doing a full three sixty. He just smiled and said, 'Ice on street.' His name is Gennady Vasilenko."

"This guy was beginning to cut a wide swath around town," Jack remembered. "There was no way in the world I would pass this up. I asked HQ for traces on him. I got a six-page womb-to-tomb report. I knew everything: his ancestry, when he joined the KGB, his blood type—you name it. He married up. His father-in-law was the father of the Soviet hydrogen bomb. I knew a guy in Moscow, Vladimir Piguzov, who had recently been recruited in Indonesia. He taught at the KGB school and had access to all the students' files, which he forwarded to the CIA. He got me the school's internal evaluation of Gennady. Piguzov was later outed by a kid I trained, Edward Lee Howard. The bastard got him killed."*

The volleyball-playing Russian was born on December 3, 1941, and from his earliest memories, Gennady Semyovich Vasilenko had a

gun in his hands, as he grew up hunting with his hard-drinking father and uncle in the volcano-encircled Siberian city of Petropavlovsk-Kamchatsky. It was a hardscrabble Russian existence at its most stereotypical: he drank pure alcohol from the age of three, his house had no electricity or gas, and he remembers his first childhood pet—a bear cub—fondly. He also remembers skating down a frozen river for two miles every day to attend grade school.

Gennady's parents had met in Podolsk, where his mother was training to be an

---

* Although many conclude that Piguzov was outed by another still-in-place traitor, Jack was adamant that Howard was responsible.

accountant. They married when his mother was still in her teens. Gennady was the only child of this union, which wasn't unusual in wartime when soldiers were off getting killed and women were often widowed or remained unmarried. "I was lucky to be born at all!" he says, laughing.

His athleticism came by necessity. He learned to ski when he was three years old just to get from place to place in the snow. He learned to fish in order to eat. Besides, there was nothing else to do in his small village, so if you were healthy, you explored or did something physical "or else you'd go crazy."

His pet bear grew so fast Gennady noticed the difference from day to day. Still, the boy counted the bear as a friend and was too young to understand mundane concepts such as the nature of the beast. One day he was playing with the bear in the river and it pounced on him, nearly drowning him. Fortunately, a soldier happened to be walking by, witnessed the struggle, and threw the bear off the boy, saving his life. When Gennady's father got home, he shot the bear. "I've always been lucky," Gennady says.

Gennady's father was born in Siberia too and was a literature teacher who wrote poetry. He was a warm man despite his lot in life, and Gennady adored him. In fact, there is not a trace of bitterness in Gennady's voice toward his parents and the harsh conditions of his childhood. As any reader of Russian literature knows, seething outrage is suffused throughout the culture over the country's hundreds of years of war, not to mention its miserable climate and woeful economic conditions. However, if the Platts had the gene for alcoholism, the Vasilenkos possessed a life spark, resilience, and practical optimism that overrode their conditions.

And, of course, there was the Vasilenko luck.

During World War II, Gennady's father was fighting the Japanese in the Kuril Islands, serving in an artillery battalion. He was shouting orders during a particularly vicious advance, and with his mouth agape, a piece of shrapnel tore through one cheek and flew out the other—amazingly damaging very little besides skin. "He was lucky he was shouting at that moment," Gennady says.

Not even World War II made the Vasilenkos angry toward their country and leadership. Gennady explained that the Russians were constantly in peril, at that time against Hitler, who had invaded the Motherland. Of course, they knew Stalin was a brutal man, but he had to be to fight Hitler, they concluded. Even when Khrushchev denounced Stalin in the early 1950s, the Vasilenkos, like so many other Russians, were skeptical. They figured the smear job was just Soviet bureaucratic nonsense. It took generations for the facts about Stalin's genocidal policies to convert from data points into accepted reality. "When the Nazis are outside your village, you hate the Nazis and fight 'for the Motherland and Stalin.'"

After the war, Gennady's father was stationed in Potsdam, where he met another woman. He divorced Gennady's mother, had another family (a set of fraternal twins and another boy), and moved to the Black Sea city of Gudauta, where he became a regional military commandant.

Gennady traveled there and met his half siblings a few times. He doesn't express a sense of trauma about the breakup of his family, shrugging it off as a common condition of Russian existence during that period. This may explain his resilience during the operatic personal life he came to live as an adult.

When he was in grade school, Gennady moved with his mother closer to Moscow, where she found a job near where her sister lived. Gennady then began to channel his raw athleticism into all manner of

Teenaged Gennady Vasilenko.

organized sports: skiing, hockey, tennis, track and field, basketball, soccer, and gymnastics. Despite the lack of social sophistication associated with his upbringing in the country, he found that wilderness children actually had an athletic advantage over city kids. Without a trace of inferiority, the increasingly charismatic Gennady came into his own in the big city.

As a young adult, the six-foot-two, athletic, and handsome Gennady was drafted onto the Soviet Olympic volleyball team in 1964 (the Tokyo Summer Games was the first Olympics to include the sport), but he was sidelined by a shoulder injury. However, the strapping playboy-athlete went on to become a member of the KGB-sponsored Dynamo team and a telecommunications and engineering major at the I. V. Kurchatov Institute of Atomic Energy, which he attended in order to avoid the draft. While he was no technology savant, this basic training would come in handy years later when he handled National Security Agency turncoat Ronald Pelton.

Gennady first saw Irina Goncharova on a bus on the way to the Institute. "I liked her from the first glance." It turned out that she had the same destination. He began searching for her at the Institute, which was a challenge given it was set on hundreds of acres with many buildings containing labyrinthine passageways. Eventually, Gennady, as always, got lucky. He spotted Irina in the Institute cafeteria and recognized some of the people she was eating with. *Goncharova?* As in Vladimir Goncharov? Royalty. The Siberian wild child deep within him had a pang of insecurity. But just one pang—after all, he was the blessed Gennady, who deserved only good things. Why not him? He inquired about Irina, arranged to be on the same bus, and walked her from her stop to her house in Sokol. They were married a year and a half later.

Upon his 1968 graduation, with wife Irina and baby daughter Julia (pronounced "Yu-lee-ah") in tow, he was successfully recruited by the KGB. Gennady chuckles. "I was the only guy who got into the KGB on a sports scholarship." That his father-in-law was such a big shot didn't hurt either.

While at the Yuri Andropov Institute at Yurlovo, Gennady specialized in telecommunications, computer studies, and engineering, instructed by many of the USSR's heroes, the very spies who had worked with Western turncoats such as Kim Philby, Guy Burgess, and the Rosenbergs. These teachers constantly referred to the US government, but not its people, as the "main enemy."

There was, of course, a great emphasis on field training at Yurlovo. In this regard, the Russians were the most intense, craftiest, and even harshest in the world. When the trainees were on a supposed break from studies, perhaps enjoying some leisure time in Moscow with no documentation, their superiors would often leak false criminal evidence about them to the local police, who would then proceed to roll them up like common criminals. "They wanted to see if you could figure it out, how you could handle tough situations," Gennady says. "If you admitted being KGB, you were out." The watchword was "Deny everything."

Upon graduation in 1974, Gennady began his first posting at the KGB's Yasenevo headquarters, Department 3, the Africa and Asia division. Nicknamed both "The Woods" and "Little Langley," the Yasenevo HQ was situated in a forest on the Volga River, southwest of central Moscow. All roads to the high-concrete-walled compound were marked with the same sign, SANITARY ZONE, while the gated entrance bore the plaque SCIENTIFIC INFORMATION CENTER. Author David Wise, the only Western journalist to be allowed to visit the "Russian Langley," wrote, "Physically, the parallels with the rival Central Intelligence Agency are remarkable. Like the CIA, the espionage directorate is out in the woods, away from the capital."

Inside the walls were a bucolic park, tennis courts, a soccer field, and a large fountain stocked with KGB chief Vladimir Kryuchkov's prized ducks. Of course, the chief had to advertise more than his soft side: he regularly ordered that crows be shot and hung by their feet from the trees that surrounded the fountain to remind potential turncoats of their fate. Much like at the CIA's home base in McLean,

Virginia, KGB agents could be seen jogging near the complex at all hours.

At the center of the park was the nucleus of the complex, a twenty-story building (described as "soulless modern" by KGB officer Victor Cherkashin) that included conference halls, a gym, and an indoor swimming pool. At Yasenevo, Gennady made many lifelong friends, especially in the Africa department, which was in a small room shared by three agents. His closest friend was fellow volleyball player Aleksandr Zaporozhsky, who would be rotated to Africa after his term at Yasenevo. Although he and Gennady would be separated by thousands of miles, they managed to keep in touch over the years as their lives played out in overlapping dramas. These dramas would collide three decades later, involving two of the century's most damaging espionage cases.

Occasionally Gennady was sent to work at the KGB's fearsome Lubyanka complex at 2 Dzerzhinsky Square, Moscow—fearsome because it housed a basement prison that was made to order for torture and summary executions, which is exactly what it was used for during the Revolution and the early days of the KGB. A local woman, who became a KGB folk figure known as the "Cellar Babushka," was hired solely to clean up the bloody messes. Similar executions had been performed at the notorious Lefortovo Prison located on the outskirts of Moscow.

In late 1977, under the guise of a diplomat, Gennady was assigned to the coveted post of counterintelligence (Line KR) agent at the KGB's Washington, DC, *rezidentura*. He took an apartment in Arlington, Virginia, for his growing family, which now included Julia's younger brother, Ilya. The romantic portrayal of espionage evaporated almost as soon as Gennady's cab dropped him off at the Soviet Embassy at 1125 16th Street NW, four blocks north of the White House. (Years later, the cheeky Americans would name the intersection "Andrei Sakharov Plaza," after the dissident Soviet scientist who had been exiled to the forbidden city of Gorky in the 1980s.) It was the largest embassy in Washington, employing more than five hundred people, many of whom came into the office at night because during the day "everybody was out spying."

Once inside the embassy, Gennady was directed to the *rezidentura*, located on the fourth floor, in the back, down a narrow, poorly lit corridor. He was instructed to always hang any coat he carried in a hallway closet in order to prevent him and any colleagues from secreting CIA-furnished spy gadgetry into the workplace. On a digital clock outside a nondescript door, Gennady typed in a code he had been given, unlocking the thick steel entrance to the enclave. That's when the dreariness of his real-world spy job hit him.

Dozens of agents were crammed into a single, eight-hundred-square-foot room. On entry into the anteroom, an agent was greeted by a large map of the Maryland-DC-Virginia area, onto which operatives had marked their next covert meetings, drop-offs, etc., signed with their code names. This map would prove to be a goldmine for the CIA when it placed its own assets inside the facility. In his memoir *Washington Station*, KGB agent Yuri Shvets described the rest of the *rezidentura*:

> Everyone...had to work in incredibly tight quarters. Thin partitions divided the residency into four extremely small rooms, tiny as birdcages, which accommodated its four sections: Political Intelligence, External Counterintelligence, Scientific and Technological Intelligence, and Technical Operations.

All of which explains why Gennady immediately turned on his heel and ran out to play volleyball at the State Department. But before lacing up his Converse All Stars, he presented himself to the recently appointed *resident*, Major General Dmitri Yakushkin, a beret-wearing, hulking, six-foot-four man of surprising refinement. With a degree in economic science, Yakushkin was a highly cultured spy from a prominent Russian family and was known to be concerned with human rights and arms control. He was also a workaholic, putting in twelve-hour days at the *rezidentura*. He and his KGB-translator wife, Irene, wary of being targeted by the "main enemy," almost never socialized. Their only known recreation was an occasional weekend visit to the recently purchased forty-five-acre Russian retreat in Centreville, Maryland, on the state's Eastern Shore—the very one President Obama would order the Russians to vacate in 2016 after they hacked the DNC's emails.

Gennady would enjoy a father-son relationship with Yakushkin, but he regularly tested his boss's nerves. One day, shortly after Gennady received a promotion, he decided to screw with Yakushkin. He borrowed an embassy security guard's uniform and on a lapel affixed the star he had received—which for a spy was supposed to be hidden away in a drawer. He then loaded up the uniform with every ornament he could find and burst into Yakushkin's office, shouting, "KGB spy Vasilenko reporting for duty, sir!" Given that the whole idea of being a spy was to be subtle, Yakushkin shouted, "You stupid motherfucker!" Gennady pretended he didn't understand why his boss was so angry. "But I went all the way back to Moscow to get this undercover uniform!" Gennady exclaimed. Yakushkin then recognized it was a joke, broke out in laughter, and opened up a bottle of Dimple, his favorite scotch. Still, he knew Gennady was a problem child at heart.

Whatever Americans have come to think of KGB agents as a result of Hollywood portrayals, Gennady did not fit anyone's image of a spy. Westerners are inclined to imagine that Russian agents are as cold as Siberia, utterly devoid of individual humanity—think assassins from an Ian Fleming thriller, like the chiseled, blond, robotic killer Grant in *From Russia with Love*, or Xenia Onatopp in *GoldenEye*, who strangled men with her thighs, her pulse barely elevated. Or Vladimir Putin. These stereotypes echoed in the American consciousness for decades, all brutality and ruthlessness.

But Gennady was all open-faced charm. Not in the unctuous

sense of a cinematic smooth operator, but with the lovability of a big brother to whom you could tell things that your parents would never understand. Despite being married, Gennady liked women and pursued them habitually—a pastime he attributes to growing up in a town where all the men had been lost during the war, leaving him with the enviable thirty-to-one ratio of women to men. And these poor women craved some attention, Gennady would argue. In fact, as a young teen, Gennady was practically preyed upon by older women on a daily basis. ("He was the village stud" was the way one friend described Gennady's childhood.) The experience taught him the power of seduction and sexuality by the time he was twelve. So, as an adult, he became a seducer at heart, even when the seduction was fraternal, not sexual. Smiling Gennady could make a traitor feel positively buoyant about betraying his country, as if becoming a turncoat were nothing more than a senior prank.

It was Gennady's Western-style warmth and intramural athleticism that made him a perfect operative to place in Washington, DC. His interpersonal talents called to mind the telltale passage in F. Scott Fitzgerald's *The Great Gatsby*:

He smiled understandingly—much more than understandingly. It was one of those rare smiles with a quality of eternal reassurance that you may come across four or five times in life. It faced—or seemed to face—the whole external world for an instant, and then concentrated on you with an irresistible prejudice in your favor. It understood you just so far as you wanted to be understood, believed in you as you would like to believe in yourself, and assured you that it had precisely the impression of you that, at your best, you hoped to convey.

Of course, Gennady's almost frenzied joie de vivre would regularly place him in the crosshairs of his dutiful Spartan boss, Yakushkin—much like another man who often ran afoul of his bosses in the SE Division, a man Gennady would come to know as "Chris," and a man who would change Gennady's life.

"After reading the dossier, I sat down with [Patrick] Matthews," Jack said. "I said, 'I can get in with him by my experience with Carlos the Jackal. He would be interested in that. Also, he's a gun aficionado, like me. Tell him my name is Chris.'" Since the chain-smoking Jack wasn't about to challenge the Russian to a game of volleyball, he had to come up with another entrée. Jack had a connection at the shiny new Capital Centre sports venue who could score tickets for him on short notice, so he checked the arena's schedule and instructed Matthews as to what to tell the Russian. Matthews, posing as a businessman, dutifully arranged the meet-up, telling Gennady, "My friend Chris can get us tickets to the Globetrotters. Bring your son." Patrick had met Gennady's eight-year-old son previously. He lied that he didn't know exactly where Chris worked. Gennady happily accepted the offer.

— 3 —

CONTACT

Halfway through the game I realized, I really like this guy.

August 28, 2005
Day four in solitary confinement in the Solntzevo police station

The FSB was at it again. New faces this time. But Gennady wasn't sure. He could not differentiate between individuals anymore. Torturers weren't people; they were teeth on a zipper, essentially identical but for the occasional variable feature of a jagged edge. How did a man survive this? What life experience could he dip into for guidance? Were there any aphorisms that could get him through this? All good things to those who wait? To thine own self be true? The truth will out? Bullshit. None of it mattered to these animals. They were in this racket because they liked hurting people under the moral cover of "love of country."

Gennady's cheekbone was on the cold concrete. There was moisture. Blood again. How much blood did a man have? How much could seep from him before there was none left?

"You want it to stop?" his interrogator asked. "Tell me about this 'Chris' person. When did you offer your services to him?"

Gennady could barely whisper now: "I never offered anybody anything, cocksucker."

They worked him over even more viciously. This was what glasnost got you. This was what friendship with an American got you. Nobody wanted peace. This was what they all liked: violence under the banner of patriotism. The violence managed to find the last reservoir of air, just enough to make him cough up one last curse.

Spring 1979

Under the guise of a Soviet diplomat, Gennady had become a man-about-town in Washington, his mission to befriend and ultimately recruit Americans—especially FBI and CIA employees—to spy for the Soviets at the same time Jack was doing the reverse. "Of course, the failure rate is ninety-nine percent, but we had to try," says Gennady, echoing Cowboy. "Maybe we'd make one good recruit in five years. Most of the traitors were walk-ins, same as at the CIA."

Gennady's modus operandi was to utilize his great athletic prowess at tennis and volleyball in order to cozy up to federal employees; he was the KGB's version of Kelly Robinson in the '60s TV series *I Spy*. Gennady proudly states that on his very first day in the US he managed to secure passes to play on the volleyball and tennis courts reserved for State Department employees and their guests.

As soon as he landed in Washington, Gennady had found out about volleyball and tennis games being played at the State and Interior departments. Identifying himself as a diplomat, he signed himself up. To his delight, in the Interior department's lobby, a bulletin board listed the names and departmental affiliations of all the players. Gennady had hit the jackpot, and at first he wrote the names down, but he soon decided that was too time consuming—so he impressed his new boss by just yanking the lists off the bulletin board and presenting them as prized inside information, which, in a broad sense, they were.

Gennady thought his career was over when, as he was removing a list one day, he heard a voice behind him saying, "Hey, don't take that!" The voice belonged to a security officer, who followed up with, "That's the old list. Here's the new one." He handed the newer list to the frozen Russian, then walked on.

Gennady, recipient of Russia's Master of Sport award, had also become the captain of the Soviet team that played in the dozen-team Embassy Volleyball League. The *Washington Post* called him "the tall, handsome Master of Sport." The Soviets, volleyball powerhouses who practiced in their spiffy new private gym at their new embassy under construction in the Mount Alto area, won the league championship practically every year. During one stretch, Gennady's team went undefeated for four years. When Brazil finally eked out a win, Captain Gennady had an answer. For the next game, he recruited two Soviet national team all-stars who "just happened" to be in town that day. Gennady's *rezidentura* teammate Igor Filin was initially peeved at being benched in order to make room for the substitutes. But when he saw them, he almost fell off the bench. "Goddamned Gennady," he said to no one in particular. "He's got ringers!"

One of the ringers, a twenty-one-year-old, six-foot-seven-inch behemoth, made a furtive move to the net every time Brazil served, preventing the serve from even crossing the plane. The *Washington Post* called it "the sneakiest Russian maneuver since the invasion of Afghanistan." *Volleyball Magazine* wrote of Gennady's secret weapon: "He has logged more air time than most TWA pilots. In career kills he trails only Joseph Stalin in the record books...He stuffs the ball well before it ever violates Soviet air space." The Soviets managed a 15–2 victory.

When the *Post* caught up with Gennady, he was hooting. "It was just a joke," he said, explaining that he was tired of the other teams complaining about the Russian players, when in fact, those other teams used many players who had no affiliation with their embassy teams. He almost gave away his real job when he added, "I know where they are working and what they are doing." Interviewed a week later, after the Brazilian ambassador's official hairstylist wrote a letter of complaint to the rec league before the next game, "the personable Vasilenko was still laughing." After beating the Brazilians a month later for the championship, Gennady took the entire Brazilian team out for beers. By the end of the night, the Brazilians were referring to "the Russian team as their great new friends."

The *Post* interviewed a Soviet specialist who pontificated that Gennady's ringer incident couldn't be a joke: "The Russians don't have a sense of humor, so I doubt it was a joke." That shows that the "specialist" didn't know as much as he thought he knew. Gennady is still chuckling about it decades later.

With rapid-fire pace, Gennady made new athlete pals all over the district. In a short time, he became good friends with a four-star general, and the two shared dinners with each other's families. It was only a matter of time, it seemed, before he would be a couple of Kevin Bacon handshakes away from every government employee who knew a jock. And so it was that Gennady's occasional tennis partner Patrick Matthews, who worked with Jack, initiated the Globetrotters gambit.

Jack snickered when he read the *Washington Post* piece about the Globetrotters' upcoming games that weekend. The paper noted that the Trotters held a slim 13,046 to 323 winning margin over their hapless perennial opponents, the Washington Generals. Elsewhere in the paper, a more sobering opinion piece by Republican senator William S. Cohen of Maine provided perspective for the gambit soon to be played out by Jack and Gennady. In his effort to show why he opposed the pending Strategic Arms Limitation Treaty (SALT II), Cohen wrote that if the US approved the treaty, "the ultimate consequence will be to stand in the shadow of a Soviet Union first-strike capability and capitulate rather than risk the instant liquidation of more than 100 million Americans." (President Jimmy Carter and Soviet leader Leonid Brezhnev in fact signed the treaty three months later in Vienna.)

It was Saturday, March 3, 1979, when Cowboy Jack got to his seat in the bustling Capital Centre outside Washington and found that Patrick had not yet arrived. The stands were filling up mostly with families. Fathers and sons predominated. Cowboy saw a father and boy of six or seven inspecting their tickets and eyeing the row where he was sitting. The father looked like a California jock—in his late thirties, tall and athletic, with brown hair parted on the side. The boy was whip-thin, like his dad, with light brown hair.

Decked out in full South Texas regalia, Cowboy stood up and introduced himself with his legend "Chris Llorenz." One reason for using the pseudonym was that the Soviets had to have a huge portfolio on "Jack Platt" from his days posted in Paris and Vienna. He also chose the bizarre venue of a Globetrotters game with trade-craft in mind. "I didn't want another routine meeting at a cocktail party," Cowboy explained. "That's how everybody else does it. Too obvious."

Cowboy was taken by the affection between father and son, having grown accustomed to the tendency of Russian fathers to be more like generals than parents with their sons, barking orders as if they were preparing for war. Simultaneously, Gennady and Ilya took note of their new American companion and his John Wayne attire. They had seen boots like these before on television and in the movies. Could this man…be…a *cowboy?*

Cowboy and Gennady exchanged carefully crafted versions of themselves. Gennady, who by now had been given the dual CIA/FBI code name MONOLITE (later GT/GLAZING), said he was a diplomat with the Soviet Embassy. Cowboy said he was with the Pentagon, once having served as a liaison with the French police to help capture the terrorist Carlos the Jackal. Venezuelan born, pro-Palestinian Ilich "Carlos the Jackal" Ramírez Sánchez had been at the time a thirty-year-old fugitive, wanted for the 1975 murders of an informant for the French government and two French counter-intelligence agents. He was further suspected of masterminding the December 1975 raid on the Organization of the Petroleum Export-ing Countries (OPEC) headquarters in Vienna, in which sixty peo-ple were held hostage and flown to Algiers before being released. His friends had nicknamed him "Carlos," and he had been dubbed "the Jackal" when a journalist spotted Frederick Forsyth's 1971 novel *The Day of the Jackal* near some of Sánchez's belongings.*

While Cowboy worked for the CIA, not the Pentagon, the liai-son reference was true. When he was posted at the Paris Station he had in fact worked with the French police on Carlos. Cowboy knew that by flagging himself as a Pentagon man, it would make him all the more appealing as a target for Gennady. And it wasn't lost on him that the Soviets also were monitoring the Jackal. The exchange highlighted Cowboy Jack Platt's credo: Be as truthful as you possibly can—too many lies can be perceived and exploited by the adversary.

Gennady thought, *If anybody gets Carlos, it'll be this cowboy.* He also surmised that Cowboy's "job" at the Pentagon was what it was: a leg-end. He suspected Cowboy's real vocation from the outset, espe-cially when Patrick started excusing himself so the two men could speak alone. "I suspected that Chris was either FBI or CIA, and my boss was certain Chris was CIA."

The incident exemplifies the inherent absurdity their jobs often entailed. Both were acting, and both knew it. "We eyed each other the way dogs do when they first meet, circling around each other," Cowboy recalled. "I was putting on a performance twenty-four hours a day in case I was being watched. I'm on a stage, but the job can be fun." Or as Gennady describes it, "You have to be a mother and a

---

* This period was followed by a string of Carlos-inspired attacks against Western targets in the 1980s that killed 11 and injured 150 people. For many years, Sánchez was among the most wanted international fugitives. He was ultimately captured in Sudan in 1994 and is currently serving a life sentence in France.

father and a friend to your recruit. You might meet them by spilling a drink on them, or denting his car, which I did a number of times."

Cowboy remembered that either Meadowlark Lemon or Curly Neal fired the ball from center court, and Cowboy slyly expressed admiration for his "shooting." Gennady made a gun gesture with his hand: "He is a shooter?" Cowboy clarified the misunderstanding, which led to a broader discussion about guns, an instantaneous bond between the men. "We both love the outdoors," Cowboy explained, "and I knew from the dossier that Gennady loved guns but had no access to the outdoors and hunting. He was usually stuck inside a cubicle. We had to get to know each other. So I had planned to lob the word 'shooter' into the conversation at some point to get the discussion started."

Gennady said that he had always wanted to shoot an American hunting rifle. He described the type of firearm, animating his arms and hands as if he were loading it, manipulating its bolt action, bringing it up to his shoulder, aiming at a carefully selected target, and firing it. Cowboy thought his new Russian contact's handling of the imaginary weapon bordered on being sexual, as if he were dancing with it or talking it into an upstairs bedroom.

"I could probably get my hands on some different guns. Maybe we could go out shooting, Gennady," Cowboy said.

"Please, Chris, you can call me Genya. Yes. Yes, let's do that."

"Halfway through the game I realized, I really like this guy," Cowboy recalled.

As the men went their separate ways after the game, they couldn't have known how similar they were at their core.

The one chink in Cowboy Jack's armor was a danger variable he himself had helped establish on his list of potential spy vulnerabilities: he was an alcoholic, and his condition in the late 1970s was *not* yet under control. Nor was it a secret to those in the intelligence community. "I thought one day the CIA might throw him out," Gennady says. "They actually came close to doing it. Then I could offer him a job at the KGB." Of course, Gennady loved his vodka, but having been weaned on it since childhood, it had little effect on him.

As different as Cowboy and Gennady were in personality and operating style, both men were patriotic risk takers. Both loved their chosen professions and had no respect for the desk jockeys and quasi academics who populated their trade. The only way to do this job, they were certain, was to be out engaging the enemy—even if that engagement included friendship—rather than just typing up reports, which was a bigger part of being a spy than most people could fathom. And they *really* loved their guns.

Both men had reputations as "cowboys" in a world of staid "agency men." It was clear that part of their bonding resulted from the fact that they were both spooks who played by their own rules, kindred spirits who validated each other's quirky approach to their straitlaced profession. So intensely did Cowboy and Gennady loathe bureaucrats that they subscribed to a theory—neither was sure who came up with it—that bureaucrats were actually manufactured in a factory by a shrewd capitalist enterprise because the global demand for them was so huge. Cowboy theorized that this factory was, for some reason, located in Teaneck, New Jersey—mostly because Cowboy didn't like Teaneck, New Jersey.

The duo had signed on to their respective spy organizations at a time when the stakes couldn't have been higher and the East-West chasm couldn't have been wider. The Cold War, after a brief period of détente, had escalated in the 1960s: U-2 spy planes were shot down, the Cuban missile crisis took the world to the lip of Armageddon, the Berlin Wall had been erected, Oleg Penkovsky had sold the USSR's technical nuclear missile designs to the US (for which he was summarily executed), to name but a few of the provocations. By far the top priority for both the KGB and the CIA was to gather intelligence to stop a nuclear first strike. The KGB even gave the intel-gathering operation a code name: VRYAN (Vnezapnoye Raketnoye

Yadernoye Napadeniye), a Russian acronym for "surprise nuclear missile attack."

Fellow KGB agent assigned to DC Yuri Shvets wrote, "The primary mission entrusted to me and my colleagues at the Washington residency, as spelled out in the KGB chairman's orders and instructions, was to prevent a sudden US nuclear missile attack against the USSR. No more. No less."

A 1990 study by George H. W. Bush's President's Foreign Intelligence Advisory Board (PFIAB) concluded that in the late '70s and early '80s the Soviets genuinely believed a nuclear first strike against them by the US and NATO was a strong likelihood, not just academic war gaming. The Soviets referred to this period as the "war scare."

The intel-gathering priority was not as fanciful as it might seem today. Other now-declassified documents show that as far back as July 20, 1961, President Kennedy's Joint Chiefs of Staff, the Director of the CIA, and others presented plans for a first nuclear strike. They answered questions from Kennedy about timing and effects, and promised further information. The meeting recessed under a presidential injunction of secrecy that has not been broken until recently. According to a memo about the meeting, Kennedy posed the following queries to his National Security Council:

- "Has there ever been made an assessment of damage results to the USSR which would be incurred by a preemptive attack?"
- "What would happen if we launched a strike in the winter of 1962?" Allen Dulles, then Director of the CIA, responded: "The attack would be much less effective since there would be considerably fewer missiles involved." In December 1962 the US would have had too few missiles, but by December of 1963 there likely would have been sufficient numbers.
- "How much time would citizens need to remain in shelters following an attack?" The president received a qualified

estimate of two weeks from a member of the subcommittee. The group was clearly talking about US citizens protecting themselves from the globe-encircling fallout following a US nuclear attack on the USSR.

At the close of the gathering, Kennedy issued a directive stating that "no member in attendance disclose even the subject of the meeting." Amazingly, the secret lasted more than half a century.

Two years after Kennedy's directive, the young president seemed to reconsider the nuclear option when he delivered his extraordinary "peace speech" at American University in which he outlined an approach for nuclear disarmament. In his commencement address, JFK decried even the consideration of the use of nuclear weapons. Additionally, he called on all the world's inhabitants to focus on their common human desires and even to sympathize with the insecurities of the Soviet Union in the wake of the horrors it had suffered in World War II. Soviet premier Nikita Khrushchev called the speech the greatest given by a US president since Franklin Roosevelt. Just eight weeks later, the Limited Nuclear Test Ban Treaty was signed. Nuke fears vanished rapidly as backyard fallout shelters were turned into playhouses for the kids. The levity would be short-lived, thanks to what might be called the "era of doctrines."

Arguably the catalyst in the abandonment of the "peace speech" spirit was the civil war in Vietnam, into which the US inserted itself, and which was viewed by many as a proxy war of expansion between the US and the USSR. Simultaneous with the United States' catastrophic invasion of Vietnam was the issuance of the Johnson Doctrine, which supported authoritarian regimes in Latin America. The Soviets replied with the muscular Brezhnev Doctrine, which led to the August 1968 Soviet invasion of Czechoslovakia. This was answered by the Nixon Doctrine, which underlined the United States' right to support their capitalist allies; followed by the Carter

Doctrine, with its call to unite countries in opposition to socialism (especially in the Persian Gulf); and finally the Reagan Doctrine, which enlarged US military potential to resist Soviet influence in the world with such tools as an arms race and an economic war against the USSR.

From the Soviet point of view, all of these presidential doctrines were thinly veiled anti-Communist—and especially anti-Soviet—broadsides. And in case the message was lost on anyone, in 1969, President Johnson initiated a massive military exercise called Reforger, in which tens of thousands of US military troops were deployed to West Germany in order to act out US support for NATO operations against the USSR. Reforger would be staged annually for the next twenty-four years, with more than 125,000 troops utilized at its peak. In a recent interview, Jack Platt's SE boss Burton Gerber opined that "[t]he Russians became concerned about US military exercises in the 1970s, which escalated tensions. They even interpreted blood drives as CIA prep for launching a war."

The "war scare" era was punctuated in 1983 not only by President Ronald Reagan's Star Wars initiative but also by military action. According to a recent *Washington Post* article by David Hoffman, a November 1983 NATO exercise was interpreted as "cover for a nuclear surprise attack by the United States." A declassified top-secret report concluded that the operation might have inadvertently pushed the superpowers to the brink of a nuclear exchange.

In the late 1970s, just as Cowboy and Gennady were receiving their respective marching orders in the US capital, their countries possessed, more or less in parity, some fifty thousand nuclear warheads. Thus the strategy: *Get the other side's agents to betray their country's nuclear agenda.* Shvets recalled an instructor saying, "I hope no one doubts that the United States is capable of wiping our country off the face of the earth...But does it have the desire and the will to do so?...This is exactly what you will have to find out when you are sent there." Gennady was a particularly attractive target for the US because he was the son-in-law of the high-ranking scientist Goncharov, who was one of the major players in the creation of the Soviet atomic and hydrogen bombs.

"So, what's your play?" Haviland asked Cowboy the day after the Globetrotters game.

"Not a coerced recruitment, that's for sure," Cowboy replied. "There's a damned good chance Genya will go back to his boss and tell him what happened."

"Genya?" Haviland said. "Nickname basis. Do I hear wedding bells?"

Cowboy chuckled. "I liked the guy. You should have seen him with his son. There's a message in there somewhere. The kid speaks great English. He likes to climb trees. The carrot here is a better life in America."

If he had to describe Gennady in one word, Cowboy said, it would be "seducer," adding that he didn't want to get back to Gennady too fast because that could smack of desperation. He decided to run into him again and then invite him to go shooting. He'd need some weapons and a place to shoot where they wouldn't be bothered. Haviland had an ace up his sleeve, too. As Cowboy and Gennady were beginning their spy mating dance, the Americans were digging a billion-dollar tunnel (code-named MONOPOLY) beneath the decoding room of the KGB's future DC *rezidentura*, in the new Soviet Embassy still under construction. Eventually, it was hoped, the tunnel would give ammunition to operatives attempting to turn their counterparts.

Back at the current *rezidentura*, Gennady, who had chosen the code name ILYA, after his son, likewise met with his superior, Yakushkin. Of Cowboy (whom he knew as Chris Llorenz at this point), Gennady said, "Chris wears cowboy boots."

"American cowboy?" Yakushkin asked. Then he pointed to Gennady and said, "Russian cowboy. You like playing with guns. You like playing with girls, too. You like to roam around and not do what you are told."

Gennady conceded to Yakushkin that he was at a loss to identify a weakness in Cowboy. "He gave Ilya a lot of attention," he added. "And he likes to shoot guns."

"Maybe you see him again by accident, maybe not," Yakushkin replied matter-of-factly.

After a suitable amount of time passed, Cowboy put word out among his Pentagon friends that he wanted to run into Gennady at a social event. Given Gennady's sports endeavors with State and Pentagon staffers, he knew this wouldn't be a difficult task. A few weeks after the Globetrotters game, a high-ranking Pentagon official threw a party in Northern Virginia. Gennady had been invited, so Cowboy, who stood out like Gene Autry at a Hyannis Port regatta, wrangled his own invitation, and it didn't take long for Gennady to find him. While Irina wasn't with him, the Russian was anything but alone; he sauntered across the room arm in arm with the host's comely twenty-something daughter. Cowboy considered the blackmail potential of what he had just seen. But an insouciant Gennady just threw out his arms and said, "Chris! I was hoping to see you. When will we go shooting?"

Well, I guess blackmail isn't going to work if this guy's just gonna be on the make all over town, Cowboy thought. He made a mental note about Gennady: *Seducer. Reckless. Human weakness, carnal. Capable of betrayal (of wife and family). Odd candor.* Cowboy told Gennady that he had located a place to shoot and hoped Gennady would be able to join him the following weekend. "I've got some weapons I think you'll really like."

After a couple months of casual get-togethers, the pretense began to loosen a bit, with both hinting that their real jobs were a little different than first described. "Gennady said, 'My job is to talk to these crazy people who come into the embassy,'" Cowboy said. "I told him I had the same job in Vienna." Indeed, many of the walk-ins were head cases that had seen a few too many James Bond movies, but some, like naval officer John Walker Jr., were the most valuable Russian assets during the Cold War.

With Jack already knowing Gennady's true employer, and Gennady virtually certain that Cowboy was either FBI or CIA, the two suggested their own version of what would become known years later as glasnost: an open discussion. They both agreed to share at least one type of intelligence that would be mutually beneficial: terrorism, the common enemy. At the time, both their countries were concerned about the possibility of an attack at the upcoming Summer Olympic Games to be held in Moscow. Gennady and Cowboy, with their bosses' consent, actually provided leads to each other. (Of course, the topic would soon be moot for the US, which ended up, along with sixty-five other nations, boycotting the games in protest of the 1979 Soviet invasion of Afghanistan.)

One weekend, Cowboy picked up Gennady at the Soviet Embassy and the two men drove to a wooded location in Maryland. The government, which owned the property, had told its supervisors that they were to take the day off and not express any curiosity about what might be occurring there.

Cowboy drove deep into the woods. Gennady had figured they would be going to an official range somewhere. "Are we in Siberia?" Gennady asked.

"Pretty much," Cowboy said, explaining, "We have to go far away from anything because one of the weapons I have is illegal."

Gennady liked the sound of that. This Chris fellow really was a cowboy.

When Cowboy got to a clearing in the woods, he popped the trunk and told Gennady to follow him. Cowboy drew back a blanket in the trunk and exposed for Gennady a cache of weapons, including

Cowboy's Smith & Wesson .357 Magnum revolver and a Smith & Wesson Model 29, the .44 Magnum revolver Clint Eastwood used in the popular Dirty Harry movie series.

"Dirty Harry!" Gennady said. He picked up the 29 and pointed it into the wilderness. In heavily accented Russian, he asked the trees, "Do you feel lucky, punk?"

Cowboy pulled back another blanket and revealed a Marlin 336, often considered a perfect American hunting rifle. Much as he did at the Globetrotters game, when he mimicked the handling of a weapon, Gennady picked up the rifle, caressed its stock, pulled back on the bolt action, and pressed the weapon's scope against his eye. Cowboy's instinct told him, *You cannot fake this.* Gennady was not faking, any more than he had been faking his love of Ilya at the Globetrotters game.

"This is illegal?" Gennady asked Cowboy, still holding the Marlin.

"Oh no. The Marlin is legal. This, however..." Cowboy pulled back another blanket in his trunk and revealed...a violin case.

"Violin?" Gennady asked.

"Not exactly." Cowboy opened up the case, and there was a Thompson submachine gun, the weapon used *by* frontier gangsters and *against* them by lawmen.

"The Tommy!" Gennady said. This was what the FBI and CIA didn't want the property's local custodians hearing. There were few things more recognizably illegal than automatic gunfire.

"Where did you get this?" Gennady asked.

"It belonged to a gangster in the 1930s," Cowboy answered. "A friend at the FBI loaned it to me."

The duo set up the targets Cowboy had brought against

wooden posts that had already been stabbed into the ground. They also propped up cans as well as an assortment of fruits along a fence. As the men obliterated tin cans, grapefruits, and watermelons, Gennady noticed that Cowboy wasn't shooting the Marlin very often. "You don't like the Marlin?" Gennady asked.

"Of course I do," Cowboy said. Playing coy, he added, "It's just that my feelings are hurt you didn't bring along one of those legendary Russian carbines we Americans hear about. Is it true that only a handful of custom carbines were made for Russian leaders?"

"I heard that Stalin, Zhukov, and Brezhnev had custom weapons made, but I never saw them," Gennady answered.

"I'll make you a deal," Cowboy said. "If you are a good boy and you get your hands on a rare Russian carbine, I'll see what I can do about a Marlin. But you must be good."

As they each schemed to get the other to betray his country, both men griped about the bureaucracies they worked for. Not one word was exchanged at this outing that even hinted at an act of betrayal by either party. There would be time for that, but both men were satisfied with their early efforts.

For the rest of 1979, the duo played it cool, meeting once a month for dinner at the Gangplank Restaurant or for the occasional target practice. Cowboy would sometimes joke with Gennady about how, if he moved to the United States, he could shoot US weapons all the time and perhaps even own a Marlin 336. One day later in the summer of 1979, Cowboy brought an unusually aggressive amount of alcohol to one of their outings. Both men drank heavily, but where Gennady's aim remained true, Jack started shooting far afield of the targets.

"Do you want to always work for the government, Chris?"

"Not as much as I used to," Cowboy said. "Biding my time. I'll take a crack at business someday. I've got three girls to put through college."

"I can get money," Gennady said in his soft, understanding manner.

Cowboy's wretched state didn't weaken his sense of duty. He slurred, "What the hell are you going to offer me? Five hours in a bread line? Nine square meters of living space in Moscow?"

"That's enough drinking, Chris. I will drive us home."

The following Monday, when Gennady got to work he reported to Yakushkin, "Chris loves his beer." Cowboy's report to Haviland Smith took a different tack and simply concluded, "Gennady likes it in America."

4

MUSKETEERS

Will you still be here when I get out?

Since Gennady spent much more time on the volleyball and tennis courts than at the target range, Cowboy informed Lane Crocker that he would need a Bureau athlete to really schmooze this guy. Shortly thereafter, an agent from the criminal division, Gary Schwinn (a pseudonym chosen by the authors), was assigned to CI-4 and the new "Get Gennady" team. Cowboy introduced thirty-year-old Schwinn, a five-letter man in college (including tennis and volleyball), to the Russian as a tennis-loving "business friend." In fact, Schwinn was also a weekend disco dance instructor (white Travolta suit included) who was called "Johnny Disco" by others on the Squad. Members of the Squad remember his go-to pickup line for female agents: "Do you Hustle?"

On the early evening of September 25, 1979, the flamboyant trio found themselves at the Gangplank Restaurant, where they met up with a CIA code clerk "Captain Dougie," who owned a houseboat that was moored nearby at the capital's only live-aboard marina. Walking toward Hains Point along the dock, Gennady's eyes lit up when Cowboy pointed out in the distance the presidential yacht the *Sequoia.* "You mean where Kennedy did all his fucking?" Gennady inquired.

Inside the Gangplank, the four-dozen patrons at the crowded upper-deck restaurant had no idea that the increasingly rowdy quartet, which was downing copious amounts of beer and vodka, consisted of two CIA officers, an FBI agent, and a KGB spy. While Cowboy and Gennady were masters at holding their alcohol—Gennady was rumored to have a cast-iron liver—Gary and Captain Dougie were having a hard time remaining upright.

Suddenly, Gary attempted to rise and blurted out to two couples at the next table, "This here is real vodka, this here is a real KGB guy, those are real CIA guys, and I'm FBI!" Cowboy flushed with the instant realization that he could be out of a job if this continued—in fact, it might already have been too late to save it. He threw a hundred-dollar bill on the table and told Gary and Captain Dougie that they had to get out of there, now. That's when Gennady and Cowboy discovered that the inebriated duo couldn't walk.

Cowboy instructed Gennady, "You take Johnny Disco. I'll take Dougie." Cowboy and Gennady proceeded to carry them to Captain Dougie's houseboat, but as the quartet stumbled down the docks, Cowboy lost his grip and the clerk fell into the channel—not the first or last Gangplank patron to do so. After Gennady retrieved Captain Dougie, Cowboy thought, *Isn't this just spectacular? A CIA officer and KGB spy carrying an FBI agent and a sopping wet Agency code clerk to a houseboat*. When Gary came to hours later, Cowboy let him have it: "You got drunk and had a fuckin' KGB officer carry you to the boat. Don't let it happen again. We have a case to work here."

The looming problem for Cowboy was a stroke of splendidly awful luck: the two couples seated at the next table had been Air Force Intelligence colonels and their wives, and the next day they reported the incident to the Air Force Office of Special Investigations (AFOSI), which passed them over to the FBI, where they were referred to Cowboy's friend John "Mad Dog" Denton in the CI-4 office. Before joining the Bureau in 1969, New Jersey native Denton had, like Cowboy, served in the Marines, where his practical jokes and good-natured irreverence earned him the "Mad Dog" moniker. Among his stunts was scaling the Marine base's fence late at night as if he were an intruder and whispering faux-foreign gibberish, throwing the sentries into a panic. Mad Dog's Marine moniker followed him into his FBI work, say fellow CI-4 members. Once he ripped out the wires of a police car radio because the siren drove him nuts. Mad Dog and Cowboy's shared "leatherneck" history and iconoclastic behavior forged a strong bond between the two counterintelligence partners. "I had met Jack at social gatherings," Denton says. "He was not only a fellow jarhead but a real nutjob."

The colonels who had witnessed the Gangplank fiasco described the supposed "CIA guy" as oddly wearing one glove on his left hand—a peculiarity that applied to only one known Agency employee: Cowboy Jack Platt. At CI-4 headquarters, a furious Lane Crocker instructed Mad Dog Denton to "see if [Gennady's recruitment] is salvageable." If that turned out to be the case, Denton would partner with Jack. "I was looking forward to working with him," Denton says.

Mike Rochford couldn't have picked a more bizarre occasion for his first day on the job with the CI-4 Squad. The twenty-four-year-old Southern Illinois farm boy had just completed Russian language training at the Defense Language Institute and was now looking to introduce himself to his new boss. "I asked to see Lane Crocker," recalls Rochford, "and I was told he was busy trying to save some CIA's officer's career." In his office, Lane was in fact on the phone to CIA headquarters and Cowboy Jack at the CIA Washington Station in Bethesda.

"Lane told me I was in trouble at headquarters," Cowboy remembered, "so I went right over to see Hav Smith and begged for my career." Smith said he'd see what he could do but made no promises. Cowboy twisted in the wind for a week until the final word came.

"The indelible date for me was October 8, 1979, when Hav told me I was about to be fired," Cowboy said. "Hav reminded me that Nixon had years earlier passed a decree that any CIA officer who refused treatment for alcoholism or drugs had to be fired. I was crying by this time."

According to one colleague, the Gangplank event was not the only infraction on Jack's card; in his zeal to "accomplish the mission," Jack had taken his work home, work that included classified documents. Thus he was already hanging by a thread when the marina incident occurred. His Williams College friend Carl Vogt, by now living in DC and a partner in Leon Jaworski's law firm, remembers a distraught Jack calling him the next day, saying, "I need to talk to someone." Jack told Carl that he had been given an ultimatum to get help immediately. "The penalty is I'll never get promoted," Jack said. "The good news is I don't get fired."

It wasn't just the CIA that was fed up with Jack; someone with far greater influence over him—his wife, Paige—had been quietly making plans to leave him. She had found full-time work and was making her own money, a core element of her exit strategy. Then, out of nowhere, Jack called Paige from work and said he needed to meet her for lunch, something he never did. As soon as Paige sat down, Jack said, "I have something to tell you: I'm an alcoholic and I'm going into rehab tomorrow morning. Will you still be here when I get out?" Paige was stunned. She had been making progress on finding a divorce attorney and now this. She doesn't remember exactly how she answered Jack other than having conveyed her skepticism that he could beat this curse. Perhaps she didn't want to commit to an assurance. Nevertheless, she stayed.

Both Jack's Agency supervisors and his wife had been correct about his problem, and he now knew it. Although he had held it together at the Gangplank, the fact was that in recent months he had been having regular blackouts. "You know you're an alcoholic when you start having blackouts," he said. "I became a ceiling-ologist. Drunks often wake up looking at the ceiling, trying to remember where they are."

Jack jumped at the chance to save his career—and his deteriorating marriage—and right after hanging up with Carl, he checked into a medical facility at the CIA's secret training center, The Farm, near Williamsburg, Virginia, where he spent twenty-eight days going cold turkey before attending Alcoholics Anonymous for the rest of his life. "Recovery is one day at a time. AA is wonderful." From that day on, Jack's go-to drink was near beer.

Once Jack had recovered and had become more forthcoming about his struggles, his daughter Leigh asked him if, in all his adventures, he had ever had an affair. Her father answered, "Yes, I had an affair. With a bottle." But never with another woman. "Dad was in a business where you work hard but get no affirmation. Dad didn't need affirmation; he just needed my mom."

While Jack was in treatment, the Bureau and the CIA shut down the "Get Gennady" operation, and Gary Schwinn received the ultimate FBI chastisement: a transfer. While Schwinn packed his bags for the Bureau's version of Siberia (Detroit), Mad Dog Denton further investigated the Gangplank incident, interviewing not only the witnesses but also Gary's and Gennady's volleyball pals in order to determine how badly CI-4 had been compromised.*

While Denton worked on the Gangplank damage assessment, FBI rookie Mike Rochford spent his first month at Buzzard Point in

---

* In a recent interview, Schwinn asserted that he wasn't drunk that night and, in fact, didn't have a drinking problem. He says he did black out from about 9 p.m. until 4 a.m., but he believes it was because someone slipped him a "mickey." Further, he says he wasn't transferred because of the incident but because he threatened to hire a lawyer—a no-no in FBI land—after he was put on probation for the incident. Jack, Mad Dog, and Gennady stand by their version of events.

frustration. He had been tasked with compiling material on one of Gennady's *rezidentura* colleagues, the idea being, as always, to determine if a pitch was possible. However, the CIA's SE Division had balked at sharing its KGB files with the Bureau. That difficulty was about to be remedied.

"I'm sitting at my desk when I see this guy dressed in cowboy gear coming into the office," remembers Rochford. "He throws a thick stack of paper on my desk and says, 'I heard you wanted these. Well, they just fell off a truck.'"

"'Who are *you*?' I asked him," Rochford recalls. "That was the first time I met Jack Platt."

It was Cowboy's first day back on the job after drying out at The Farm. A week later, Mike Rochford was assigned to share his government car with none other than Cowboy and Mad Dog, chauffeuring them around town. Rochford was, however, not deemed ready to associate with their main target, Gennady.

Soon Denton concluded that the Gennady case was indeed salvageable, but supervisor Lane Crocker nevertheless decided to put the project on ice for the time being. However, Mad Dog's Gangplank investigation yielded unforeseen benefits regarding the Russian's local contacts, information that would change Crocker's mind and culminate in a major overture to Gennady. One of Gennady's closest friends, Denton learned, was a colorful Ukrainian-born radio engineer named George Powstenko, who was clearly the Russian Cowboy's "uncle"/confidant. Powstenko had been a US citizen for two decades, but "George looked like a Cossack, with his moustache and ushanka hats," recalls Denton. "He was a stereotypical Eastern Bloc character—everything revolves around drinking together."

Powstenko, whose company—Smith and Powstenko—serviced radio and TV transmission needs, was a force of nature in his own right and could be found most mornings at Blackie's House of Beef, already sipping on B and B (brandy and Benedictine). Having immigrated to the US in 1949 after the USSR absorbed the Ukraine, Powstenko had become one of the leading voices of the millions of fellow Ukrainians living in US exile.* He had originally connected with Gennady through the men's volleyball team he founded, Chaika, which included amateurs from many government agencies and was called "Washington's Yankees" by local players. When George and Gennady weren't chasing errant volleyballs, they indulged in their other mutual passion: chasing skirts. (Unbeknownst to George, Yakushkin had ordered Gennady to keep an eye on the Cossack engineer also.)

After one of his three-martini working lunches with Powstenko, Mad Dog Denton was witnessed under his Washington Field Office desk, feet sticking out for his fellows to trip over, while warbling "The Star-Spangled Banner" at full volume. When he was first asked to become a source for the Squad, Powstenko replied tersely, "I won't help the FBI—it is a fucked up organization." To which Mad Dog answered, "You're absolutely correct." Powstenko, obviously appreciating Denton's candor, then turned on a dime. "Okay, I'll help you."

Powstenko said he was happy to discuss any KGB business he picked up in the local Russian community so long as his friend Gennady was untouched. Cowboy and Mad Dog agreed, but Cowboy still believed he needed to recruit an athlete to get even closer to Gennady, and he hoped Powstenko would point him in the right direction. More often than not, Powstenko had salacious Gennady tales to relate, including the time Powstenko was walking down 16th Street and pulled Gennady out of a car, where he had been screwing the eighteen-year-old niece of a high-ranking member of Jimmy Carter's administration.

---

* Powstenko founded the three-day Festival of the Art of Ukraine, held at DAR Constitution Hall and attended by twenty thousand. The *Washington Post* referred to the "rugged" Powstenko as an "indefatigable impresario of the art, song, poetry, and dance of his native land."

While waiting for a good lead from the Ukrainian, Cowboy and Mad Dog continued socializing with Gennady, taking the Russian, who openly defied Yakushkin, for all sorts of get-togethers: lunches, family dinners, shooting and fishing excursions. "We often went camping in Fredericksburg, Virginia, near where the Rappahannock River meets the Rapidan," remembers Denton. "It was all shooting, fishing, and practical jokes. We were like three overgrown kids." One night, the trio was out shooting in the woods when they walked into a clearing and came upon concerned campers with flashlights. The FBI men flashed their badges and explained to the citizens that they were on a top-secret government mission to neutralize space aliens who had been caught creeping through the forest. "We got 'em all," the Feds explained to the anxious campers.

Eventually, Powstenko delivered the goods, telling Cowboy and Mad Dog about Tom Welch, an Arlington-based regional executive with IBM *and* a top-flight volleyball player-coach. Powstenko told the pair that Welch was coincidentally just now forming his own six-man AAU volleyball team in Virginia and was, like Gennady, a thirty-seven-year-old bachelor—Gennady in spirit, at least. More importantly, Californian Welch liked girls and vodka.

By the spring of 1980, Cowboy and Mad Dog had convinced their respective bosses to restart what they formerly called "Operation Gennady" (now officially called DOVKA, an anagram of "vodka"). Time was short, they told their superiors. Gennady had told the team that he was due to be rotated back to Moscow after his US posting expired in 1981. Cowboy and Mad Dog succeeded in convincing Lane Crocker at the WFO to back an entrée to Welch, officially making him part of the operation. It wasn't long before Cowboy and Denton showed up at Welch's IBM office in Arlington.

"One day my secretary came into my office with a concerned look on her face," said Welch.

"There are two strange men who want to see you," she said.

"Who are they?"

"They won't say."

"Where are they from?"

"They won't say."

"That's it?"

"One of them is dressed like he's with a rodeo."

"Hell, show them in."

On entering the office, Cowboy spoke up first. "Mr. Welch, would you mind if we closed your office door?"

Welch agreed while Mad Dog gave the secretary his best "Get lost" look. She closed the door behind her. According to Welch, Cowboy and Mad Dog made no pretense about where they worked, displaying their FBI and CIA credentials.

Again, Cowboy spoke up. "There's a gentleman working at the Russian embassy, a fellow volleyball player named Gennady Vasilenko. We want you to play volleyball with him, take him out, have fun, anything you want. Basically, entertain Gennady and tell him why he should defect. We'll set up a bank account for you to use with him."

"So the CIA needs better volleyball players that bad?" Welch half joked, drawing no response from either Cowboy or Mad Dog. "I made it crystal clear to them that it's not my job to recruit spies," remembers Welch.

"Okay, then just party with him—on our tab," Cowboy countered. "Let him know how great America is. We'll do the rest."

A bit of a carefree, adventurous type himself, Welch agreed—the idea of partying on the government's dime, with no quid pro quo, was an offer he couldn't refuse. Of course, the whole gambit would only go forward if he liked the Russian, Welch said.

"Don't worry," Cowboy said. "Everybody likes him."

Soon, an operational funds account of $5,000 ($14,000 in 2017 dollars) was set up for Welch with the Bank of Virginia. To put the plan into motion, Powstenko was contacted and told to suggest to the unsuspecting Gennady that he try out for Welch's new team.

"I remember when Gennady first showed up at our practice," Welch recalls.

"I want to play for your team," Gennady said in his thick Russian accent.

"I already have a team," answered Welch, feigning disinterest.

"Just give me one set," Gennady pleaded.

At that point one of Welch's players inserted himself. "What the hell? Let him play one set." Welch relented and was glad he did.

"He was amazing—far better than the best player on our team," Welch says. At a team meeting the next day, Welch took the temperature of his players regarding whether one of them minded being benched for a Russian former Olympian. "I don't give a fuck," said team captain Antonio. "Put him on the team."

Over the next few months, Welch and Gennady partied on the government's dime, attending fancy embassy parties and the best Georgetown bistros. Welch remembers he and Gennady often practicing two-man volleyball together, and drinking hard after. "Whenever he'd call me up for a practice, he'd always end by saying, 'Tom, bring alcohol.' Of course, Gennady always came well stocked anyway, with five-star Russian vodka. After just our second drink together, he told me that he was KGB and the vodka was part of his official allotment for recruiting."

Welch harbored a vague sense that hanging out with a Russian spy might be dangerous in theory—an exploding fountain pen, perhaps—but he never imagined that the hazard would come in the form of anything as banal as Gennady's driving. Late one night, Welch picked up Gennady and two other foreign volleyball players in his clunky old Mercedes for a road trip to a meet in North Carolina. As they crossed the state line after midnight, with Antonio and Juan sleeping in the back, Gennady's frustration with the pace of things took root.

"Tom, you drive too slow," he said. "I'll drive now." Once behind the wheel, Gennady hit the gas and sped the Mercedes to well over 100 miles per hour.

Tom grabbed the armrest and the window, shouting, "You're going to kill us!"

Gennady shrugged. "Don't worry. I do this all the time."

Within minutes they were being chased by one of Carolina's finest, all lit up and siren screaming. Gennady accelerated to about 140 miles per hour, the engine straining as the cop vanished in the rearview mirror. Gennady paid a compliment to German engineering and brought the car back to about 100.

A few miles later, the volleyballers came upon a constellation of whirring red lights and found themselves confronting twenty police cars blocking the highway. This got Gennady's attention, and he hit the brakes. Tom instructed his foreign friends to pretend they couldn't speak any English. The cops demanded that Gennady, Tom, Antonio, and Juan raise their hands above their heads and get out of the car. Tom pleaded with the officers, explaining that they couldn't be arrested because they were embassy employees with diplomatic immunity. The threesome displayed their IDs. Tom told the disbelieving cops that they were on their way to a volleyball tournament. "Prove it." He slowly popped open the Mercedes's trunk to reveal four balls and about twelve bottles of Gennady's best vodka.

Furious that the "diplomats" were beyond his reach for arrest, the lead cop gave Gennady a speeding ticket for going 140 in a 60 mile-per-hour zone. As the cops walked away, Gennady spoke out, now in perfect English: "Nice to see you, Officer—and *fuck you!*"

When the summer of 1980 rolled around, Welch was preparing a trip home to California to visit his parents and attend an Al Scates Summer Camp in La Jolla. A coach at UCLA since 1959, the legendary

Scates had personally reinvented the way volleyball was played,* going on to have, in a fifty-year career, an 81 percent winning record, three undefeated seasons, and twelve national championship rings (two more than UCLA basketball legend John Wooden). His nineteen national titles are the second most of any college coach in *any* sport.

Welch had a passing acquaintance with Scates and phoned him at UCLA to see if he would like a former Russian Olympian to give a clinic or two at the camp. Scates said he'd be happy to have him. "I thought Southern California would be a great way for Gennady to experience the best of America," Welch says. "Great weather, girls on the beach, the whole nine yards." Of course, the notion rested on the assumption that Gennady could wrangle a sign-off from Yakushkin.

Cowboy and Mad Dog were immediately on board with the California idea and began making their own travel plans. The mission was to party hard with Gennady in California after Welch had handed him over. "The reason for the California trip," says Denton, "was that it's always important to get a potential recruit away from his controls. They have a terrifying hold on their officers."

Gennady was ecstatic about the Welch invitation, as Al Scates was well known to him—as were California bikinis. Back at the embassy, Gennady approached Dmitri Yakushkin with his request to spend a week in Southern California. Although Gennady suggested to his boss that the trip might yield some recon intel on Southern California military bases, as well as the future US Olympic team, his actual, unstated goal was to check out those "California girls" he had heard so much about. When he informed a hesitant Yakushkin that all expenses were to be paid by Welch, the chief caved but sternly warned him that he had a seven-day pass, not one minute more.

Soon thereafter, Gennady met Cowboy at one of their regular

---

* Although they are staples today, Scates's ideas about quick sets to inside hitters and sophisticated combination sets, in which two hitters are sent to the same area, overwhelming the opposing blocker, were considered revolutionary in the '60s.

haunts, bristling with excitement. "Guess what?" he said. "I'm playing volleyball in San Diego, California, in August." To which a poker-faced Cowboy replied, "What a coincidence. I'll be in LA at the same time for a conference. I'll try to come down and see you."

There was only one more piece of the puzzle that needed to fall into place before the trip: a critical addition to their merry band. With Gary Schwinn long gone and Mad Dog soon to be transferred to Knoxville, a new FBI CI-4 case officer was assigned to the Gennady DOVKA operation. Dion Rankin was chosen, according to Denton, because "Dion was the guy who was most like Gennady." Some might call that an understatement.

Dion (pronounced "Dy-on") was a thirty-four-year-old native of Augusta, Georgia, where his father bred walking horses (and sold one to their neighbor, soul icon James Brown). He was also a master tracker, having learned the skill in the wilds of Malaysia, where as an army first lieutenant he volunteered to study at the British Jungle Warfare School. After Malaysia and then Vietnam, Dion got his degree in psychology before joining the FBI in 1972. He achieved Bureau acclaim when he helped track James Earl Ray, the assassin of Martin Luther King Jr., after his 1977 escape from Brushy Mountain State Penitentiary in Tennessee. He also provided key tracking assistance during the 1975 Pine Ridge incident in which two FBI agents had been murdered by Indian activist Leonard Peltier, still on the run when Dion arrived on the scene. Known among his colleagues as a man who didn't suffer fools, Dion had worked in seven different FBI field offices as an interrogator, polygrapher, and firearms instructor before joining CI-4 in 1977, where he had been involved in the successful roll-up of CIA turncoat David Henry Barnett in 1979. In that investigation, Dion and his colleagues had obtained the key evidence from Vladimir Piguzov, the same man who had helped Cowboy gather background on Gennady. Dion had met Cowboy in 1978 at a mutual friend's party. "He had a good line of bullshit," remembers Dion. "He had a foul mouth, but endearing."

Operation DOVKA now officially included the acknowledged cowboys from their respective agencies—the CIA, FBI, and KGB—although Cowboy, Dion, and Gennady preferred to call themselves the Three Musketeers (and even had matching shirts made to that effect). Mad Dog, soon to be transferred, was an "honorary" Musketeer. Driver Rochford soaked up their collective "spook wisdom" like a sponge. "All these type A personalities together," recalls Rochford. "How they all got along was fuckin' beyond me."

Rochford bonded with all the men but grew to love the externally gruff Marine Cowboy Jack. "The first time I met Jack's family told me a lot about him," says Rochford. "It was a Christmas party at his house. Jack noticed that my three-year-old, Megan, was all alone, shy. He sat beside her and held her hand, takes her over to the tree. 'Anything there you like?' Jack asked her. Megan pointed to a stuffed bear as big as she was. Jack grabbed it and gave it to her: 'Merry Christmas.' It was his daughter Michelle's bear. Megan has it to this day, thirty-eight years later."

The California trip, Mad Dog's last CI-4 assignment before his transfer, was perceived by Crocker—and especially Jack's current SE boss Dave Forden—as a pitch operation. The Musketeers promised their superiors they would put recruitment, or at least defection, on the table in San Diego.

Gennady and Welch took a red-eye flight in order to have a full day available when they got off the plane. On the first day, after checking into a hotel in Santa Monica, the duo headed straight for the beach and took on its local two-man volleyball hotshots. Gennady crushed them. "He told me, 'Move over,'" says Welch. "He took over ninety percent of the sand court and destroyed the locals almost single-handedly." That night, Welch threw a welcome party for Gennady—courtesy of the FBI—at a swank Beverly Hills restaurant with about fifty attendees.

Meanwhile, on their plane to San Diego with Mad Dog, Dion

and Cowboy strategized about just when and how they were going to pitch Gennady. The Musketeers quickly agreed to defy their marching orders. "Fuck Forden," Cowboy said. "Let's just do it like the Russians—take your time, be patient." One of the many things that bonded Cowboy and Dion was their shared impunity regarding rules from above.

"We both concluded that it was easier to ask forgiveness later than to ask for permission in advance," Dion recalls. Thus the only plan they hatched was to introduce Gennady to Dion and Mad Dog, and do everything possible to create a lasting bond, all the while showing Gennady how much fun he could have in the US of A.

Mike Rochford summarizes what was happening between the team and their target, Gennady: "It had nothing to do with recruitment. We didn't care if he got recruited. It was simply that access meant opportunity. The Russians have a word for it: *blat*. It means 'favors through networking,' the magic of relationships. Bureaucrats push for recruitment, like it's a quota thing. But that's stupid. It's about trust, friendship, and patience."

Jack agreed, adding, "I knew he loved his country, but perhaps he didn't love his government." With that calculus, it was decided that recruitment was unlikely, but perhaps Gennady would one day relocate to the US and help in ways yet unforeseen.

The Musketeers checked into the high-end Hotel del Coronado on San Diego Bay. Regarding the first-class accommodations, Dion explains, "This operation was a high priority for the Squad. They spared no expense." No sooner had Jack thrown his suitcase on his room bed than he called Gennady at his Santa Monica hotel and set up a get-together for the next day—no time to waste since Gennady had only a seven-day pass. Jack next called Welch and arranged a tête-à-tête for later that day, with Jack and Mad Dog making the drive north.

Welch took Gennady back to the beach, where he rightly assumed he would become engaged with a bikini or two, affording Welch the opportunity to sneak away to meet Jack and Mad Dog at the well-known Santa Monica burger joint Father's Office. "Jack wanted to know how it was going," says Welch. "I told him that Gennady was having a blast." The trio made plans for the handoff in La Jolla after Gennady gave his clinic at the camp.

Driving south to La Jolla the next day, Gennady told Welch that a friend had called and that they were going shooting together after the camp broke. Welch feigned surprise; at this point Gennady wasn't aware that Jack even knew Welch. On the way to the camp, there was a massive Marine amphibious exercise on the beaches and just offshore at Camp Pendleton. "Gennady yelled, 'Stop the car! Stop the car!'" For the next ninety minutes, he photographed the exercise from a promontory for his boss, Yakushkin, his California getaway now justified.

Back in the car, Gennady sought to reassure Welch.

"Tom, you're a good man," he said. "No worries. America is a great place. You don't have to worry about Russians. Worry about Chinese."

At Scates's camp, Gennady found himself in volleyball heaven, giving a clinic and scrimmaging with future Olympic legends Sinjin Smith and Karch Kiraly, who were working as assistants to Scates. After the clinic, Cowboy showed up, and Tom handed Gennady off before driving back to LA. "And these guys have the most amazing

Volleyball legend Al Scates (l.) with Gennady (c.) and unidentified assistant coach.

toys!" Cowboy said, contorting and shaking his arms to mimic an automatic weapon. *"Puh-puh-puh-puh-puh-puh-puh."* Gennady's eyes lit up. He was in; the combination of a guilt-free conscience and the chance to hang with American gunslingers was sheer bliss.

The next morning, Cowboy, Dion and Mad Dog climbed into a Bureau sedan and set out from their hotel north on I-5 to the UCSD dorms in La Jolla. Denton remembers that Cowboy, mindful of his recruitment scheme, was so anxious to see his pal again that he rushed out without his one black glove. Halfway to La Jolla they had to turn around and retrieve it. "The glove never made any sense to me," observes Mad Dog. "It was just as good an identifier as the missing finger. Go figure." Still using his "Chris" cover, Cowboy introduced Dion and Mad Dog as the FBI agents they were. "The fewer lies the better," Cowboy said.

"Gennady was guarded and a little nervous on meeting us," says Dion. "But we loosened him up real quick." That night the foursome wined and dined at a swanky oceanside Mexican restaurant, where Dion concluded that "it is impossible to get Gennady drunk."

The two new FBI guys on the case soon realized why Gennady had been seen as a possible recruit. According to Denton, "He was different from most Russians—Western tastes and a sense of humor. Cowboy called him 'the KGB's oldest teenager.'" He loved Western clothes, guns, and especially Western women. But unlike clothes and women, guns were all but prohibited in the USSR. Denton made a call to the San Diego Field Office to see what armaments he could line up for the KGB spy, a request he was certain he had never made before.

Soon the Musketeers were driving back down to the Coronado, where a Bureau Chevy Blazer had been left for them, and off they drove into the desert toward the Escondido Police range. Mad Dog remembers, "On the shooting range, we laid guns out on a table like a smorgasbord for Gennady. His eyes were the size of baseballs." Dion also noticed the first sign of unease from the Russian. "He seemed a little nervous to be around all these armed FBI guys," Dion says. "He calmed down when we all started obliterating the targets. It broke the ice."

After blowing the targets to smithereens with some of the highest-powered weaponry at the Bureau's disposal, the guys piled back

Gennady appears to be a KGB assassin taking aim at Dion.

into the Blazer and attacked the desert sand dunes with childlike abandon. Cowboy took a photo of Gennady wearing Mad Dog's FBI badge. They sensed that the Russian felt totally free for the first time in his life.

Denton recalls that the craziness subsided the next day, when Cowboy asked to be driven to the City Heights area of San Diego, known to locals as Little Cambodia. "I've got to go see some people," Cowboy said. He had an address that took them to a two-story apartment complex that held perhaps twenty units. "It was full of Cambodians and Laotians that Jack had helped relocate after the war," Mad Dog Denton says. "The entire complex emptied and rushed out to hug him. It was Christ-like, or like a scene out of the movie *Lord Jim*."*

Later that day, all four Musketeers met up with a retired local FBI agent who owned a deep-sea fishing boat. While on the excursion, Dion did a little bit of his own human reeling in. He purposely sat by

---

* This was in 1980, when the concept of refugee resettlement bore a much different connotation than today, when those fleeing war-torn countries were welcomed into the US. According to the *Oxford Research Encyclopedia of American History*, after the passage of the 1980 Refugee Act, "refugees were seen as people who 'voted with their feet' as they escaped from countries ruled by oppressive Communist regimes; hence, such 'freedom fighters' should be welcomed into the United States." And they were definitely welcomed by Cowboy Jack Platt, an old-school Republican.

himself on the bow, hoping that Gennady might get curious. "Twenty-five miles out to sea, Gennady approaches me on the front of the boat—he wants to talk," Dion says. "He was nervous. He just wanted to get to know me, feel me out. 'Where are we going with this?' he asked.

John "Mad Dog" Denton, Cowboy Jack, and Dion.

Just fun, no business, I told him. So we just talked about family." It was the beginning of a lifelong friendship.

As the sun beat down on their scalps, Jack appeared at the front of the boat and chimed in. "Look, Gennady, this has been a great trip, and it was a great trip because we weren't screwing around with the mission. My view: there shouldn't be a mission anymore, at least not with each other. The truth is, I'm CIA and you're KGB. I still think you would be happy in America, but if you don't know that by now, it's not a car I can sell you." Jack's statement wasn't pure virtuousness; one of the cardinal rules of tradecraft was "Don't harass the opposition," at least not to the point where you might chase away a target. If Gennady would come over to the American side, it would be evolutionary, not via tactical intervention.

Gennady agreed. "Let's have a good relationship. Let's forget about the task. That is the agreement. That is our deal."

The deal was their friendship. More than three decades later, Jack and Gennady still referred to this trip as "the dealmaker." They then turned their attention back to detonating marine life. They were having such a blast, literally, that they lost track of time while they were alternatively fishing and trying to blow up anything in the water that moved with firepower from the deck. Suddenly, Gennady realized he had to get to LAX. His boss had been explicit about his getting back to the *rezidentura* on time. At full throttle, they steamed the yacht back to the harbor. The four men climbed into Mad Dog's FBI car and headed up the coast to Los Angeles.

"On the way to LAX," Denton recalls, "I thought we were lost, so I pulled up alongside a Cheech Marin hippie type in a VW microbus on my right." Dion, in the passenger seat, rolled down his window and asked, "Do you know how to get to LAX?"

"Yes," the hippie answered cheerfully. Then he pulled away.*

"That was it. I was burnt out," Denton says. "Dion took over." Dion clarified nearly four decades later: "Denton drove like an old lady."

Encountering traffic at a construction standstill on the 405, Gennady began to sweat. "If I don't make my plane, I am in big trouble." Dion, whom Jack was now calling Tracker, pulled a red police beacon from under his seat, plugged it in, and slapped it on the roof of the car. Blaring the horn, Dion pulled onto the shoulder and floored it.

When they neared LAX, a police car spotted the vehicle roaring down La Cienega Boulevard and gave chase. "Shit! Cops!" Jack said. Employing an old favorite tactic of underworld wheelmen on the run from the Feds, Tracker Dion diverted the vehicle onto a side street and cut in front of a line of cars waiting at a car wash, waving his badge out the window. "Move!" As the other patrons surely wondered why the hell an FBI agent needed a car wash so urgently, Dion hid their car between two giant brushes and cascades of water. When they thought they had lost the cops (even though two of *them* were cops), the gang pulled out of the car wash and drew down on LAX, the engine beginning to overheat. With smoke whistling out

---

* Denton finds it amusing that a hippie had just dissed three government agencies at once (CIA, FBI, and KGB) and didn't even realize it. "It was what I would call a grand slam," laughs Denton.

of the hood, Dion barreled into LAX, popped the trunk, and they all got out.

"We raced past the airport lines, screaming, 'This is a diplomat! This is a diplomat!'" says Denton, who had earlier presented the diplomat with a parting gift. "I gave Gennady a clip of bullets to use as a paperweight. He got them on[to] the plane. It was a different time, that's for sure." Gennady used every bit of his athleticism to sprint to his plane, which he made just as the door to the gate was closing.

"After he gets on the plane, we go back to the car, which is smoking, brakes wrecked," says a chuckling Dion. No one remembers what happened to the abused FBI car or what excuse was given to headquarters as to its miserable state—but it was clean!

Back in DC, the men reported to their various bosses and dutifully filed their operational reports. "In our shooting range report we called Gennady 'orgasmic,'" remembers Denton. "We were promptly ordered to clean up our language." Cowboy received a serious dressing-down from Forden for not pitching his Soviet target. But Cowboy knew he was playing the Russian right, and Forden's tongue lashing didn't register one whit.

For his part, Gennady met with Yakushkin, who ordered him to end all contact with Platt and the others, a directive that also went in one ear and out the other. Soon thereafter, Gennady called his "uncle" George Powstenko for lunch—the same uncle who, unbeknownst to Gennady, helped set up the "coincidental" road trip.

GENNADY: I just had a great time in California with FBI guys.
GEORGE: Oh, really?
GENNADY: You should meet them. We'll get lunch and drink vodka.
GEORGE: No way! We'll get killed!

After the lunch, Ukrainian George called Mad Dog Denton, imploring, "Don't hurt [Gennady]. He's a good guy." From that point on, Dion used George as a conduit to reach Gennady at the embassy. When Gennady initiated the contact, he used a code, assuming he was being monitored. Dion recalls, "When Gennady wanted to get together with us, he'd call George and say, 'Let's go to the junkyard. I need car parts' or 'I need some Visine' or 'I want to go look at a Chevy Blazer that's for sale.'" The references were all too clear to the Musketeers: the junkyard referred to Gennady's actual trips with the others to get cheap car parts, the Blazer recalled their jaunt in the California desert with the Chevy Blazer, and the Visine was Jack's joke, a treatment to "get the Red out."

Dion remembers a typical getaway with the Russian: "We were in Gennady's car going to lunch in Arlington, where he was living. We were near the Washington Monument—I remember it like it was yesterday. All of a sudden, Gennady slows down and a car pulls along his driver's side. I recognized the passenger as a KGB guy I'd been following. It was unclear if he recognized me. Still, I'm thinking, *It's a setup. We're done for.* Just then Gennady reaches into the back seat and grabs a paper bag and hands it to the KGB guys through the window. They pull away. It was an arranged handoff."

DION: What was that?
GENNADY: Just a bag of bullets.

On still another excursion, Jack, Dion, and Gennady were with Powstenko in his Mercedes, on the way to Powstenko's house in Bethany Beach, Delaware, when a car bearing "R" diplomatic tags (KGB) approached them from behind. "This time it was Gennady's face that went

George Powstenko and his prized Mercedes.
(Courtesy Tamara "Tami" Powstenko)

white, and he slumped down in his seat," says Rankin. "But they didn't stop. They just passed us without giving us a glance. It was just a coincidence. They were probably going to the Soviet retreat house on the Chesapeake. It was one of the rare times that Gennady didn't shrug it off."

"Jack's wife, Paige, finally met Gennady at a Cherry Blossom Parade in downtown Washington," remembers Dion, who was there with his wife, Jenny. "She posed as Jack's girlfriend, using the bizarre masculine cover name 'Thomas Gordon.'"

Jack worried how they would find Gennady in the huge crowd. Paige had no such worries. "He's a trained KGB spy. If we just stay in one place, he'll find us—you know, like dogs do." He did.

Shortly thereafter, Gennady defied Yakushkin, who had forbidden him from seeing Dion, the nemesis of KGB agents like Alexander Kukhar, and showed up at the FBI man's home in Crofton, Maryland, for a dinner party.

"Gennady's wife, Irina, brought their kids, Ilya and Julia. This was before they turned fourteen and were forbidden from living abroad. Ilya found my credentials and badge on the microwave, put it on. 'This is our secret,' I told him, and he agreed. Of course, he immediately went down to the basement where everybody was visiting and announced, 'Mister Rankin and I have a secret!'" Dion took Gennady outside and suggested, "You should talk to your son about this."

Introducing Gennady to the Platt family was fraught with a different sort of peril. Upon escorting Gennady into the Platt family residence for the first time, Jack reminded the randy Russian to stay away from his wife and three teenaged daughters. According to Jack, within three days Gennady had hit on all of them. Of course, in Gennady's mind, he was just being friendly.

But despite the growing mutual trust and Gennady's obvious taste for Western culture, it was, according to Mad Dog Denton, also beginning to dawn on the Americans that Gennady would never be recruited. "The family would have to be sent back to Russia soon, and by Russian law at the time, they couldn't come back with their kids. If it weren't for that, we might have eventually gotten him," says Denton. "In those days, kids over fourteen couldn't join their parents overseas. They were like hostages to guarantee that their parents wouldn't defect."

As the Musketeers steeled themselves for the departure of their great new Russian friend, they knew there was a good chance they'd never see him again.

They couldn't know that their greatest adventures still lay ahead.

— 5 —

THE IOC

Do not tell your mother!

August 27, 2005
Solntzevo police station

By his third day in solitary confinement, there was no part of Gennady's body that didn't ache from the kicks and beatings, with thick-soled military boots being the weapon of choice. Lying on the stone floor of his cell, curled in the fetal position in his thoroughly blood-soaked FBI sweatshirt, he was certain his left knee was broken. He felt a gash in his forehead and, in his dizzy exhaustion, remembered that this one was not new; it was from the 1988 beating he had endured from his comrades in Havana. Could the bastards have drilled a second divot into his skull?

Gennady had yet to be given a glass of water, let alone any food, and had lost all sense of time, but it was still dark when a jailer proffered a metal can of water through a portal in the cell's bars. Struggling to sit up, Gennady took and quickly spit out the vile liquid.

"What, you don't like piss?" The guard chuckled as he walked away.

Before the jailer disappeared down the hallway, an FSB thug carrying a tray full of food took his place. The jailer returned to let him into Gennady's cell and provided the agent with a chair. Instead of offering any to Gennady, the agent slowly teased him by eating the eggs and toast himself, quaffing it down with a large glass of juice. Gennady begged him for something to drink.

"Oh, I'm sorry. How rude of me," replied the FSB man. "Ivan," he called to the jailer, who appeared with another full tray, setting it just outside the cell bars.

"I just have a couple of questions before we dine together." The man smiled, then placed his tray on the floor, out of reach of Gennady's arm (his other injured in his arrest), and pulled a thick leather whip off his belt. "Don't worry, it's the soft one," he said as he unleashed a flurry of strikes.

"When did you introduce Chris to Motorin?" Crack.

"To Martynov?" Crack.

"Your food's getting cold, traitor Vasilenko." The heel of a hurled boot hit him in the lip.

"I don't know what you're talking about," Gennady barely uttered. *"It was all a coincidence. You've got to believe me."*

"So just how does a man with no pension afford a dacha in the country? Was it FBI money? CIA money? How much?"

Crack.

"I never took their money! I swear it on my children's lives!"

October 1980

Upon his return to Washington, Gennady gifted Yakushkin with a UCLA baseball cap. The token, meant to make the stern *rezident* smile, was immediately tossed in the trash without comment. Within days, Gennady found that his sundry duties now included socializing in a veritable DC institution. Harry Truman, John F. Kennedy, Lyndon Johnson, and Richard Nixon all had held court in the dark and cozy wooden booths at Martin's Tavern on Wisconsin Avenue in Georgetown. On this day, a different breed of Cold Warrior was ordering up an oversized brunch at Martin's: Gennady

Vasilenko and *rezidentura* newcomers Valery Martynov and Sergei Motorin.

Briefing the new arrivals, Gennady explained the purpose of the large map in the *rezidentura* anteroom, the first thing an agent saw upon entering. Gennady happily showed the men around town, pointing out, especially to the gregarious Motorin, where the cutest girls could be found. Motorin, a known skirt chaser and prankster, had more in common with Gennady than did the straitlaced Martynov. They were both six-foot-two, womanizing tennis players and neighbors in Arlington. Motorin was also something of a Western music fan. In time, he would share another bond with Gennady: they were both regularly on Yakushkin's shit list for general insubordination.

Then Gennady moved on to the subject of lonely girls in the pool of secretaries in the Soviet Embassy. Gennady and Motorin eventually would joke "Let's raid the refrigerator" when they encountered a dry spell of American talent. Time would demonstrate that Motorin was as reckless as Gennady when it came to the ladies. One time he smashed up his car while squiring a prostitute around Washington. The FBI learned about it from the insurance adjustor assigned to estimate the damage.

Valery Martynov had a young family similar in age to Gennady's. In time, he would come to share Gennady's growing fondness for America to the point where he worked harder than other KGB agents to master English, not only for spying purposes but because of his genuine affinity for the country.

Although Gennady spent as little time as possible in the *rezidentura*, when there, he shared a cubicle with other spies who would alter his life, as well as the history of espionage, in major ways. One was, like Gennady, another fan of American music: a young B. B. King–loving officer named Anatoly Stepanov (pseudonym), who was a KGB legacy, the son of another LINE KR officer. "He was a squirrelly guy," remembers Gennady, who remembered Stepanov from the days when they both worked at Yasenevo. "Not really a team player, out for himself." At the moment, Stepanov's self-serving attitude was just a minor irritation, but it would come to haunt Gennady in the decades ahead.

For Gennady, the cubicle boredom was finally broken when a suspicious walk-in arrived at the Soviet Embassy in the spring of 1980. Ronald William Pelton was a recently retired, highly placed official with the famously impenetrable—pre–Edward Snowden—National Security Agency. One day in 1980, Pelton walked off the street and into the embassy to volunteer his services. After a debriefing by Gennady's colleague Vitaly Yurchenko, Gennady's boss decided Pelton was a snare—a double agent—and he didn't want to waste his time with him. "Let me try with this guy," Gennady offered. It made sense: both men were schooled in technology, and it was hoped that would give them a starting point for friendly conversation. For Gennady, the Pelton recruitment was a perfect case in point to showcase his seducer's modus operandi. During their meetings in pizza parlors and at malls, Gennady saw opportunity and cheered Pelton on, sympathizing with his financial struggles, the urgent repairs to his house he couldn't afford to make, and the NSA bosses who didn't appreciate his many gifts.

In a few months, Gennady was squiring Pelton around Vienna, Austria, for clandestine debriefs—easier to soften a target to the notes of Mozart and Beethoven than those of John Philip Sousa, and it was a nice upgrade from pizza parlors. But the payoff was huge: Pelton eventually compromised, among other things, Operation Ivy Bells, the US scheme to monitor Soviet military communications, including submarine activity. He helped the Soviets uncover the bugging operation, which allowed them to take countermeasures, including passing potential disinformation. The *rezidentura*'s counterintelligence chief, Victor Cherkashin, summarizes Gennady's success: "Washington…had spent hundreds of millions of dollars on the operation…Pelton shut down the whole project for $35,000." Gennady had delivered big-time.

Gennady's important assignments with Pelton and other walk-ins put his intricate dance with Jack and Dion on the back burner for the time being. The Musketeers' soft recruitment gambits were seemingly to come to an end in 1981, when Gennady and his family were routinely rotated back to the Soviet Union. Before the Vasilenkos' June departure, Dion went to his supervisor, Lane Crocker, with a last-ditch ploy. "I talked to Lane about the idea of offering Gennady an inducement to stay in the US," Rankin recalls. "Jack and I thought that we couldn't get an outright recruitment, but perhaps a defection." With Irina, Ilya, and Julia here, the team believed this would be their best chance. Crocker, who supported both Dion and Operation DOVKA completely, quickly got his CIA counterpart's concurrence on the overture. "I was given a large brown shopping bag containing four green cards for Gennady's family and forty thousand dollars in cash," says Rankin, which is the equivalent of more than $100,000 today. "That bag sat in my house for a week or so, until I could coordinate a meeting with Gennady. My wife, Jennifer, was a nervous wreck."

George Powstenko arranged the meet-up at Blackie's House of Beef in DC. There, Dion hauled his precious brown bag up to a private room arranged by George for the sit-down with Jack and Gennady. Before lunch, Dion gave George "the look," which told him to disappear for a few minutes, after which Dion and Jack showed Gennady the booty with the clear implication that it represented just an initial show of good intentions. "We let him know that there'd be much more where that came from," says Dion.

"All we want is for you to stay in America—no spying, just a better life," explained Rankin.

Gennady responded predictably: "Just take out enough for lunch and a bottle of champagne." As he said this, he was mindful of personal issues that trumped his love of Western stuff and these new friends. "I need to go home," he explained. "Irina's father is not doing well, and I do love my country. Now let's eat." An hour later, as the trio stood in the parking lot, Gennady added solemnly, "I don't want to hear from you guys. I'll help you find me when I get out."

Dogged Dion made a few more attempts to change Gennady's mind at social gatherings, but it was clear he was getting agitated, so Dion let it be, and the two said their goodbyes.

Soon thereafter, it was Jack's turn to say a final farewell to his Russian Cowboy counterpart, driving the Vasilenkos to Dulles Airport. At the gate, after Irina and the kids had disappeared down the jetway, Jack gave his friend a "Russian bear" hug. One more time, Jack asked, "Are you sure I can't get you and your family to stay?"

The refrain to switch sides had become more of a squabble between an old married couple at this point rather than an enticement to commit treason. Gennady just replied, "Would you stop with that already?"

"Call me when you get settled," Jack said.

"No way," Gennady replied. "That's not how it works in Moscow for KGB. But we will see each other again. This I promise. Like I told you before, I'll help you find me when I'm out of the country. Tell all the American girls to wait for me." He laughed as he boarded his plane.

When Jack returned to the parking garage, he noticed that Gennady had left a long box in the backseat of the car, to which a handwritten note had been affixed:

Chris, they only made seven of these. Don't ask how I got it. Of course, this means I can still chase girls! Until we meet again, GV.

Opening the box, Jack saw a custom Russian carbine, sporting a gorgeous hand-carved walnut stock. Jack would later learn that this was a rare MCC 551, designed for a former Communist Party bigwig.

For the next three years, Gennady was back at "Little Langley," the KGB's Yasenevo First Chief Directorate headquarters, working a desk job in the massive North America department, which consumed half the main building's fifth floor. Gennady's friend "Chris" was similarly assigned at the real Langley, where for the next five years he was tasked with updating the Agency's field operations training—another blessed reason to be out of the building as much as possible. Some colleagues have opined that Agency bureaucrats still didn't trust Jack in the field given his former alcohol problems. Others disagree, explaining that Jack was selected because he alone had inherited his mentor Hav Smith's operational trickery, devised for the vicious Berlin front. Additionally, Jack's experience included all that he had learned at the feet of his Laotian colleagues, Brian O'Connor, George Kenning Jr., and their "Black Thai" operatives, the Kangaroos, and all of that combined expertise was needed now more than ever. An espionage storm was brewing that would soon make the Musketeers' carefree days but a distant memory.

In the 1980s, Cowboy Jack and his CIA colleagues were dealing with the harsh new reality of Iron Curtain espionage. According to a 2008 study by the Department of Defense, US spies saw a 30 percent drop in successful "espionage attempts" after 1980. Divorce rates among operatives doubled during the same period, and CIA field officers were being routinely identified and expelled from the "denied areas." But most importantly, the work had become exponentially more dangerous than ever before—indeed deadly.

Haviland Smith once summarized the challenge starkly: "What most Americans don't ever consider is that the job of CIA case officers who work overseas in human espionage operations is to break the laws of the countries where they serve. During the Cold War, when we met a Soviet citizen in Moscow who was one of our agents, we were breaking Soviet law by that simple act. There is no other nonmilitary organization in the US government whose job it is to break other countries' laws."

The KGB was always more adept at the craft of espionage, due in large part to the USSR's closed-society history and the free rein given to its defense and security apparatus. By the '80s, its home-turf surveillance had become downright smothering—not just on suspected spies but on all non-Soviets. Camera and microphone factories likely ran three shifts per day in order to keep up with the KGB's demand that every conceivable Moscow hotel, restaurant, and museum be covered. Anya Schmemann, the daughter of Serge Schmemann, a reporter for the *New York Times* who had brought his family on his Moscow assignment during this period, recalled that her family was under relentless surveillance, including being followed, having their phones and apartment tapped, and having their mail opened. The Schmemanns accepted as fact that their government-provided housekeeper was providing the KGB with updates on the family's activities—and they behaved accordingly.

Field operatives obtained evidence that the KGB was even resorting to the use of the dangerous tracking tool known to the CIA as "spy dust" and to the KGB as *metka* (Russian for "mark"). This substance—nitrophenyl pentadienal (NPPD), sometimes combined with luminol—was sprinkled on a target as a fine, invisible-to-the-eye powder. When a KGB agent shone a special light on the surface of the CIA operative's clothes, the particles illuminated, making for easy tracking at night and in a crowd.

But the KGB wasn't flawless. For the better part of a quarter century they failed to realize that a GRU general, Dmitri Polyakov (CIA code name BOURBON), had been spying for the CIA. Polyakov's bosses had denied him the opportunity to take his gravely ill young son to the United States for medical treatment. The boy died, so Polyakov sought his revenge by furnishing the CIA with valuable information about Soviet battlefield weaponry and the state of the tenuous relationship between his country and Communist China. Some in the spy community believe that Polyakov's information, coupled with a dose of Ping-Pong diplomacy,* helped pave the way for President Richard Nixon's breakthrough outreach to China in 1972. A veteran CIA officer described Polyakov's reports as being "like Christmas." Said former CIA Director James Woolsey, "Polyakov was the jewel in the crown." Polyakov was executed for treason in 1988.

Often a spy's detection came down to something as simple as a staple: meticulously detailed CIA-made fake passports were routinely spotted as such by KGB-trained customs officers due to the fact that the documents' bindings were held together with staples made of superior American stainless-steel-coated wire, whereas a true Soviet passport began falling apart as soon as it was put together, due to inferior copper-coated Russian staples that began corroding immediately. But more likely their discovery came as a result of the KGB's brilliant surveillance, brutal interrogations, and seemingly endless supply of agents on the streets. US spies referred to this oppressive—and brutally effective—Soviet-style espionage as the "Moscow rules" (commandments for operating in "denied areas"), and in order to deal with this dangerous new world, CIA executives decided by 1980 that field operatives required better training.

Up until this time, field case officers relied on the training that all new personnel received at the CIA's then-secret facility called The Farm, situated between Interstate 64 and the York River, near Williamsburg, Virginia. Disguised on maps and signage as a fictitious

---

* In 1971, the US national table tennis team was in Japan for the world championships. US player Glenn Cowan made friends with the Chinese team, which led to the US team visiting China a week later, easing tensions between the two countries. The "Ping-Pong diplomacy" led to the restoration of Sino-US relations, which had been cut for more than two decades, formalized by President Nixon's trip to China a year later. This triggered off a series of other events, including the restoration of China's rights in the United Nations, and the establishment of diplomatic relations between China and other countries.

military base named "Camp Peary," with a gated security entrance sign bearing the words ARMED FORCES EXPERIMENTAL TRAINING ACTIVITY, the nearly ten-thousand-acre complex is actually owned and operated by US spymasters.

On the property sits a barracks, warehouse, gym, target ranges, and even a private airstrip labeled "Camp Peary Airstrip" on Google Maps. Rookie officers spend their first four months completing the Agency's Operations Course (OC), where they learn to shed surveillance, recruit and handle agents, master disguises, and perform basic paramilitary functions. The Farm's training program certainly had been adequate for the first decades of the CIA, which was founded in 1947, but considering the KGB tactics developing behind the Iron Curtain—and the CIA's losses—it was found clearly wanting. Thus it was decided that officers heading into that particular maelstrom needed additional preparation, beyond the OC.

The origins of the OC involved Hav Smith's time in Berlin in 1961 when the Wall went up. Having to send so-called rabbits into the Soviet Sector had required a whole new approach. It hadn't been so much about guarding the rabbits; it had been about protecting their assets. If the enemy was able to follow a case officer to a meet-up, the officer would be arrested, perhaps briefly roughed up, and then exiled back to the US. But the hard-won asset would almost assuredly be killed.

Hav went back to the US to formulate the OC. Dave Forden was one of his first students. They trained in New York City's Grand Central Station, where the "rabbits" were set loose, and Hav stood on a second-floor balcony so he could watch the action. The new brush pass technique was perfected there, going up and down the station stairs.

The idea for new human-contact tradecraft had been firmly resisted by Deputy Director of Plans Richard Helms in the 1960s, but in the 1980s, with "Moscow rules" in effect, it was clear to all that even more involved training had to be done. To head up the development of an additional course, Dave Forden—by now the SE Division chief—needed someone who was as tough as nails, could think subversively, and possessed years of experience in hostile "denied" overseas environments. Unsurprisingly, Forden turned to Marine Jack Platt, whose mentor, now-retired tradecraft master Haviland Smith, had taught him many of his best surveillance-detection creations. As Jack told trainee-author Michael Sellers in 2010, "We stood on the shoulders of great men and women who ran the course before us."

Working with Haviland's successor, Gus Hathaway, Jack took on the mission of creating the additional CIA field-training program, the Internal Operations Course (IOC). The IOC would be required, pre-assignment preparation for all young officers, code clerks, secretaries, and NSA monitors assigned to work behind the Iron Curtain and other denied areas. (It had been decided that using experienced operatives was actually a drawback because the KGB likely had identified them already. Therefore only rookie field officers would be used.) Observed and handpicked by all of Langley's division chiefs, the "first draft" of OC grads always went to the critical SE Division, of which Jack was a veteran. The draftees nonetheless had a large washout percentage in Jack's grueling IOC, which took place on the streets of Washington, in its suburbs, and in surrounding rural locales.

Years later, Cowboy Jack summarized his strategy: "I wanted to turn the CIA into a mini Parris Island. The goal was survival, survival, survival. You're being sent into hell, a police dictatorship. They'll wreck your car, break into your house, anything. The only way to learn to live with that is to be harassed yourself. I made sure every single one that was going overseas got arrested by the FBI. I said, 'I want a real arrest, throw them on the fucking ground, put them through a ninety-minute interrogation. Make it as tough as you can.' Over the years I trained three hundred forty officers, only six were women."

Cowboy called them "pipeliners." They were young spies hoping to be assigned to "the action," which consisted largely of the Soviet and Eastern Europe hot zones. Pipeliners, more formally called Zephyrs, were an elite group of new operatives selected from the best OC graduates of The Farm. Cowboy enlisted a group of CIA and FBI instructors, whom he referred to as the "Dirty Dozen," to whip the young ones into shape. Among these instructors were men such as Jim "Horse" Smith, Bob "the Beard" Miller, Gene Lassiter, and even occasionally his Musketeer pal Dion Rankin. Over the course of six weeks, the rookies would dutifully report every morning to the Agency's Ames Building on North Fort Myer Drive in Rosslyn, Virginia, where they soon learned not to make any personal plans before midnight for the nearly two-month duration.

On the first day, Cowboy told the pipeliners they were going to be pushed to their limits. It would be harsh, unfair. "You're going to hate us," he warned. It would be a crucible. Zephyr Mike Sellers called the course "organized mayhem," perhaps accounting for the participation of his wife and six-week-old son (Cowboy awarded the infant a "youngest graduate" diploma). Sellers relates an exercise in which his team's job was to retrieve a milk carton strategically abandoned at a Washington, DC, marina. When he picked it up, "Fifteen FBI guys threw me facedown on the floor. I thought we stumbled into a real drug bust." Some people couldn't withstand the trauma of arrest. In the end, there was no course grade, but Cowboy would discreetly meet with his bosses upon the course's conclusion and inform them who wasn't fit for fieldwork.

By far the most important facets of the program involved spotting and evading hostile surveillance ("dry cleaning"); making dead drops, brush passes, and moving car deliveries (MCDs); and defeating harsh interrogation. One of the IOC instructors, Tony Mendez, in his 2002 book *Spy Dust*, recalled how the Moscow rules were inculcated into the aspiring operatives by making the Soviets "think it was their fault that they had lost you, not vice versa, because KGB officers knew better than to report their own mistakes."

Mendez also described how he drilled a mantra into the trainees, a slogan that is prominent in Ian Fleming's James Bond thriller *Goldfinger*: "Once is an accident; twice, a coincidence; three times, an enemy action." The surveilled hoped to emulate Hav Smith's momentary "gap" from their pursuers, only long enough to drop off a document—or a human. One of the more cinematic evasion techniques Jack taught his charges was the coincidentally nicknamed "jack-in-the-box" (JIB). It consisted of a low-cost piece of gadgetry that Ian Fleming's Q would never be seen with: a flat cardboard cutout of a human torso that, when a lever was pulled by a vehicle driver, would pop up from a box (or in one real-life case, a hollow cake) and appear to the KGB pursuers, usually trailing two blocks behind, as a passenger. Of course, the operative who had been in the passenger seat would have jumped from the car during a "gap," whereupon the driver would deploy the JIB, going so far as to pull puppetry strings to make the cardboard move occasionally. The escaped passenger also would have put on a disguise before jumping so, even if spotted by the enemy, he could walk right past them undetected. One soon-to-be infamous pipeliner, Edward Lee Howard, would later admit that he often used his JIB for distinctly non-CIA business: partaking of the Dulles Airport area's high-occupancy vehicle lanes.

But not even a JIB could protect Howard and his wife, Mary, from the searing pressure of Jack Platt's training course. On one occasion, the Howards were tasked with engaging in a dead-drop pickup of valuable microfilm near a Washington marina. FBI agent Courtney West was assigned to observe the Howards, and he did so undetected. "We chased them down to make the arrest, when all of a sudden, Howard floors it on the George Washington Parkway, eventually going over one hundred miles per hour," recalls West. "Suddenly, he spins around, making a one hundred eighty degree U-turn and races past us, yelling 'Fuck you' through his open window." That's when Cowboy Jack got on the radio and ordered West to "Pull that bitch over!" Eventually, Howard was captured and hauled down to the Washington Field Office in Buzzard Point.

The couple was separated and aggressively interrogated. "Through all this, Mary remained tearful but silent," says West. "Even when the FBI agent came into the interrogation room with the 'results' of the lab tests of the powder that indicated pure heroin, which came with a lengthy prison sentence, Mary did a great job and didn't break cover after her arrest. But her husband was a different story." West remembers that, under interrogation, Mary began wheezing, the result of an asthma attack. She asked West to obtain the name of her medication from her husband, who was being questioned in another room. West was stunned by Howard's icy reply: "Fuck her." Mary may have never broken cover, but the terror of that confrontation never left her, even after she was informed that the ordeal had been an exercise. "I remember Edward Lee Howard very well," Cowboy recalled. "I trained both he and Mary. I liked Mary a lot." West remembers that Cowboy wrote a negative report on Edward Lee Howard. "They never should have kept him at the CIA after that report," West says. Had the Agency dismissed Howard, lives would have been saved and the Moscow Station wouldn't have been set back twenty years.

On occasion, case officers who had experienced Moscow rules firsthand lectured the Zephyrs, and one of the most notable was Martha "Marti" Peterson. Thirty-five-year-old Marti Peterson had been the CIA's first female field officer stationed in Moscow, in 1975. Like Cowboy, she had lived in Laos, where she was the wife of John Peterson, a former Green Beret who joined the CIA after his discharge. While stationed in Laos for the Agency in 1972, John was killed in action in a helicopter crash. (One of the stars on the CIA's hallowed Memorial Wall is for John.) At just twenty-seven years of age, the crushed Marti was already a widow. In part to honor her hero husband, she joined the Agency in 1975.

In Moscow, Marti encountered Moscow rules at their worst, and Cowboy had her impart what she had seen on the Zephyrs. She talked about the nonstop harassment, including phones ringing at all hours of the night. The US Embassy, where she had had a cover job in the clerical pool, was bombarded with microwave radiation to jam electronic communications, resulting in a number of deadly cancers contracted by Marti's fellow officers. It was also a lonely job since all officers were forbidden from having contact outside the station.

Marti spent eight hours a day at her cover job, where embassy clerical work was mostly performed by women. She likely hadn't known that she had been handpicked for the Moscow posting precisely because she was a woman. The station chief had concluded correctly that, due to the overt sexism of the time, all the KGB officers would assume Marti couldn't be a spy. That allowed her to use her lunch breaks and after-work hours to make covert drops and pickups with one of the CIA's greatest assets ever. Code-named TRIGON, KGB agent Aleksandr Dmitryevich Ogorodnik over the last few years had given the "main enemy" huge caches of photographed secret diplomatic cables, providing key insights into Soviet policy and negotiating positions. Many of his purloined documents were sent to the Carter White House daily. Among other things, Marti had also arranged for TRIGON to receive a special pen that contained a cyanide capsule for use in the event of his capture.

For over a year, Marti conducted successful dead drops for TRIGON around the city, often of spy-camera film. On July 15, 1977, after she returned from a late-night drop, more than a dozen KGB men jumped from a van, threw her in, and took her to the dreaded Lubyanka Prison for three hours of harsh interrogation. Although male KGB officers groped her until they found a radio receiver in her bra, she was released, having admitted nothing. The next day, Marti took the first flight out of Moscow, never to return.

Hours of deceptive maneuvers, including entering and exiting three subways and walking miles to shed any surveillance, still hadn't been good enough, or so Marti had thought. Years later, the CIA discovered that the operation had been sold out by a crooked CIA contract translator who had given information to the KGB about a traitorous diplomat fitting TRIGON's profile. Thus TRIGON, whom Marti had never actually met, was also rolled up, and when he was forced to sign a confession, he grabbed the pen Marti had supplied him with and bit down on it, breaking the cyanide capsule hidden inside. He died instantly.

At Cowboy's SE Division, many tears were shed for their lost asset. Marti would eventually receive the William J. Donovan Award, an intelligence honor named for the founder of the CIA's predecessor, the OSS, and the George H. W. Bush Award for excellence in counterterrorism.

Drawing on her experience, Marti put Cowboy's trainees through a simulated arrest and interrogation. "Part of what you don't know about yourself, until the time comes, is how you'll react in a bad situation," she told them. She also advised, "Always speak English so you know what you're saying—and remain calm." But by far the lasting impression left on the Zephyrs was the bone-deep sorrow they would endure if one of their assets were to be lost.

After the basics had been taught, the rookies were assigned a test mission in the field, where their performances would be graded. Zephyrs usually operated in husband-wife teams since that was the preferred deployment overseas. Typically the teams would be instructed to arrive at a package drop-off point, after having spotted and shed any surveillance over many hours of movement, pick up a package, and deliver it at another drop-off point, again undetected. The difficulty lay in the fact that some two-dozen men and civilian surveillance experts (from the Special Surveillance Group, or SSG)—often retired FBI agents disguised as the most unassuming shoppers, elderly couples, sailors on leave, etc.—were placed along the route between the Ames Building and the package location (frequently the CI-4 hangout Gangplank Marina).

Occasionally Cowboy and instructor Bob "the Beard" were not present for the 8 a.m. release of the pipeliners. That's because they would stop by Rockville High School to take the Platt twins, Michelle and Diana, out of class for a seemingly reoccurring family problem. The actual reason was not some domestic melodrama but Cowboy's desire to have extremely hard-to-detect spotters—kids—chasing down his rookies. The SSG participants were great at disguises, but none of them could look like actual sixteen-year-olds. The logic was that no one would suspect a kid of being a spy. Cowboy would admonish his IOC students for having the preconceived notion that spies were white males of military bearing.

Diana Platt grins broadly as she remembers her father exploiting her twin-ness to train and test his students. The students who realized they had been followed got a bronze star. The students who realized they had been followed by a young girl got a silver star. One student, however, sheepishly reported back to Cowboy, "I think I was followed by a young girl and…um…this may sound crazy, but I think she may be twins." Cowboy was delighted, and this student got a gold star for his perceptiveness.

Michelle and Diana never busted an actual package retrieval, but they had other successes against the Zephyrs, getting close enough to overhear their strategies. "We overheard conversations they should not have been having," Michelle recalls. "They discounted us due to our age." The girls, of course, had a blast playing hooky from school in order to play spy versus spy on the streets of Annapolis or Georgetown. As for their father, he had to keep this ploy secret not only from the pipeliners but also from his CIA superior Dave

Forden, and even more so from his ultimate superior. "I remember that Dad was very emphatic about one thing," Michelle says. "Do *not* tell your mother!" As for Cowboy's employer, Michelle opines, "The CIA would have been pissed that Jack was using his kids for surveillance. But it was this risk taking and flouting of the rules that made him effective. And you could take risks like that back then—there wasn't constant oversight and political correctness the way there is now."

One time, when she was in her early twenties, Diana was caught by a police officer as she was rustling around in the bushes near an Arlington, Virginia, shopping center. The cop arrested her for solicitation, as it was an area known for prostitution. Witnessing the arrest, Cowboy's team leader, Jim "Horse" Smith, a tough Marine sharpshooter, intervened and explained to the cop that he had walked in on a CIA training program and had just busted the daughter of a legendary CIA operative. "The cop was pissed," Diana says, "but he let me go."

The trainees had been told how to slip their coverage by running mundane errands, entering large department stores where they might slip on a disguise before taking a back exit, or performing an MCD if they created a slight gap in coverage. All the while, Cowboy and his instructors—like Hav Smith at Grand Central Station years before—would watch the action from above, usually a rooftop. Should the trainees spot a pursuer they couldn't elude, they were instructed to abort the operation, which was graded highly since it was also the right thing to do in the field.

Trainee Jason Matthews recalled for *Men's Journal* how Cowboy's instructors also played mind games with the Zephyrs in order to prepare them for hostile KGB surveillance and interrogation. On one occasion, operatives broke into Matthews's house, defecated in his toilet, and poured anchovy oil in his car's engine block. "It's sort of the psychic equivalent of Hell Week for SEALs," Matthews said—except it lasted for eight weeks. "They want to see who can handle it and who can't." Brant Bassett recently said, about training for an assignment in Budapest, "The training was daylong and nightlong. Pressure was applied to see if you'd crack. At the end of a day we'd meet in a bar or restaurant and Jack would tell us how we did." Cowboy wanted to find out how observant the pipeliners had been: How many agents were there? Could he describe them? What kinds of cars did they use? License plate numbers?

Jack Lee, Cowboy's longtime friend and colleague at SE, remembers watching Cowboy at these skull sessions. "Despite a gruff, Marine external demeanor, Jack was disarming to colleagues because he was very understanding of people, empathetic with their problems. People wanted to please him. If you fell short, he would not admonish, he would work to improve you. This contrasted with the tough nature of the Internal Operations Course, which was daunting, but Jack wanted you to succeed. Everybody loved Jack."

However, Burton Gerber, who during this time replaced Forden as SE chief, recalled that Jack had trouble restraining himself with his foul language, which was a problem with some of the wives being trained. Nonetheless, Gerber knew that Jack's IOC was a great success. "Jack was a treasure to the CIA because of his contribution with IOC," Gerber recalls. "He was energetic and tough but encouraging. In short, he was a great motivator and leader."

On their final day of testing, the Zephyrs were even tracked by planes. The IOC was a big-ticket budget item for the Agency, but the cost was an indicator of how much espionage behind the Iron Curtain was a priority.

For that last all-important IOC mission, the one that would determine if the rookies had the right stuff, the Zephyrs spent eight to ten hours on the streets, running a gauntlet of disguised volunteers in order to lose them, and eventually made their pickups (or aborted the mission if spotted), only to be arrested by the FBI on the way back to Rosslyn. The trainees were handcuffed, thrown onto the floor of a Bureau vehicle, and hauled off to a jail in downtown Washington. The trainees, in fact, were taken not to an actual jail but to the basement of the Washington Field Office in Buzzard Point—something Cowboy hoped they might notice on the way in. Few did.

Dion (l.) and his FBI team bust Jack's IOC trainees.

There, they were informed that the package they had been carrying contained cocaine. Next, the husband and wife were separated and subjected to harsh, often physically intimidating interrogation lasting hours. The men were forcibly strip-searched, and both husbands and wives were told that the other was cooperating. Eventually, Cowboy entered the room and announced that the arrest was part of the training, a KGB-like detention to determine who would crack and say they were CIA. If they had copped to that fact, they would likely become supporting benchwarmers overseas, a major humiliation.

Jack Lee, an occasional IOC instructor, remembers, "People in [the] IOC often thought a real operation was going down. They didn't know it was training. [The] FBI would actually arrest people, to see if they'd crack. If you said, 'I'm CIA,' thinking it would help you, you failed. You had to keep your cover. Only a few could do it." The phony arrests were the big secret of the IOC, the ultimate test of a Zephyr's mettle. "We were sworn to secrecy as far as telling future trainees what happened," says Brant Bassett.

Bassett was one of those who made the grade. He recently described the benefits of the IOC experience, especially how he and his wife endured grueling training with their three small children in tow. By the time the Bassetts arrived for their assignment in Budapest, they were "dry cleaning" aficionados who had never been caught, which was a huge victory given the stakes. Among the things Bassett learned from one of his agents was that the entire US battle plan for fighting World War III in Europe had gotten into Soviet hands before the Pentagon brass even saw it. As a result, the Soviets changed the locations and assignments of their land and air forces. Given Bassett's freedom to operate, he and his CIA colleagues were eventually able to nail the US traitor Clyde Conrad. Bassett says, "Thank you, Jack Platt."

Clyde Lee Conrad, while stationed in Budapest for the US Army in the 1980s, was a highly paid traitor who sold top-secret NATO war plans to Soviet-bloc Hungary for over a decade. As Bassett implies, Conrad was caught in Operation Iceberg and sentenced to life in prison thanks in part to Jack's training of investigators like Bassett. At Conrad's sentencing, the presiding judge noted the importance of his capture: "If war had broken out between NATO and the Warsaw Pact, the West would have faced certain defeat. NATO would have quickly been forced to choose between capitulation or the use of nuclear weapons on German territory. Conrad's treason had doomed the Federal Republic to become a nuclear battlefield."*

Author and thirty-three-year veteran of the CIA's clandestine Directorate of Operations, Jason Matthews, himself a grad of Cowboy's IOC, recently added, "It's something not many people at the Agency can do." However, those who graduated entered the Langley-to-Moscow pipeline as prepared as humanly possible. One of Cowboy's trainees would also utilize the techniques taught him in IOC

---

* Conrad died of a heart attack in prison in 1998. By coincidence, Cowboy Jack wasn't the only Musketeer whose skills influenced the Conrad roll-up. In December 1988, FBI director Louis Freeh gave Dion Rankin an incentive award for his stateside work apprehending Conrad's cohorts. Dion's expert back-and-forth interrogations between suspects led to a full confession by Kelly Church, who, while stationed in Germany, funneled classified intel to Conrad over an extended period of time. She was sentenced to fifteen years.

to evade detection when successfully making a dash to defect to the KGB.

Cowboy Jack regarded his work with the IOC as his greatest achievement at the CIA. To everyone who knew him in those years, it was clearly his passion project. When asked about Jack's all-day, all-night course, SE chief Burton Gerber wondered how he ever saw his family: "Jack seemed to never take vacations."

Despite the vast training improvements designed by Jack, Iron Curtain operations were still getting busted, and assets killed. Due to its now improved training course, CIA executives were certain that tradecraft, including blown surveillance detection, wasn't the problem. As CIA Director William Casey would eventually ask his Deputy Director for Operations (DDO), "What about the human penetration? Do you think there's a spy in here?"

6

THE QUISLING

I told you I knew how to fucking train people.

In 1984, Gennady was finally relieved of his tedious desk job at Yasenevo and posted to the Caribbean country of Guyana, which had opened diplomatic relations with the USSR fourteen years earlier. "Headquarters had promised to send me to New York," Gennady says. "But at the last minute I was sent to Georgetown [Guyana]— some sort of security emergency." Gennady wasn't happy and told his superiors as much. Nevertheless, he knew, for his career's sake, that he ultimately had to accept the post. His boss added that they would make it up to him.

The "Land of Many Waters" was seen as a strategic Soviet partner in Central America and the Caribbean, a base for operations against US strategic missile submarines as well as for sabotaging lines of communication in the mid-Atlantic and South Atlantic Ocean. The small country also had prime deposits of bauxite, a main source of aluminum (a major Soviet industry) and an ore in short supply in the USSR. Yet all of this looked more impressive on paper than it was in reality.

"We had a big station in Georgetown, but no counterintelligence function," Gennady explains. "More work needed to be done to protect the embassy—and to spy on Americans. They promised they'd only put me there for a year before sending me to New York."

Another DC posting was against procedure, but New York would have allowed Gennady to be close to the other Musketeers. At this point, he had been out of contact with them for three years, and he missed them. It would have been career suicide, if not actual physical suicide, for him to make contact while working in Moscow.

Gennady may have been unhappy with the new posting, but he made the most of it, as only he could. One of his regular responsibilities was accompanying the embassy accountant to the bank, where he made deposits or withdrew large sums. On one such visit, Gennady noticed and then fell hard for a gorgeous young teller named Sherry. One day, he offered to "give her a lift." ("I ended up giving her a lift for one year," Gennady says with a sly grin.) He began dating Sherry and invited her to volleyball matches. At some point the Soviet ambassador pulled Gennady aside in the embassy and admonished him for dating a woman so young. "Now, knock it off or you'll get thrown in jail and cause an international incident." Did he knock it off? "Of course not," Gennady says. "Well, not right away." He saw her a few more times, then dropped her.

Almost as important as the girls was his friendship with the other Musketeers. Soon he hit upon a way to make contact. Among Gennady's other routine duties in 1984 was to liaise between the Soviet ambassador in Guyana and the Soviet UN mission in New York. According to Cowboy, during phone calls to the UN representative—calls Gennady knew were tapped by the NSA for the US Embassy in Guyana, located a mile west along the seawall—Gennady broke the cardinal rule of tradecraft and announced himself with his real name (not his cover, ILYA) in a stage voice that would have been crystal clear to even the most dunderheaded American phone transcriber:

GENNADY: Hello, this is Gennady Vasilenko—that's G-E-N-N-A-D-Y, V-A-S-I-L-E-N-K-O. I'm calling from the Soviet Embassy in Guyana. G-U-Y-A-N-A. I used to work at the

Soviet Embassy in Washington from 1977 to 1980. That's right, Washington, DC.

For good measure, Gennady added that he needed "some Visine and parts for a Chevy Blazer," the Musketeers private code for "Come get me!" The secret code also guaranteed the Musketeers that the caller was indeed Gennady, not some imposter provocateur. The Americans traced Gennady's location, and the conversation was quickly relayed to the men it was actually intended for: Dion Rankin and Cowboy Jack. In Gennady's version of the story, his whereabouts likely had been discovered already by Jack and Dion's friend McKim Symington, who worked at the US Embassy in Georgetown, Guyana.

Word of Gennady came first to the Washington Field Office and Dion Rankin, who had continued to believe that Gennady's parting words in DC left the door open to possible recruitment, or at least defection. He immediately called Jack, who took leave from the IOC in Rosslyn and drove to Buzzard Point, where Dion read him the transcript so Jack could decide for himself whether it was a provocation. Dion had barely gotten the words out of his mouth when Jack shot back, "Genya's in Georgetown. Let's go!"

Dion agreed with Cowboy's faith in Operation DOVKA and quickly broached with his superiors the possibility of a trip. "I never had any problems with Crocker when it came to the Genya thing," Dion says. "When I asked permission to travel to Guyana he immediately said, 'Okay, go.'"

If only it were that easy, an envious Cowboy Jack thought. In fact, Cowboy's cobra-mongoose relationship with Agency executives on the seventh floor would prove a major stumbling point. They had come to think of the whole operation as little more than a boondoggle for juvenile delinquent spies who liked to drink, shoot squirrels, and generally screw around on the government's dime. Enough was enough. Both SE chief Burton Gerber and Counterintelligence Director Paul Redmond had made it clear to Cowboy that they were finished funding the Musketeers' personal vacations, disguised, in their view, as Agency business. Gerber, in a recent interview, recalled that he felt that the friendship was just a personal thing, and he saw no strategic or tactical value in the cultivation of Gennady. It was a friendship, period. While Gennady was promising in theory, Gerber was not interested in financing the international target-shooting getaways of good buddies. Gerber also vetoed the purchase of a hunting rifle for Gennady for the same reason—not because he was anti-gift or anti-gun but because he saw no value in it. "I don't see what you can do there," Gerber told Cowboy. "I don't see that he's recruitable."

Dion accompanied Jack as he went around Gerber and took his trip request to Redmond on the seventh floor. It was an encounter he'd never forget—and it was typical Cowboy. "Jack and I sat on a small couch facing Redmond's desk," Dion remembers. "It was a narrow room, and there were two of his junior execs sitting off to the side. When Redmond first indicated he was against the Guyana thing, Jack, who was decked out in full Cowboy regalia, slowly and dramatically pulls a cigarette out of his vest pocket—he was a chain-smoker at this time." Of course, smoking was against the rules in the executive offices, so everyone's eyes were riveted to that Marlboro. "So he continues making his case for the trip as he lights up. Except for Jack's voice, you could hear a pin drop." All eyes were on Jack's cigarette because they were wondering what the hell he was going to do with it in the ashtray-less suite.

Dion couldn't stifle laughter as he recounted how Jack proceeded to speak ever so slowly about Gennady in Guyana, all the while tapping his ashes onto Redmond's polished tile floor. "It went on for twenty minutes," says Dion. "It was like a comedy bit, but just for my benefit. Redmond and the other two never said a word. They were horrified. But Jack just kept on talking until there was a pile of ash on the floor." Finally Jack threw the cigarette on the floor and squashed it under his boot. "For his encore, he threw the butt under

Gennady's Dynamo Volleyball Team (Gennady third from left).

Major Gennady
Vasilenko, KGB.

Gennady's Komsomol
(All-Union Leninist
Young Communist
League) Membership
Card.

Jack Platt is promoted to Second Lieutenant in the USMC, with the participation of Jack's father, John Cheney Platt II, and wife, Paige.

Polly and Jack. *(Courtesy of Sashy Bogdanovich)*

The Platt sisters in Laos.

Dion Rankin.

John "Mad Dog" Denton.

George Powstenko
and Gennady.
*(Courtesy of Tamara
"Tami" Powstenko)*

Vitaly Yurchenko (l.)
with Gennady (r.) and
unidentified colleague.

Gennady (l.) and
Dmitry Yakushkin (r.).

Gennady (center) with Irina (4th from right) and Sergei Motorin (3rd from right) at the old Russian Embassy in Washington.

Gennady at the Seawall in Georgetown, Guyana.

Dion and Gennady have a very secure picnic in Guyana.

Jack and Dion in Georgetown, Guyana.

The Four Musketeers in San Diego.

Deep sea fishing with "Mad Dog," Genya, and Cowboy. *(Courtesy of John Denton)*

The Gangplank Marina, restaurant in background (early eighties). *(Courtesy of Linda Herdering)*

The Air Rights Center Building on Wisconsin Ave. in Bethesda, MD, home to the CIA's DC "Domestic Station" in the seventies and eighties.

The old Russian Embassy on 16th St., before its relocation to Mount Alto on Wisconsin Ave.

"The Center"—Lubyanka, the former KGB Headquarters and prison, Moscow.

"The Woods"—Yasenevo Spy Center, eleven miles from Moscow, home of the Russian Foreign Intelligence Service (SVR) Former First Chief Directorate HQ of the KGB.

The killing courtyard at Lefortovo Prison, Moscow.

the cushion of Redmond's sofa. Then he said, 'Thanks for your consideration,' and we walked out into the hall."

"What the hell was that?!" Dion asked as they entered the elevator.

"Fuck 'em!" Jack said in the elevator containing a half-dozen shocked secretarial staff. Jack just smiled and said, "Good morning, ladies."

"You had to love him," Dion says.

Of course, not everyone on the seventh floor agreed with Dion. Although Burton Gerber admired Jack, he was also aware of many fellow executives who weren't amused by Jack's brusque manner. One CIA colleague expressed it more candidly, saying that Agency management was just plain afraid of him. "His personality became a problem for Jack at the CIA," Gerber says. "He could have advanced further if he had gotten it under control." To which Jack would have replied that he had no interest in advancement—he just wanted to be left alone to do his patriotic duty. Semper fi.

Dion and Jack concluded that the Agency was concerned with more than the company expense account; they worried the overture was actually a provocation, and they didn't wish to take the risk. But Jack thought—*knew*—that his superiors were missing the big picture. Who knew what kind of information was hibernating in Gennady's brain, especially considering that his father-in-law had been one of the Wise Men of the Soviet nuclear program? Didn't the suits understand that cultivating sources wasn't like dropping a coin in a vending machine, then pulling a knob to release an order of nicely packaged treachery? Didn't the suits trust Jack to not fall for a provocation? Although Jack had a personal interest in seeing his Russian friend, he and Dion also held out that Gennady would someday end up living in the US, and when that time came, he would be a great asset for both their agencies.

As it was, Jack went back to Rosslyn and continued to train others for overseas action while Dion spent six weeks at the CIA, training and learning about Guyana. Dion then made the trip alone and checked into the Pegasus Hotel in Georgetown as a diplomat named "Donald Williams." The Pegasus overlooks the Caribbean and the 280-mile-long seawall that protects the below-sea-level country. It was the hotel of choice for visiting government employees since it was located just two blocks from the US Embassy. Ironically, it also attracted a decidedly nongovernmental crowd. "It was like a scene from *Casablanca*—all spies, drug dealers, and con men staying there," remembers Dion. "But it's the only decent hotel. All the water in Guyana made you sick—you had to down a cocktail before the foul-water ice melted. The hotel buffet was dried toast, dried bacon, and egg whites—just whites because the chickens were malnourished. A plate of eggs looked like a plate of snot. The people were poor as shit there."

Dion proceeded about a mile east to the Soviet compound, which took up a large square block where Pere Street abuts the Caribbean. The complex included a basketball court, a tennis court, a large pool, and a volleyball area. Dion pictured his old friend spending a good deal of his time at these recreations. Once inside, Dion had the receptionist page Gennady. "In a few minutes he walks into the conference room where I was waiting," Dion says. "We both played it cool, knowing we were being watched. I told him I was staying at the Pegasus. Later at the hotel I get a message to meet him by the jagged seawall at ten that night. When the cab dropped me off and drove away it was pitch black. I walked for two miles to lose possible surveillance—Jack would have been pleased—until I arrived at the beach location. Gennady showed up right on time. We got reacquainted, but I still played it cool, no pitch. The first thing he said was 'Where's Chris?'"

About an hour later, Gennady drove Dion to within a few blocks of his hotel, and Dion proceeded back on foot. He stayed a week in Georgetown, where the duo met each other every day, often shooting targets from the seawall. Dion laughs. "One thing was clear. Gennady hadn't changed a bit. He had at least two girlfriends there, including a pharmacist. One day I went to his apartment and I saw Irina, who was there for her twice-yearly visit. She was screaming at him." Ilya and Julia weren't there—they were no longer permitted to leave the USSR because they were teenagers. Irina could leave because she was the wife of a "diplomat." "But Irina was

Gennady, Irina, and Dion in Guyana.

frightened that Gennady would get into trouble by hanging with me," Dion says. The truth was, Gennady didn't need anyone's help pissing people off.

After the two men parted ways each night, they were likely at their typewriters, simultaneously writing up their reports. Gennady's Yasenevo superior, fully aware of his officer's history with the other Musketeers, was furious. "He warned me not to talk to either of them. He said it's a provocation," Gennady says. "I told him to fuck off. 'If you don't trust me, send me home. I don't want to be here anyway.'"

For the rest of the week, Gennady and Dion continued meeting. Thus once again Gennady had allowed his friendships with the Musketeers to force him to deceive his own agency. These deceptions would prove to be monumental mistakes, but, like Jack, Gennady felt the friendships were worth the risk. When Gennady bid Dion goodbye on his last day, he said, "Tell the Cowboy to get his ass down here!"

Dion returned to Washington and immediately called Cowboy, to whom he reported that their friend was well and had asked for him repeatedly. Cowboy knew that Burton Gerber was nearing the end of his rope with Operation DOVKA, so he came up with a new argument for the need to travel to the country. Guyana had vaulted into public consciousness in 1978 when an American Communist cult leader named Jim Jones convinced more than nine hundred of his Peoples Temple followers to commit mass suicide by drinking Flavor Aid laced with cyanide. Jones died along with his followers at his "Jonestown" commune by a presumably self-inflicted gunshot to the head—the US authorities had been investigating his cult, and the maniac had been hearing footsteps. Nearly all of those who died were Americans. Later reports indicated that many of those who "drank the Kool-Aid" might have done so at the gunpoint of Jones's Marxist henchmen. The deaths immediately followed the assassination of US congressman Leo Ryan, who had traveled to Guyana to investigate reports of Americans being held against their will.

Cowboy knew that the CIA and the KGB had been interested in this small Caribbean nation for some time. In fact, its current president, L. Forbes Burnham, had been installed as prime minister with CIA support in 1964. Regarding the Jonestown incident, both the KGB and the Kremlin tied the nine hundred deaths to American decadence and sickness; however, they did so without mentioning their own secret links to the cult. It was soon learned that Soviet representatives had visited the Peoples Temple on a number of occasions. Survivors told journalists that Jim Jones had met regularly with the local KGB contingent. Immediately after the deaths, Burnham released memos detailing the local KGB contacts, noting discussions to relocate the compound to the Black Sea. Letters were made public, showing that $7.2 million of Jonestown money had been delivered to local banks with the Soviet Embassy in Georgetown empowered to withdraw the funds.

While no one truly believed the Soviets had had a hand in the Jonestown massacre, if nothing else, the tragedy became a flashpoint for motivated CIA operatives to pay closer attention—and to visit— Guyana. Nobody wanted another Jonestown on his or her hands. *Whatever works*, Cowboy thought. After nonstop harassing from Cowboy, Gerber finally relented and signed off on Cowboy's trip to

Guyana in February 1985. As Gennady saw it, his life in Guyana had consisted primarily of waiting for something to happen—and it was about to.

The February 1985 Guyana Musketeers reunion was set to be a surprise, a celebration of Jack's birthday that month and, belatedly, Gennady's December birthday. For this trip, Jack used his overseas cover name, "Charles Kneller," while Dion once again went by "Donald Williams." After checking in at the Pegasus, Jack stayed behind while Dion walked to the Soviet Embassy, where he made a point of *accidentally* running into Gennady and invited him back to the hotel for a drink after work.

That evening, Gennady appeared at Dion's small room, but before they could settle in, Dion took a camera from his suitcase and asked the Russian to pose.

"What, the FBI doesn't have enough pictures of me already?" asked Gennady.

"Well, this is going to be a special shot," answered Dion.

Then Gennady was jumped from behind by someone (a thug?) who had been hiding in the closet, as Dion clicked away on his Nikon. *Was this a setup?* Gennady thought for a second. When he looked down and saw that he was being hugged by a man with half a finger missing on his left hand, he broke into a huge smile, captured by Dion's camera.

Jack surprises Gennady in the Pegasus Hotel, Guyana.

"Cowboy! What took you so long?" Gennady laughed. "I mean to come out of the closet." Now the two were hugging each other face-to-face.

"You never call me anymore," Jack feigned like a spurned teenage girl.

"Okay, ladies, break it up," Dion interrupted.

The trio caught up in the following hours, solidifying plans for the rest of the four-day trip. For the next few days, Jack, Gennady, and Dion met down at the seawall, where they picnicked, shot at tin cans, or wined and dined at the best bistros Georgetown had to offer. At the end of the trip, the two American Musketeers dutifully filed their reports, while the Russian did not. No recruitment had been attempted by any of the friends. But Jack and Dion held to their gut feelings that by merely gaining Gennady's friendship, something good would happen one day.

Dion and Gennady have a Caribbean picnic, spy style.

Back in Washington that spring, Dion and Jack found their professional worlds in upheaval. While the irrepressible Russian Cowboy was left to play volleyball and sun himself among the bikinis on Guyana's "63 Beach, Berbice," Dion and his CI-4 Squad, and Jack and his SE Division, were considering much more sobering business: recently there had been a marked uptick in Americans spying against the US. In 1985 and 1986, there would be fourteen traitors arrested. A report written years later by top CIA mole hunter Sandy Grimes concluded that some thirty CIA operations against the Soviets had been fatally compromised.

The KGB busted Moscow case officers Michael Sellers and Eric Sites, both of whom had to be exfiltrated back to the US. The cover of GRU (Soviet military intelligence) colonel Sergei Bokhan was blown, forcing him, after ten years of working for the Agency, to be essentially smuggled to the US. At one point in 1985, the CIA lost six Iron Curtain assets (foreign penetration agents) in six months—either known executions or "disappearances."

Then there was the loss, after five years of hard work, of a valuable CIA-NSA joint technical success. Code-named GT/TAW, it involved the planting of a sophisticated tape recorder and electronic bug in a sewer on the main landline cable that connected the KGB's headquarters in Moscow to its nuclear weapons research institute south of the capital.

"This whole place is falling apart," Paul Redmond, the CIA's legendary chief of Counterintelligence, concluded. "Everybody's getting rolled up." Although experienced CIA officers had planned their Moscow operations fastidiously—utilizing Russian clothes, Russian language, and the latest in Ian Fleming–type gadgets—they were routinely bested by their KGB opponents. The mystery was *how*.

But the Americans were not alone in their travails. The Soviets had their own losses to repair, especially the losses of John Walker Jr. and Ronald Pelton, the NSA asset cultivated by Gennady.

CIA director Casey had been correct when he speculated about a turncoat, except that he had seriously underestimated: there was more than one. Cowboy Jack would soon learn that one of the worst was among his own Zephyr IOC graduates. In late August 1985, during a regular visit to see Musketeer Dion and Lane Crocker at Buzzard Point, Jack got the sobering news that a couple he had put through the pipeline gauntlet was suspected in the exposure of one of the CIA's best Soviet assets. Jack was crestfallen. He not only had prepared them for a Moscow Station posting but had developed a special father-daughter bond with the woman under suspicion. The couple in question was Edward Lee and Mary Howard. "Ed was always a problem, but I would have been stunned to learn that Mary had done such a thing," Jack said.

The Howards had both joined the Agency in 1981, after meeting in the Peace Corps years earlier and marrying in 1976. Edward had a love of James Bond movies; however, like Bond, he had a fondness for alcohol and, unlike Bond, a recreational interest in pot, hashish, cocaine, LSD, and Quaaludes. In hindsight, most at the CIA say he never should have been recruited in the first place. But incredibly, both Edward and Mary Howard were not only hired but also assigned to the elite SE Division, where they were groomed to relocate under deep cover to the most demanding station: Moscow. Most significantly, Edward was briefed on Adolf Tolkachev, a Soviet engineer who for the last five years had been a valuable CIA source of Soviet fighter jet radar defense systems intel—for a CIA fee of $200,000 per year placed in an escrow account for him. When Howard landed in Moscow, he would likely become Tolkachev's case officer.

After completing Jack's training, though, and before the couple was dispatched to Moscow, Howard was fired, in May 1983, after failing four polygraph tests (tests were a once-every-three-years routine for CIA personnel). He was found to be deceptive on questions regarding his drug usage and theft. Five months later, Howard, who had relocated to his New Mexico birthplace, traveled to the Soviet Consulate in DC and gave them a letter of introduction, in which he stated that he was a disgruntled ex-CIA employee. Over the next year and a half, he repeatedly visited Vienna, Austria, where he supposedly had contacts with KGB handlers.

By 1984, then drinking heavily, Howard told a number of former colleagues that he had "been fucked" by the Agency. It got back to HQ that Howard, who was living in El Dorado, near Santa Fe, was not only drinking but admitting to his Soviet Consulate visit—a toxic combination for the CIA, which hadn't yet known about the Vienna trips. Howard possessed too many of the Agency's most closely held secrets about Moscow Station.

But perhaps the greatest loss was the highly classified asset

Edward Lee Howard had been preparing to handle. On June 13, 1985, engineer/asset Tolkachev missed his scheduled meeting with case officer Paul "Skip" Stombaugh. Instead of passing a cache to Tolkachev, Skip was arrested by KGB agents at the drop site and taken to Lubyanka Prison. Tolkachev had been arrested weeks earlier and taken to Lefortovo Prison, to be executed a year later.

This was all playing out at the same time temporary KGB turncoat, Gennady's colleague, Vitaly Yurchenko was cooperating with the CIA. He not only informed them that Ronald Pelton had given up Operation Ivy Bells;* he also had SE Division chief Burton Gerber (a constant thorn in Jack Platt's side, and vice versa) convinced that Jack's pipeliner Edward Lee Howard was working to help the KGB blow up Moscow Station. Yurchenko was persuasive, but the CIA had another problem child. Howard's best friend at the Agency, Bill Bosch—who had been fired one year after Howard for currency fraud and incompetence at the Bolivia Station—was reporting some disturbing information about Howard back to his former employer. The men had stayed in close touch, and at one get-together, Howard had suggested the two buddies, both unfairly dismissed, should get revenge. With a strategy employed twenty years earlier by Lee Harvey Oswald, Howard planned to go to the Soviet Embassy in Mexico City and tell them everything he knew about the Central Intelligence Agency. Bosch said he'd have to think it over. Instead he got word to the SE Division that Howard's drinking was escalating and he was suggesting a joint espionage caper.

In August 1985, now armed with the vital news, Jack warned Lane Crocker and others at the Washington Field Office that Howard had taken the IOC course, so only the FBI's best personnel had a chance of catching him if he made a dash. Local field office agents dispatched from Albuquerque began watching the Howards from a distance,

---

* The FBI rolled up Pelton soon after the Yurchenko disclosure. He was convicted of espionage and sentenced to three concurrent life sentences and a hundred-dollar fine. However, he was released from federal prison in 2015 at age seventy-four.

usually through electronic surveillance aimed at their home. On September 10, the Bureau learned from Howard's psychiatrist that he would likely crack under the pressure of an interrogation. Along with a half dozen other Washington-based agents, Dion Rankin, a seasoned interrogator and polygrapher, packed his bags for the trip to New Mexico.

Two CIA officers were also packing their bags. One was Howard's former supervisor at SE, Tom Mills, whom Howard respected, though in his enraged state after being fired, Howard had screamed at him in Mills's driveway. Mills was designated to convince Howard to cooperate with the Bureau. The other Agency man going west was Cowboy Jack Platt, assigned to use his special rapport with Mary to convince her to do the same. Additionally, since Jack knew both the Howards, his expertise might prove critical in predicting their response. Plus, for Jack it was a chance to be in a place where his personal dress code was both appropriate and accepted.

Dion studied the Howard case file and spent many hours preparing his polygraph questions for Bosch and the Howards before meeting Jack at Dulles Airport. "Jack and I flew down to Albuquerque together," says Dion. "The plan was for me to polygraph Edward, then fly down to South Padre Island, Texas, to do Bosch. Jack would stay with the team in Santa Fe and babysit Mary." On September 19, 1985, two agents called Howard and asked him to come to the Hilton Hotel in Santa Fe so they could talk. Meeting him in the lobby, the FBI men took him up to room 327, which shared a wall with room 329, where Dion and Jack waited silently with another agent for the signal to come next door to conduct the polygraph.

Ears to the wall, Jack and Dion heard the discussion quickly escalate, as Howard began screaming at his inquisitors, refusing to be polygraphed. Clearly his drinking and bitterness over his dismissal—or perhaps the prospect of being caught spying—had him on the edge. "Howard got so aggressive that the other agent in *our* room pulled out his gun," remembers Dion. "He had it inadvertently aimed at my stomach. Jack and I made him holster it before one of us got shot accidentally. We laughed about that for years." Jack and Dion stayed in their room until it was clear that Howard had left the scene.

Later that day, Howard actually bumped into a member of the FBI's surveillance team in a Santa Fe supermarket. He was now calm, telling the agent that he was willing to discuss another meeting. The startled agent advised Howard that his hotel interrogators were waiting for him back at the Hilton. In a brief preliminary encounter at the hotel, Howard said he'd take the polygraph on Monday (four days later), but he would be lawyering up over the weekend. The agents breathed a sigh of relief, believing they had just scored a breakthrough.

That night, Dion took a three-hour flight to Texas with local FBI agent Bill Koopman to polygraph Bill Bosch, while Jack stayed behind in Santa Fe, continuing to observe Howard and advise the Bureau. On Saturday, Dion and Koopman spent eight hours questioning, and ultimately polygraphing, Bosch at the Bahia Mar Resort on South Padre Island. "We told him about how one of our assets, whom Howard had handled in Moscow, had just been executed in that same city," Dion remembers. "He admitted everything. He told us about how Howard admitted to accepting money from the KGB in Europe and about how Howard wanted Bosch to join him in the espionage." Toward the end of the long day, Bosch began to fall apart under the strain. "He began hyperventilating, became almost hysterical," says Dion. "But we had already poly'd him, and he passed easily." Dion relayed the news to Lane Crocker at the Washington Field Office, and Crocker set the arrest for Monday—two days were needed to acquire the warrant. But that would prove two days too late, as Howard was already on the run.

That very Saturday night, the Howards enlisted their regular babysitter to watch their two-year-old son, Lee, while the couple went out to dinner. That was a cover story. In truth, the pair had spent the previous night rehearsing every evasion trick they had learned from Jack. After Edward Howard kissed his son goodbye, possibly forever, he and Mary drove away, and by sheer happenstance, their Bureau minders were looking the other way.

Wrongly assuming that the G-men were on their tail, and with Mary at the wheel, the husband and wife spies left their home at 4:30 and proceeded to have that last dinner. From there a tearful Mary drove her husband to a drop-off point they had scouted earlier in the day. The drive from the restaurant was a master class in the evasion techniques Jack had taught them in their time as Zephyrs: creating a "gap" in surveillance with hours of driving, the jack-in-a-box (JIB), and the moving car delivery (MCD) in order to lose the Bureau's best surveillance team. Of course, no one was actually following them, so it was doubly embarrassing for Edward when he jumped from the moving car and almost broke his arm. Mary deployed the JIB and returned home. US authorities never laid eyes on Edward Lee Howard again.

Still reeling from the knowledge that one of his trainees had betrayed his country, causing the execution of a good man and a priceless asset in Moscow (Piguzov), in addition to Tolkachev, Jack spent the next few days with Dion, hoping to learn that the woman Jack had bonded with and believed in was not also a traitor. While Jack called Mary and asked her to meet him at the High Mesa Inn, Dion prepared his questions for the polygraph session. Mary, who arrived with her mother, didn't agree to a polygraph right away, but eventually, with Jack and a female FBI agent flown in from Los Angeles reassuring her, she relented. Additionally, she likely knew that if she failed to cooperate, Lee might be left with no parents at all. "Once she had relaxed, Mary told me everything," Dion says, adding that she passed the polygraph test easily.

After Mary opened up, she became a dream witness, giving up

details that Jack, Dion, and the rest could never have anticipated. One evening, she mentioned that Edward possessed a Swiss bank account and had made a large deposit ($150,000, the Bureau would later learn from Swiss sources). Did she have the account number? No. Anything else? Yes. Mary said she was with him when he buried an emergency stash in the New Mexico desert, and it should still be there. She could take them there sometime if they'd like. The agents responded in unison: *"We're going now."*

Dion remembers driving at around eleven at night in the pitch-blackness of a moonless desert night across a small stream with Mary pointing the way to a particular tree. One team member had brought a small shovel, and Dion held a flashlight. According to author David Wise, who interviewed Mary for his book *The Spy Who Got Away*, Mary was sobbing as the agent broke ground. He dug for only a few minutes when he hit upon a green military ammo box, crammed full of silver bars, US currency in varied denominations, Canadian coins, and two gold Krugerrands, all totaling about $10,000. Dion remembered that it also held an envelope containing a deposit slip bearing the number of the Swiss bank account.

Before jetting back to Washington, Jack and Dion experienced another mini drama with Mary. In one of their last conversations, she disclosed that her husband had told her she would hear from him at a specific time, at a specific place, a few days after his MCD jump. Neither Jack nor Dion recall the exact day, but the place was a telephone booth in a park near her home where the couple often played with little Lee. When the phone rang precisely on time, Dion squeezed into the booth with Mary and put his ear up to the receiver. Dion can't say for certain, but he thinks Jack had his ear up against the glass booth.

"He's with us" was all that was spoken from the other end, in a distinctive Russian accent. In fact, Edward Howard wasn't in Russia yet. He was just beginning a nine-month, nine-country odyssey, looking for a place to land. The route, according to Howard, went like this: Tucson, New York, Copenhagen, Frankfurt, Munich, Helsinki, Latin America for six months under an assumed name, Vienna, Budapest, and finally Moscow in June 1986.

Jack and Dion returned to New Mexico in late October 1985 to make certain they had obtained everything Mary could offer. Once again she was polygraphed, and once again she passed. Soon came the question of whether to charge Mary as an accomplice. Jack had long ago concluded that Mary was a good person trapped in a bad place with an alcoholic. Knowing a thing or two about alcoholics himself, Jack lobbied forcefully on Mary's behalf. "She was the codependent of an alcoholic and she got caught up in his craziness," Jack remembered. "She was a victim. We had to let her go. Plus she had a child to raise." Jack added that Edward Lee Howard had been a handful, given the reports he received about his attitude and performance both at The Farm and in the SE Division. Mary was never charged.

In 1983, Howard had been psychologically destroyed by his failure to ever make it to Moscow for the CIA, especially after two years of rigorous preparation. When he finally got there in 1986, it was courtesy of the KGB. In exile, the man Jack had trained coincidentally spent a good deal of his leisure time playing volleyball at Gennady's former home, the KGB's Dynamo Sports complex. After a few visits to Edward in Moscow, Mary eventually divorced him in 1996. Jack continued to stay in touch with her for years to come. Howard died at age fifty on July 12, 2002, breaking his neck in what some consider a mysterious fall. Dion Rankin, remembering what Jack had told him about Howard being a handful, is among the suspicious: "I think he was pushed," having outlived his usefulness.

Until the end of his life, and in his memoir *Safe House*, Howard proclaimed his innocence, asserting that he was outed by Yurchenko in order to waste precious FBI and CIA resources so that a real double agent—or double agents—would go undetected. To which Jack said, "Bullshit. The fucking quisling sold out the entire Moscow

Station for $150,000. He gave up everyone's true identity, including the asset [Vladimir Piguzov, or JOGGER] who gave me the initial background dossier on Gennady." Jack's anger was aggravated by his strong hunch that there was another US double agent out there.

Soon after Howard vanished in 1985, Jack pranced into Burton Gerber's office to deliver one terse sentence about Howard before turning on his boot heel: "I told you I knew how to fucking train people."

— 7 —

SOFTLY, SOFTLY, CATCHEE MONKEY

What are you guys doing to my friends?

August 2005, Solntzevo, Russia

His captors were moving him around from cell to cell, without warning, forcing him to adapt to different environments on a dime. The objective was disorientation: to make him feel a glimmer of hope that the next room would be better, the next inquisitor would be kinder. The dashed expectations, in theory, would leave him so lost that he would do—or say—anything to achieve a return to normalcy.*

For now, Gennady was groggy, tired enough to crave sleep, but anxious enough to know his sleep would be sabotaged by a boot, a slap, or, at this moment, a cold bucket of dirty water thrown at his face. He spit out the water and coughed to catch his breath.

"Terrorists don't sleep well in Russia," the gray-faced FSB man lectured Gennady. He removed his thick-soled boot and whipped it around by its fraying laces, moving it closer and closer to Gennady's face.

---

* This was a mild prelude to what Gennady would face in the years ahead, when the FSB would move him from prison to prison, forcing him to constantly renegotiate sleeping arrangements with a fresh host of thugs. The choices weren't pretty: thin, coarse, puke-stained mattresses versus urine-puddled concrete floors.

"You know that I am not a terrorist!"

"You had the bomb residue on your fingers," the interrogator shouted, the air from the rotating boot feeling cold against Gennady's wet cheeks.

"You put it there!"

"Listen to the conspiracies from the terrorist!" the interrogator said, now lowering his boot onto a steel table. "We'll start out nice, shall we? How did you convince your friends at the rezidentura *in Washington to join the Americans?"*

Gennady had no idea what the man was talking about. "Who joined the Americans?"

"You know, comrade. You worked together."

"I worked with hundreds of people," Gennady said.

"I'm not talking about hundreds. I'm talking about two in particular."

"I don't know who you—"

Before Gennady could finish his sentence, he felt the boot hit the bridge of his nose, blood now dripping on his upper lip. Two in particular? What were they talking about? Did they mean Jack and Dion? Nothing made sense except the pain. The pain was perfectly clear.

December 1986

For all his gruff demeanor and gun-slinging antics, Cowboy had a deliberate, strategic side. "Softly, softly, catchee monkey" Cowboy liked to say to explain his modus operandi. He knew he would never turn Gennady with a sledgehammer and had been frustrated that Gerber, whose intellect he admired, didn't seem to appreciate that his romancing of the Russian was part of a gradual campaign. So when Cowboy decided he wanted to travel once more to Guyana and learned that Gerber would be out of the office late in the year, he schemed to approach his substitute SE chief, Milt Bearden, and angle for permission.

Cowboy entered Bearden's office—decked out in his best rodeo attire Bearden recalls—demanding a quick sign-off on both a trip to Guyana and the purchase of a special rifle.

"You're going to have to tell me who you're going to kill before I sign off."

"It's for Gennady Vasilenko," Cowboy informed him.

The two sparred for twenty minutes over the advisability of such a request. Like Gerber and Redmond before him, Bearden knew that Cowboy had met with Gennady dozens of times without a hint of success. "Why try again?" Bearden asked. "Is this thing going anywhere? Or are you and Rankin just jerking each other off?"

Yet Bearden finally relented and signed off on the foray. Gerber says that when he found out what Jack had done, he wasn't upset; he just laughed at Jack's cheekiness.

Before leaving, Cowboy and Dion went to a local custom T-shirt shop and had gifts made for Gennady, the embassy staff, and their friends at the Pegasus. The shirts bore a map of Guyana and Gennady's favorite new expression: GUYANA: IT'S NOT THE END OF THE EARTH, BUT YOU CAN SEE IT FROM HERE. Gennady hated it there so much, Dion explains, that he retains the shirt to this day.

After their arrival in Georgetown, Dion and Cowboy kidnapped the third Musketeer, taking him to the Pegasus, where they were anxious to make a presentation.

"Happy birthday, Commie." Cowboy laughed as he handed Gennady the long, thin package.

"It's my cowboy gun!" Gennady rejoiced on receiving his prize, kissing the stock of the deer-hunting rifle. The lever-action Marlin 336 chambered in .30-30 was—and remains—among the quintessential American hunting rifles, the kind audiences routinely see in movies made during Hollywood's golden age of Westerns. But in the suspicious eyes of the KGB, it would prove to be a potent symbol of Gennady's betrayal of the Motherland.

Cowboy had gone down to Guyana with the Marlin packaged neatly in a felt-lined case along with fifty rounds of ammunition. He had arranged to procure it through McKim Symington, who knew more about firearms than anyone else Cowboy was acquainted with. A colleague of Symington's had put the weapon up for sale at roughly the same time Cowboy was in the market for one for Gennady.

"I have a confession," Cowboy said to Gennady. "My name isn't Chris."

"Let me guess. Jack Platt?" Gennady responded with a sly grin.

"You knew?"

"Only since the second time I saw you."

"You son of a bitch. How—?"

"Please, Chris. Show some respect for the KGB. Your little students aren't the only ones who know how to follow people. In fact, I think my people perfected it. Besides, I like the name 'Chris.' But who the fuck cares what your name is?"

"Who the fuck, indeed."

Spring 1987

Cowboy, now fifty-two and having revamped the Agency's field training operation, decided he'd had enough of working for the government. For years he had felt disillusioned with the Agency's bureaucracy and its ceaseless loss of assets. "He just didn't belong in meetings," Paige recalls. He had also felt betrayed years earlier by President Jimmy Carter and CIA Director Stansfield Turner when they fired more than six hundred Agency employees in October 1977—the "Halloween Massacre." It was getting very hard for a spy to, well, spy. As far as he was concerned, the Clandestine Service was dead. Years later, Cowboy would express bitterness over the way his legacy IOC training was treated in his absence. "The FBI still uses the course, but the CIA shut it down in 1993," he recalled. "'The Cold War is over,' they had said. I'm glad I got out of that fuckin' place when I did."

Upon his retirement, Cowboy was honored with the Distinguished Career Intelligence Medal at a small ceremony held on the sixth floor of CIA headquarters. But the only government people who actually threw him a retirement party were his friends at the Bureau, chiefly Dion Rankin and Mike Rochford. When asked if it was rare for FBI agents to throw a party for a retiring CIA case officer, Dion just laughs. "Are you kidding? We hardly associated with them. But Cowboy was different. When the Bureau people heard they were throwing a lunchtime party for Jack at the Fish Market Restaurant in Old Town Alexandria, about thirty not only came, but we all pitched in to buy him a gift." Dion knew that Cowboy coveted a Thompson submachine gun, and he located a nice six-hundred-dollar replica at Arlington Arms, which Rochford picked up and to which they affixed a plaque with Jack's name and the epigram OUTSPOKEN, OUTLANDISH—OUTSTANDING. "Roch" remembers, "It was a rare thing for us to buy a gun for an FBI retiree, let alone a CIA. But when they heard it was for Cowboy, all the Squad members pitched in." One of Jack's IOC trainees, Mike Sulick, who was to become Deputy Director of Operations at the CIA, summarizes the feelings of many: "The key thing about Jack's career was that Jack was among the first to recognize the value of cooperation with the FBI."

FBI director William H. Webster, who was in the midst of transitioning to CIA Director, sent a letter of congratulations to Jack. It read, in part:

> *I want to take this occasion to thank you for your many contributions over the years to a number of significant achievements which involved joint operations between the FBI and the CIA. In*

addition to the vital assistance you have provided in the training
of FBI personnel, your zeal and professionalism have also greatly
strengthened the long-standing working relationship between our two
agencies.

With a reference to his upcoming post at CIA and to Jack's legendary scrapes with authority, Webster handwrote a cheeky postscript: "Please leave the Agency on time. I will not come aboard as Director until you have gone. [Signed] WHW."

Soon after retirement, Jack created a training and security consulting firm, Hamilton Trading Group (HTG), based just a mile from the CIA's McLean headquarters. In this new venture, he partnered with veteran CIA officer Ben Wickham, who explains, "Jack had the idea for a security company. We named it after Alexander Hamilton because he was good with numbers but a bad shot." Everything with Jack was tinged with mischief.

Wickham and Jack hadn't known each other when both were actively working for the CIA. They had met the same year they started the company, introduced by a mutual colleague, and were drawn to each other's complementary skills. Successful local real estate agent Roy Jacobsen helped provide capitalization, and retired FBI agent Bob Olds also joined the founding team. Jacobsen took the lead on pitch meetings, the wise and stolid Wickham concentrated on the business details, and Jack exercised his street skills to serve clients. This was a prudent division of labor because Jack's business graces were obviously not his strong suit. "Our first receptionist only lasted one day around Jack and his coarse language," Wickham says, adding that Hamilton once lost an account because Jack's repeated invocation of the f-bomb to describe the firm's offerings ("We offer the best fucking tradecraft") offended female executives. It didn't help that Cowboy's leave-behind business card read: "You can count on us. We don't fuck around."

HTG contractor and former FBI man Harry Gossett, who had known Jack since 1980 in the Washington Field Office, was there when the company lost a big State Department job thanks to Jack. "A young State Depart-

TRUST   EXPERIENCE

HTG Hamilton Trading Group, Inc.

You can count on us,
We don't fuck around

Jack Platt
Vice President
6724 Old McLean Village Drive
Suite 200
McLean, Virginia 22101
(703) 821-3535

DEPENDABLE   CONFIDENTIAL

ment clerk came by to deliver the news that Jack had offended someone by using 'the *f* word,'" Gossett recalls.

"What *f* word was that?" Jack asked the timid messenger.

"You know…"

"Oh, you mean 'foreign'?" Jack asked, toying with him.

"No, sir."

"Was it 'federal'?"

No response.

"Well, what the fuck was it?" Jack bellowed, cracking up everyone but the clerk.

"We did it for the fun of it," remembers Jacobsen. "It has never been about money for any of us. We're all crazy that way." Jacobsen's contacts provided the first income. "Ben didn't like pitch meetings, and Jack…forget it."

"Jack just didn't care about money," Paige remembers, "and he hardly took anything out of Hamilton." He just liked keeping busy and working with people he liked and on projects that he found challenging. Jack would often come home and tell Paige, "You know, I really love my boss," referring to himself. Paige would roll her eyes.

HTG exploited Jack's strong relationships with the FBI to get contracts, which included training the aforementioned State Department's Regional Security Office and FBI agents in surveillance detection on the streets of the Bureau's "Hogan's Alley" city replica in Quantico, Virginia. Jack also tapped Williams College classmate and ex-FBI man Dave Cook, who now headed security for the International Monetary Fund, to help land a lucrative contract. HTG secured training contracts with the FBI's Academy Counterintelligence Investigations Corps (CIIOPS) as well as the DoD's Joint Counterintelligence Training Academy (JCITA). For this contract alone, Jack traveled to eighteen cities to train agents of the Bureau's Special Surveillance Group (SSG) and Special Operations Group (SOG).*

CIA losses continued to mount, including assets Boris Yuzhin, Colonel Leonid Polishchuk, and Vladimir Potashiv. Jack remained convinced that turncoats were still out there, and if there was one thing he hated, it was traitors to the United States, the "precious experiment," as his father had always called it. The country's survival was a subject that could bring Jack to tears, both because of his fear for the nation's well-being and because it brought back memories of his discussions with his beloved old man. He was determined to hunt the traitor down and punish him ("Gimme five minutes alone with the bastard") and believed that the answer to the puzzle would ultimately lie with Gennady's contacts.

On Halloween in 1987, it was back to Guyana again for now private citizen Cowboy Jack and recently (albeit temporarily) retired Dion. The Bureau hadn't given up on Gennady, and neither had his friend Cowboy, who always believed that Gennady would one day live in the United States, whether as a Soviet defector/asset or just as a private citizen. Thus Cowboy worked out a contract arrangement with the Agency so that he could play out Operation Dovka as long as

---

* The difference between the two surveillance groups is that SOG agents are armed and have law enforcement authority. They are assigned surveillance of targets who are considered armed and dangerous.

possible. The Three Musketeers had continued to meet in Guyana approximately twice a year since 1985, and it was always the same routine: target shooting on the seawall and closing the bars every night (Cowboy sipping near beers, of course).

"Each meeting got us a little more into the case," remembers Dion, who at that time was working just this case for the Bureau, also as a contract operative. "Gennady told us he had handled Pelton and how he had snuck him out the back entrance of the Soviet Embassy in coveralls after shaving his beard. He told us innocuous things that we already knew, like who else the KGB had been targeting in Washington. He also gave me a Makarov .380 on one trip. I asked him if he stole it from a Soviet cache that he routinely transshipped to Cuba."

"Of course," he laughed. "Fuck 'em."

There was something halting in Gennady's laugh, however, but Cowboy had learned not to press him on every little errant expression. Indeed, belying Gennady's pleasure at the reunion with Cowboy and Dion was a bleak reality he couldn't shake, but he had to find the right moment to bring it up. One day at the seawall, Cowboy noticed Gennady brooding uncharacteristically and shrugged at him, as if to say, "What's wrong?"

Gennady set down his Marlin rifle. "What are you guys doing to my friends?" His voiced choked.

"What friends?" Cowboy asked. He suddenly felt defensive and his mind raced over whom the uncharacteristically confrontational Gennady may be referring to.

"Motorin and Martynov were killed!"

Cowboy and Dion looked at each other, genuinely shocked at the news. They were aware that Gennady must have known his two Washington *rezidentura* KGB mates (especially Motorin) but hadn't been aware of how close they had been. At the same time, the Americans knew that Gennady had no idea his pals had been working for the FBI. And they weren't about to tell him. Despite the way he had phrased the question to Cowboy and Dion, Gennady hadn't assumed the CIA had literally murdered his friends—both US and Soviet intelligence weren't exactly known for killing their "main enemy" espionage adversaries—but there was a traitor deep inside whom the Americans had better deal with, and fast.

"Believe me," Cowboy replied to Gennady, "this is the first I've heard of it. But I'll find out." He wasn't kidding.

No one in the US intelligence community had known about the two KGB officers' fates before Gennady confronted Cowboy and Dion in Guyana. Gennady's emotional outburst about Martynov and Motorin was precisely the kind of information Cowboy had hoped to glean through his sustained, deliberate contact with Gennady, even if it fell short of turning his Russian friend. *Softly, softly, catchee monkey.*

But who on the American side had turned? The traitor, whoever he was, had tipped his KGB handlers that Martynov and Motorin were owned and controlled by US intelligence. In response to this valuable report, the KGB decided to bring the traitors back home for a little visit. But they needed to deploy a ruse in order to get them there with their guards down—while keeping the Americans in the dark.

Gennady's former DC *rezidentura* colleague, Valery Martynov, had done quite well for himself since the day Gennady had taken him and fellow new guy Sergei Motorin out for their welcome brunch at Martin's Tavern. Martynov, whose photo reveals a serious-looking, dark-haired man in his thirties with a full lower lip, had been assigned to "scientific espionage"—primarily trying to ferret out weapons technology secrets, including nuclear arms.

At one science conference, Martynov met a member of the CI-4 Squad, who in a very short time convinced him to spy for the Americans for the paltry fee of four hundred dollars per month. For the next three years, he met with FBI men approximately twice a month at a safe house in Virginia. Years later, his former boss Cherkashin concluded that Martynov turned traitor for two reasons: to provide for his family and to experience the James Bond excitement of it all.

Things seemed to be going well when Martynov received a particularly interesting assignment: he was to accompany re-defecting KGB agent Vitaly Yurchenko back to Moscow. Yurchenko had famously defected to the West in Rome in August 1985, giving up Edward Lee Howard. Then, after three months of debriefing in Washington, he re-defected back to the USSR after his mistress, the wife of a Soviet diplomat based in Toronto, broke up with him.

The day before Yurchenko boarded the plane, his Toronto mistress jumped twenty-seven stories to her death. Svetlana Dedkova was depressed due to not being able to see her fifteen-year-old son back in Moscow, part of the USSR's policy of holding the children of spies hostage by preventing their parents from having any contact with them. This was considered the second most dissuasive threat to would-be traitors after execution and imprisonment. Gennady had paid close attention to these developments.

Valery understood his role to be a member of an "honor guard" that would return Yurchenko to Mother Russia. It was a KGB trick. The honor guard swindle was the only way the KGB felt they could fool Martynov into returning to the USSR. Shortly after the Aeroflot jet landed at Moscow's Sheremetyevo Airport, KGB officers jumped Martynov as he got off the plane. A rare photo of the incident—surely released by the KGB to send a message

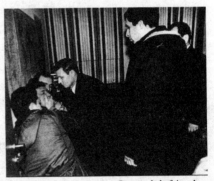

KGB enforcers arrest Gennady's friend, Valery Martynov, May 28, 1987.

to aspiring traitors—shows Martynov being braced against a wall by five hulking security men. One of them has his hand cupped over Martynov's mouth in a gesture that served as a morbid coda to the US asset's adventures in espionage. Martynov's eyes gaze upward, oddly passive, as if he had known this moment was coming.

Like Martynov, Sergei Motorin had been greatly enjoying life in the United States. Gennady describes him enthusiastically as a friend he had known better than Martynov. Tall, athletic, and sandy haired with a wispy blond moustache, Motorin betrayed the slightest hint of a Californian. In 1980, Motorin stopped into an electronics store in the affluent DC suburb of Chevy Chase, Maryland. His eyes fell upon a high-end piece of combination television and stereo equipment. His cash on hand fell short of the retail price, nearly $1,000—a significant sum. The retailer presented Motorin with an offer: he could make up for the shortfall with a case of Russian vodka. When Motorin brought the vodka, he could take the stereo.

There were two problems with this arrangement. The first was that the KGB expressly forbade Soviet officials from selling Russian goods to Americans because they were to be used exclusively for compromising traitors—and for fear it might compromise *them*. (It turned out the latter was a good assumption.) The second problem was that the FBI had filmed the whole transaction, and they vowed to send pictures of their thus far fruitless meetings to Victor Cherkashin, the *rezidentura*'s new counterintelligence chief, to which Motorin responded, "Fuck off." A real Americanized wise guy, like his friend Gennady, who had probably seen too many Hollywood flicks.

The FBI kept working on Motorin, "bumping into" him at least eight more times over a period of months, all the while being photographed by the Bureau's surveillance team. It wasn't that Motorin's sins were unforgivable in and of themselves; it was that he didn't want to go back to the Soviet Union, which is exactly what would have happened if his bosses saw the photos. They would surely conclude that nine meetings couldn't be a coincidence. One fellow KGB agent states, "He lived in mortal fear of being recalled... He preferred a well-fed America to a Soviet Union on a permanent diet."

What Motorin failed to do next ultimately sealed his fate. KGB rules dictated that any approach by a foreign operative must be reported. But Motorin knew what that meant: a busted covert agent was immediately shipped back to Moscow. It was a sentence Motorin couldn't accept. Soon he was studying the central map in the *rezidentura*, the very one that Gennady had briefed him on years before, and memorizing the day's dead drops, with code names. Then Motorin reported the details to his FBI contact, roughly seventy-five times over the years. This allowed the Bureau to go directly to KGB meetings at the exact time, thereby avoiding the expense of trailing operatives for hours while they ran their surveillance-eluding routes. In his five years as a spy, Motorin essentially gave up the Soviet's whole Washington, DC, operation for some high-end American electronics.

Whereas Martynov was taken down in the elaborate "honor guard" charade, Motorin just disappeared. Stories vary on precisely how he was rolled up, but one report indicates he was arrested in the winter of 1986 on his way to meet a CIA contact. He was taken to the dreaded Lefortovo Prison in Moscow.

On occasion, firing squads did the dirty work in the prison's courtyard. (Wild rumors ran rampant about the prison's massive meat grinder, which, like in a scene from the musical *Sweeney Todd*, mashed the bodies of the tortured before disposing of them in Moscow sewers. The specter of such a fate was the historic backdrop against which Gennady—and all other KGB agents—perpetually worked.) Martynov and Motorin were tortured at Lefortovo for a damage control assessment of their betrayals. The men stuck to their much-rehearsed stories to no avail. Soon they were introduced to the Lefortovo "method." Gennady later said, "Lefortovo was called the 'Killing Prison'; traitors were led down a dark basement corridor. Gunmen hid in niches; they would emerge behind them in the dark and shoot them in the back of the head. The prisoner is not even told he is going to be killed."

Both Motorin and Martynov had been in their early forties in 1987 when they were executed, leaving young wives and children behind. It had taken the Americans decades to cultivate assets as helpful as they had been. Yet after a few short years, they were gone. The midpoint of this lethal time period, 1985, was known in the intelligence community as the "Year of the Spy."

In Guyana that October 1987, all cards were now on the table, with Cowboy and Dion doubling down on their plea to have Gennady stay in the West. The definition of their friendship agreed to during their "dealmaker" trip to San Diego was now forgotten, as this plea came with a desperate warning, especially given what had happened to Gennady's two *rezidentura* colleagues. Cowboy told him that Vitaly Yurchenko might have also placed him in jeopardy with the KGB.

"Gennady, we asked him repeatedly about you, whether you might defect," Cowboy told his friend. Cowboy and Dion didn't tell Gennady that Yurchenko had blown Gennady's biggest success, Ronald Pelton.

But Gennady would have none of it. "I have always been a patriot, and everyone at the Center [KGB headquarters] knows it," he said. "And how would you propose to get my family over here? Now come watch my volleyball championship game."

At the time, he was playing volleyball for the Guyana national team. Cowboy and Dion sat with bank teller Sherry, directly across the court from the bleachers that held the KGB contingent. The Soviet *rezident*, Gennady's good friend Boris Kotov, pointed out

Cowboy and Dion to Gennady, saying, "Look at that. They look like two Americans. What are they doing here? Gennady, try to find out about them."

"Right after the game, sir," came Gennady's reply.

That evening back at the Pegasus, Cowboy and Dion filed their report about their day with Gennady. They noted the revelations about Motorin's and Martynov's executions, how Gennady had handled Pelton's escape, and even Gennady's strong "friendship" with Sherry. They added that they had made one more pitch to the Russian, citing that Yurchenko might have compromised him. After delivering the memo to the CIA station in Georgetown, the duo packed their bags for the trip home. The day before, Dion had gifted Gennady with a souvenir: a dark blue jacket with FBI ACADEMY on

the front. They had all laughed as the Russian modeled it.

This vignette would not be amusing for long. Six thousand miles away in Mother Russia, Gennady's KGB bosses would soon deliver other "gifts" to him; Dion and Cowboy's report—this seemingly harmless piece of paper—had inadvertently set Gennady's terrible fate in motion.

The two Musketeers had made vague plans to return to visit Gennady again in early 1988 to celebrate Cowboy's birthday in February. As that time drew closer, FBI deputy Chief of Station Bob Wade called Cowboy to say that an Agency source reported that

Gennady had disappeared. "Don't bother going. Your friend Gennady has fallen off the face of the earth," Wade informed a crestfallen Cowboy.

"We had lost so many people by 1988 that I had a fear of what had happened to Genya," Cowboy said. "I was really upset. I was more than concerned. But there was nothing I could do."

— 8 —

HAVANA TAKEDOWN

*I should have listened when they told me to
stay away from the son of a bitch.*

In January 1988, Gennady was summoned from Georgetown, Guyana, to Havana for a routine meeting with a KGB colleague visiting Cuba. One of Gennady's assignments was to type up a report documenting his observations about significant political events taking place in South America, of which there were few worth recording. It was the equivalent of cobbling together a grade school book report about a boring piece of literature. While Guyana's climate was appealing, Gennady had been growing bored with the monotony and could no longer delude himself with notions of the country's strategic importance. There had been no more Jonestowns or flashy proxy showdowns between the Americans and the Soviets. After all, a place can be strategically important but tactically boring as hell. Besides, how much more of a suntan could a kid from Siberia get?

Still, Gennady was looking forward to the Cuba trip. He had been there before for the *rezidentura* and knew a thing or two about Cuban women, Havana nights. The legends of the decadent 1950s had outlived the demise of the American Mafia's casinos, and as far as he was concerned, female beauty could flourish just as easily under dictator Fidel Castro as it could mobster Meyer Lansky. The report for the file would be the price he paid to experience la dolce vita. Gennady had become an old hand at grinding out some garbage memo and pretending it was of global historical significance. And the great bureaucracy that was the KGB knew it was all nonsense, too.

At the Havana airport on January 11, 1988, Gennady met a KGB officer—not the agent who usually picked him up when he delivered diplomatic pouches—who explained they had found a private place for Gennady to stay during his visit. The two went straight from the airport to a nondescript house. Tired from the trip, he entered the little house and followed his KGB greeter out to a terrace. Suddenly, the world went black and he was falling. Several comrades had attacked him from behind. He fell forward, unable to block the fall with both arms because they had pinned one behind him. The fall gave him a concussion and broke his arm. Gennady still has the scar on his forehead—more of an indentation where his hairline used to be—from being smashed to the floor.

The KGB goons dragged him into another room and threw him onto a chair. The lead interrogator began with two words: "Chris Llorenz."

"What about him?" Gennady asked.

"You tell us."

"There is nothing to tell."

Gennady felt the sting of a slap to his cheek. "What have you told Llorenz?"

"I've told him to aim a little lower when he shoots his Smith and Wesson," Gennady said. "That way he can hit the tin cans better. He always aims too high when he shoots."

Another crack across his face. "You think this is a joke?" his interrogator shouted.

"I think *you* are a joke!" Gennady shouted back. "I told my superiors every time I met with Chris! Is that what a clever traitor does?"

The chair Gennady was seated on was kicked over onto the floor, inflaming his concussion. He felt as if his skull had been shattered into a hundred pieces and fragments were swirling around his brain.

His statement wasn't entirely true. Yes, Gennady had dutifully informed his superiors about *most* of his meetings with Jack, but he found any implication that he had been a traitor so preposterous that he hadn't bothered to tell them about every contact he had had with the rough-and-tumble American. It wasn't as if the meetings had even been clandestine: *they had been shooting high-powered rifles on public seawalls!*

"Maybe that's your traitor's cover."

"When I told my boss I would see Chris and my boss said no, sometimes I said, 'Fuck you.' That's my traitor's cover."

The thugs kicked him as he lay curled up in a ball on the ground.

"What about Dion Rankin?" the lead interrogator asked.

"What about him?" Gennady answered.

"Did you meet with him?"

"Yes, of course I did. And I told my bosses I did. *That was my job!*"

"But you admit you saw Llorenz and Rankin after you were told not to?"

"Damned right!"

"Don't be clever! Did you know his real name? Jack Platt? Did you expect that we wouldn't figure that out?"

"I knew Chris wasn't his real name, but I never talked about it. Tell me something," Gennady said. "How exactly do you think I could recruit a man if I never meet with him?"

This stopped the beatings. For a bit.

The questioning and physical abuse went on for days, and almost every query came back to one thing: his friendship with "Chris"— Jack—the man he had been tasked with recruiting as a spy. Not only had Gennady failed to "turn" Chris; the KGB believed they now had evidence that Chris had turned him. The KGB, however, never got anything new from Gennady because, as he recalls it, "[t]here was nothing to tell."

But Gennady also knew that a lack of evidence was far from a guarantee of his survival. "I knew the KGB's history of executions," he says. "I believed I was dead. Even if they knew the arrest was a mistake, they'd shoot me to cover up the mistake. So I thought, *Why not jump off the deck and just kill myself?* Then I thought about my wife and kids."

Gennady knew it was hopeless when they didn't even bother chaining him inside the dark compartment they transferred him to, below deck on an old KGB freighter that left Havana hours later. They had already worked him over and they would do so again. It occurred to Gennady that enduring another beating might perversely be the only thing that would convince his comrades he had been telling the truth about his allegiance to Mother Russia.

Gennady's KGB comrades let him wander alone around the rusty deck at night, hundreds of miles from anywhere. Yet, this brief illusion of freedom was worse. Had they tortured him below deck there was always the chance they would figure out that he was innocent and set him free. *No*, Gennady thought, *my comrades have made up their minds. They think I belong to the Americans.* They used to tease the handsome and fun-loving Russian that he carried himself more like a California jock than a dour KGB spook. He was, after all, a professional sportsman.

There was another reason why the KGB failed to get anything more out of Gennady during those harrowing days and nights at sea: every night, seated with his hands tied behind him, Gennady was punched in his ears with the fists of his captors. As time wore on, he literally could not hear what he was being asked. His partial deafness is a disability that lingers to this day.

Gennady ran the facts through his throbbing head as he held the railing of the freighter, once again contemplating an easy hop overboard into the darkness. Which would be better: the cold black sea or Lefortovo Prison's "method"? Gennady envisioned his future in that high-security hellhole, the interrogation center of the KGB. The "Killing Prison." How long did he have before he took that final walk? Would he even know the KGB assassin who would descend

bat-like from the darkness and put a bullet in the base of his skull?
He figured if he hopped overboard he would drown in the frigid
water within an hour. A bullet to the brain in Lefortovo would kill
him in a split second, but he could be there—and be tortured—for
years. No easy answers, only terrible options.

KGB agents, suspected of being CIA operatives, had been turning up dead throughout the 1980s; Soviet justice had no place for
traitors in its prisons, only its anonymous cemeteries. Some of them
had been his friends and office mates, like Martynov and Motorin.
The KGB had a traitor burrowed deep inside the US intelligence
infrastructure, a sociopath willing to out his fellows to the Russians
for blood money. The Soviets vowed to do anything to keep the traitor in place, including cracking down on their own spies, who were
getting too cozy with their Western counterparts. In Gennady's
case, he was not only disobeying orders by fraternizing with Platt;
a document recently obtained from an asset appeared also to finger him as another KGB turncoat, a betrayal so severe that trials
were not needed, only elimination. Gennady was innocent, but he
knew that when the bureaucracy panicked and couldn't nail who was
guilty, they nailed whomever they could grab. *My guilt need not be genuine*, Gennady thought. *It need only be plausible.*

As the freighter groaned toward Russia, Gennady suspected from
the clues in his interrogation who had betrayed him: his CIA "friend,"
the Cowboy. Whoever the hell he was—Jack or "Chris"—both he
and Gennady had failed in their recruitment schemes, but then again,
most spy games end in failure. Still, one party always fails worse than
the other, and Cowboy must have played the game just a little less
badly; somehow he had seen a dividend in giving up the Russian.

I should have listened, Gennady thought. *I should have listened when
they told me to stay away from the son of a bitch.* As the freighter pitched
and rolled in the ocean, his head in a fizzy netherworld from his
beatings, Gennady thought of the photo he had taken with Cowboy

on a hunting trip, a photo he had once cherished. *How could I have been so stupid?*

His thoughts returned to jumping overboard. But he didn't jump. Why should he? He was innocent. He had a family he loved. He would survive and reinvent himself, or at least try.

Gennady had indeed fallen off the face of the earth; although, unbeknownst to Cowboy, he was still breathing. "After a while the guys on the ship were friendly," Gennady says. "Once they got to know me, they came to realize that there must be a mistake." Nonetheless, his captors told him he'd have to stay at "Hotel Lefortovo" until the investigation was completed. "But I knew the system," Gennady says. "Eight other KGB guys had just been shot."

It took two weeks for the freighter to make its way across the Atlantic, through the Aegean and Black seas, and finally arrive in Odessa, Ukraine. From there it was more blackness, inside a KGB van traveling northeast for days to Lefortovo.

Upon his arrival, he was taken into an interrogation room where, on a table before him, was the very Marlin lever-action rifle Cowboy had given him in Guyana. "Remember this? Famous American hunting rifle?" a fresh new inquisitor asked. "A nice Russian one wasn't good enough?"

How the hell did they get the Marlin? Gennady wondered. He hadn't brought it to Cuba. They must have raided his place in Guyana.

"Here's another gift from your boyfriend." The goon picked up the gun and smashed its stock into Gennady's chin, knocking him to the ground. Gennady, concussed and nauseous, drifted off into purgatory on the cold Lefortovo floor.

It was the last time he saw the Marlin.

When Gennady awoke, he was in a new cell, one of several he would occupy during his stay at Lefortovo. The first of his cellmates—all of them were strategically placed by the KGB in order to attempt to extract information from Gennady—told him that Soviet intelligence operatives had said his CIA friend had been recording their meetings. Gennady rolled on his fetid mattress with his face turned toward the wall. The last thing he wanted right now was to make a new "friend" after what he thought the last one had done to him. Gennady seethed in the darkness: Had Cowboy Jack really recorded their meetings? If so, what had Gennady said? Had Jack reframed their relationship to his benefit somehow? Bureaucrats did stuff like that, sexed things up in reports to get ahead, keep their jobs. Gennady thought of the puffed-up memo he had recently cobbled together in Guyana to make his posting seem strategically significant. Could that be what Jack had done—written a report that had been misinterpreted by somebody who thought to sell it as something it wasn't?

That's when his interrogators started reading aloud from a document they wouldn't show Gennady. "They knew exactly what I told Jack, word for word," Gennady says. "That's why I came to suspect Jack had lied. Either that or someone in the CIA sold the report to the KGB." Gennady thought Jack may have stabbed him in the back. "I was angry at Jack, but at the same time I didn't want to believe it."

Gennady recoiled at the alternating silence and strange sounds he perceived from his cell, coming from the dreaded Lefortovo catacombs where his friends Martynov and Motorin had been executed not long ago. He was hearing their souls scream. Was this what he was hearing or was the nightmare all in his head? His nerves were fraying.

Weeks went by. New cellmates came and went. Gennady considered that his disobedient attitude and contempt for bureaucracy had finally caught up with him. Did he really have to tell his bosses to "fuck off"? Had it been absolutely necessary for him to go target shooting on a public seawall with a CIA officer and an FBI agent, flashing an American hunting rifle? He could have been seen—and filmed—from every direction by the KGB. Probably was.

As he stared at the gray ceiling in the small hours of one morning, it occurred to him that there was a flaw in human self-perception that had not exempted him. That flaw was believing others saw you as you saw yourself; believing that because you knew you were a patriot, this self-image could be transfused to others. Not only did this quirk of logic fail to account for differences in perception from person to person; it also failed colossally to factor in the role of organization agendas and political crosscurrents. For the first time, he considered the awful possibility that perhaps his captors didn't give a damn whether he was a stalwart Leninist or a snake-in-the-grass capitalist. Maybe they just needed some poor jackass to take the pinch. Maybe he was that jackass.

Once the KGB realized that Gennady's story wasn't changing and that the cavalcade of "good listener" roommates didn't fool him, the beatings decreased, as did Gennady's weight. In the six-by-twelve-foot cell he shared with another prisoner, he began thinking of his family again. The only thing steady in Gennady's mind was a memory of Cowboy specifically stating that he would never record their meetings. Honor was a big thing with Chris/Jack/Cowboy—regardless of what he called himself. He had come clean about being CIA, and when Gennady had told him to back off, he had. When Cowboy came back at him with a proposal to come over to the Americans and Gennady pushed back, Cowboy had held his hands up in surrender. Not once had Cowboy ever tried anything with Gennady besides a front-door pitch topped with a cool toy, like the Marlin or the San Diego gun extravaganza.

But the worst possibility kept entering his mind: Had Cowboy's friendship been a swindle all along? Gennady considered his own possible stupidity: *a KGB officer betting his life on the trustworthiness of his nemesis, the CIA.* He knew that for men like Cowboy, patriotism trumped friendship. And what about Dion? Dion's job, after all, was to unmask KGB men so they'd never return to the United States.

Although these questions tore at him, Gennady was certain of one thing: his comrades couldn't have a damned thing on him—because he hadn't done anything. Regardless, the KGB was under its own searing bureaucratic strain and needed to put Gennady through the wringer because they had to show they were doing everything to stop their own internal hemorrhaging of assets. What was the downside for them? Nothing. When in doubt, they would do something tough and somebody was bound to be impressed with the sheer theater of it all. What did those Wall Street guys call it? Being a "big swinging dick." Gennady would stick to his position that nobody had a recording of anything, because there had been nothing to record.

SASHA

Look at your enemy and give them what they want.

Gennady was in hell, precisely where Baba Yaga wanted him. In the twilight of the Cold War, he had come to think of his tormentor as a ghost, like the Baba Yaga he had been told of as a boy. Baba Yaga was, in Russian lore, a witch—a grotesque one-eyed death goddess of the countryside who could turn small children into stone with one glance and would later thaw them out and eat them. In his rational moments, however, Gennady never imagined Baba Yaga would be an actual being, let alone a man—*one* man—and a bureaucrat no less, the singular puppeteer of his crucible: Aleksandr "Sasha" Zhomov.

Sasha, the KGB's thirty-four-year-old chief mole hunter in the Second Chief Directorate (internal counterintelligence), could throw a man's life into suspended animation as easily as a telephone operator could put a call on hold. Sasha's CIA counterpart, Milt Bearden, wrote, "Aleksandr Zhomov directly supervised the people who watched the Americans twenty-four hours a day," and he "vowed to stay on the job until he [had] his quarry in shackles in Lefortovo Prison." He was a hands-on boss known to supervise interrogations of Soviet traitors. The CIA's Burton Gerber mused that the Agency would occasionally hear something about Sasha's rise through the KGB ranks and then hear nothing about him for years.

From the 1980s to the dawn of the Age of Putin, Sasha would

come in and out of Gennady's life in terrible ways, although Gennady did not know his name until 2005. In the meantime, the CIA was hemorrhaging assets, knew there had to be a reason for it, and was hell-bent on finding out what that reason was.

And there *was* a reason, a big one. Sasha Zhomov's job was to make sure the Americans never found it. Bearden once noted Sasha's piercing gray eyes, thick black hair, and caterpillar eyebrows, so bushy they would have been comical if the eyes beneath them didn't have a way of flickering out into blackness when engaged on his favorite subject: destroying US spies by any means necessary. "He was a shorty," says Gennady, with a round face that at first glance feigned softness. Sasha's nervous tic was fingering a silver crucifix when deep in thought or when interrogating a suspected traitor. In the only known photo of Sasha, he is cuddling a cocker spaniel. A hint of a smile has descended across his lips. The dog looks worried.

Panicked in the wake of the 1985 Year of the Spy losses, the CIA assembled a mole-hunting team to investigate how and why they were losing valuable assets. Gus Hathaway, the CIA's counterintelligence chief, tapped Jeanne Vertefeuille, Sandy Grimes, Dan Payne, and Diana Worthen. On a whiteboard in the basement at Langley, they drew up three possibilities for the debacle:

1. Tradecraft (The skills and techniques employed by the CIA somehow were faulty.)
2. Communications (The Soviets were intercepting CIA correspondence through technical surveillance.)
3. Double agent (There was a traitor inside the US intelligence services.)

Sasha didn't need to have a spy in the CIA's basement to know which possibility the Agency was leaning toward. He did, however, understand the CIA's institutional vanity and intuitively appreciated what they *wanted* to believe, which was that the first two options were far more desirable than the possibility that one of their own was a traitor.

The young and ambitious Sasha received his formal orders in a Moscow bar in 1987: his boss, Valentin Klimenko, ordered him to disabuse the CIA of any notion that they might have a double agent in their midst. Klimenko also wanted the playbook on how the Americans exfiltrated their assets. This extraordinary opportunity appealed to both Sasha's hatred of the decadent capitalists and his desire for advancement. If he could pull this off...

After dawn one morning in 1987 on the Red Arrow Express, a train that traveled from Moscow to Leningrad, seasoned CIA case officer Jack Downing went to the caboose for a cigarette. He had done this countless times before and enjoyed the respite from sitting in his cramped compartment. It was May and just pleasant enough in the Soviet Union to smoke outside in the fresh air as the train whooshed through the countryside. As he exhaled, a smallish man with penetrating eyes emerged through the smoke and handed Downing an envelope. The man then disappeared back into the caboose. Downing thought, *KGB*. The man's eyes had been old enough to betray experience, but his movements had been fluid, vital, youthful. Such a man might actually know something.

Sasha Zhomov was not yet in the delegating chapter of his career. Besides, this mission was so important that even if he could have delegated it, he wanted to handle it personally. He wanted to be on that train. Plus, he enjoyed the tactile pleasures of screwing with the Americans himself.

Downing did not remove the envelope from his pocket while on the train, knowing full well that the KGB almost surely had surveillance equipment in his compartment. He was heading to the CIA's office in Leningrad. The suspense was excruciating. With all the losses the CIA had endured, perhaps this envelope contained some long overdue answers. Incredibly, the Year of the Spy had left the CIA without any working assets in the Soviet Union.

When he got to the CIA station in Leningrad, Downing carefully opened the envelope and found a photo and a letter. The photo was of Downing himself and his wife in Moscow. *All right*, Downing thought, *Mr. Caboose has some surveillance chops. I'll give him that.* The letter confirmed that Mr. Caboose was indeed KGB and that he was unhappy in the USSR, had vital information to share, and wanted to defect to the United States. He didn't give his name, but there was enough information in the letter to lead Downing and his CIA colleagues to be almost certain that the man they soon knew was Sasha Zhomov was a heavy hitter inside the KGB. But was he a traitor or a "dangle," a too-good-to-be-true disinformation agent?

So began the CIA's adventure with PROLOGUE (the code name given to Sasha), which quickly yielded an astonishing explanation of the Agency's string of losses. Wrote Grimes, "It was a rundown of the activities of our Moscow Station in the 1984–86 period, and it indicated that those losses that had taken place in Moscow were the result of our poor tradecraft." Of distressing interest was Sasha's information about the fates of CIA assets like Martynov and Motorin. Still, rather than reacting with a sense of closure, Grimes and her colleagues remained suspicious. For one thing, Sasha was telling the CIA things they already knew: both that there indeed had been serious losses and the specific names of those lost assets. While Grimes hadn't had confirmation of the assets' executions, was Sasha's intelligence really that helpful? Besides, Sasha was ascribing these losses to lousy CIA tradecraft without providing any specifics. What exactly had the CIA been doing wrong that had led to their assets being exposed? For somebody who supposedly knew so much, Sasha didn't have any answers.

Despite Grimes's skepticism, the desperate CIA became enthralled with a resource who had all—or most of—the answers. But Grimes and her cohorts kept thinking, *Why does Sasha want the CIA to believe so badly that it had botched its tradecraft?*

Grimes proposed asking Sasha questions that would get to the core of what was important to the KGB—security issues—rather than swimming around in a soup of things the CIA already knew, or would have found out soon enough. Put differently, she wanted his handlers to force him to betray intelligence that would strike at the core of what the CIA wanted to know about KGB operations. The answer she got from her superiors depressed her: "We don't want to make him mad."

It wasn't as if Grimes didn't understand the Agency's logic. Cowboy Jack Platt had often stressed the importance of caution and the "long game," which is how the Russians played things. The Russians, to the ceaseless frustration of the Americans, seemed to have all the time in the world. After all, as Cowboy admonished, "they've had eight hundred years of war." But what bothered Grimes and Vertefeuille was that the CIA had reacted with childlike enthusiasm to Sasha because of the convenient *conclusion* he had reached about the Agency's losses rather than any actual data he was providing.

And then Sasha did something that stumped the CIA and hardened its position in his favor: he said he wanted to be exfiltrated to the United States. This was huge. After all, if Sasha wanted to leave the Soviet Union, this strongly suggested that once he was in the US he would deliver the mother lode of information about KGB operations. *See*, Bearden thought, *this guy has been a diamond in the rough all along.* Furthermore, Sasha's desire to defect validated the possibility that he hadn't been lying about poor tradecraft being to blame for the CIA's losses. Why would someone lie to the very handlers who would be fully responsible for the well-being of him and his family? Maybe it had been poor tradecraft all along, and the CIA had been chasing its own Baba Yaga with their paranoid double-agent theory.

The seduction dragged on and on, with Sasha promising that fresh agents were about to descend upon the CIA. In a matter of months, it seemed as if everybody with a Russian accent had decided to betray the KGB. This ploy had the effect of jamming up the Agency so much in the vetting of new recruits that it couldn't differentiate between the fake walk-ins and the real ones.

The more Grimes dug into Sasha Zhomov, the more skeptical she became that he was a turncoat. Despite his protests about leading a miserable life, other CIA assets began to report that he had a stable marriage with a daughter he adored. As a guideline, happily married and upwardly mobile KGB officers with children were unlikely to want to disrupt their rewarding lifestyles. Plus, there were indications that Sasha was a man on the move, not some low-level functionary destined for a windowless basement cubicle in a Moscow suburb.

Grimes thought she knew exactly what Sasha was doing with this espionage version of Ding Dong Ditch: creating a distraction to buy time so the CIA would be further diverted from its real problem, an agency traitor, and get all caught up in its knickers as it searched for its tradecraft mistakes. Grimes seethed as the PROLOGUE/Sasha farce played out month after month, then into the years. The CIA might as well have named it Operation Sitting Duck, because that's what Sasha was making of the CIA.

By the spring of 1990, Sasha decided that he was finally ready for exfiltration. Maybe Grimes and Vertefeuille had been too antsy all along. The CIA proceeded to share with him its detailed plan for exfiltration, going so far as to provide him with a US passport complete with an extensive—and fake—travel history. CIA operatives descended upon Helsinki, Finland, to facilitate Sasha's trip to the West. They waited for ferry after ferry, but he was a no-show. The Agency considered that something had gone wrong and Sasha had thought it better to wait for another opportunity. That signaled good judgment, and the case officers held out hope. They took a gamble that he might return to a familiar place, like the Red Arrow train.

They were right. In July 1990, a little more than three years after

PROLOGUE began, Jill Cline, wife of the new Moscow COS Mike Cline, thought she recognized Sasha (who by now had also earned the moniker "The Phantom") on the Red Arrow. Indeed she had. Sasha walked toward her in a passageway. *The operation was alive!* As he approached, Cline's sense of anticipation was piqued. In one deft and minimal move, Sasha handed her an envelope. *Okay,* Cline thought, *perhaps just a change of plans.* Sasha wouldn't have bothered showing up at all if it was a complete goose egg.

Back at the Leningrad Station, CIA personnel gathered to read Sasha's furious and whiny letter, complaining that the Agency had put him in danger and that it was not safe for him to exfiltrate now. A black cloud of failure fell across the station, not to mention the rest of the CIA's Soviet counterintelligence team.

Finally, Milt Bearden and his colleagues reached the conclusion that Sandy Grimes and Jeanne Vertefeuille had come to much earlier: Sasha Zhomov had been the Lord of the Dangles. As the swindling of the CIA reached its desperate denouement, Grimes and company doubled down on their operating theory that not only did the CIA have a traitor in its midst who was responsible for the Year of the Spy but he was likely closer than anyone had imagined.

Meanwhile, the victor, at least for now, Sasha Zhomov, was about to sink his teeth into another sitting duck.

"It was wonderful!" Grimes remembers, the humor in her voice betraying a sense of the absurd. Sasha "read the CIA perfectly." The CIA had evangelical faith in any scenario *except* that it had a traitor in its midst. "Look at your enemy and give them what they want," Grimes says, summarizing Sasha's game plan. The KGB had long wanted to know precisely *how* the CIA exfiltrated its Soviet agents and now not only did the Communist spy service have the CIA's plans; they also had the *actual documents* that would have facilitated Sasha—or any traitor's—lawful emigration to the US. They would be in an unprecedented position to detect and foil Agency mischief going forward. The KGB was thrilled with Sasha's performance, which helped him vault to the top of its ruling team and, says Grimes, "we were the ones who helped him get there."

But it wasn't as if the CIA had learned nothing from Sasha. For one thing, they now knew that the KGB would stop at nothing to protect an asset, almost certainly a traitor, or traitors. That the Soviets so badly wanted the CIA to believe their leak was due to poor tradecraft confirmed that it was not. They also had been enlightened about the nature of their new nemesis: Sasha was an audacious son of a bitch more concerned with hurting the Americans than he was with any quaint notions of credibility or future collaboration. This guy was a bridge burner—and a cagey one at that.

Yet back in 1988, the central antagonist in Sasha Zhomov's already years-long engagement was Gennady Vasilenko.

After six months in prison, Gennady hadn't changed his story once. The slew of "cellmates" the KGB had sent in to befriend him had yielded squat. Nor had the KGB found any evidence in the form of equipment or data to indicate Gennady was a traitor. No one in the KGB, in fact, actually believed Gennady had turned. Well, then, what was he still doing in Lefortovo? He knew that those who committed acts of treachery didn't last long in the Soviet prison system. If they were lucky, within a day or two of arrival, they were "tried" in a kangaroo court and dispatched to the Lefortovo basement, and after a few short steps… Yet Gennady's captors had done the unthinkable. They had kept him alive.

After all the interrogations and beatings, Gennady started to reason with his captors, and after one particularly sleepless night, he thought of an unimpeachable argument: "If I was cooperating with Platt, wouldn't I have given him Pelton? Check the Pelton file. I was his handler!" In fact, Ronald Pelton, the ex–National Security Agency employee/turncoat, had been a functioning Soviet asset for Gennady while Gennady was associating with Jack in the US—one of the most valuable assets in years. The KGB had no good answer for Gennady.

To Gennady's surprise, another thing that helped save him was the very thing he hated most about the KGB: its stifling bureaucracy. It was a strange new time. Glasnost. Perestroika. Gorbachev. "I was lucky Gorbachev was in charge now; otherwise, I'd have been killed instantly," Gennady says. Apparently, before one could pop somebody in the Lefortovo catacombs, he had to fill out new forms, neatly typing out the evidence against the accused. Maybe the KGB was going soft, Gennady reasoned. Or maybe everybody was just getting tired of the killing.

As the KGB was finalizing its Gennady Vasilenko file, another interesting thing happened: Gennady's fellow KGB officers unanimously spoke out on his behalf. The popular colleague was a patriot to his core, they professed. Finally, it wasn't lost on the KGB brass that Gennady was the son-in-law of a big shot. If the KGB could drag Gennady to the Lefortovo basement and put a bullet in his head with no evidence, what would they do to other worthy operatives without such connections? No one wanted to find out.

The good news was that Gennady would be freed—alive. But it wasn't as if he'd be leaving Lefortovo with a gold Rolex and a Montblanc pen. In July 1988, after six months in stir, the KGB cited him for a vague charge of not filing the proper reports while meeting with hostile parties (Cowboy and Dion). In one last cruel joke, his captors dressed him in a fresh KGB uniform and marched him out to Lefortovo's killing courtyard. They lined him up against the wall that held so many firing squad bullet scars. After a long minute of silence, the guards walked up to him and ripped his ceremonial epaulets from his uniform, before escorting him to the prison's exit gate and throwing him out on the street—with literally nothing but the clothes on his back. On October 14, he was officially fired from the KGB. His hard-earned pension was taken away: "A couple of months after my release they called me back for a private meeting," Gennady recalls. "They didn't want all my KGB colleagues to know what they were going to do. They demoted me, then they fired me." Gennady knew that it wasn't just Gorbachev who had saved him; it was the incontrovertible fact that Gennady had never told Jack about the KGB's prized American turncoat Ronald Pelton. In fact, when he returned to Moscow in November 1985, Yurchenko admitted to the KGB that it was he, not Gennady, who had sold out Pelton. "Ronald Pelton saved my life," Gennady concludes.

Gennady had nothing now, except a family to support. On the one hand, he savored freedom. On the other, he was going to do what he had to do. While he didn't want to believe that Cowboy had betrayed him, he resented the pain and suffering their friendship had caused him. Nor was he certain that Cowboy or someone close to him hadn't been sloppy with the knowledge of their friendship.

As the months lurched by without contact from Gennady, Cowboy sat in his private study, glancing at the photo of Gennady and himself back in the day when they both drank themselves silly; a twelve-pack seemed to be whispering in his ear, *I'm here if you need me.* His conscience was clear in the sense that he hadn't sold Gennady out, but he knew their friendship had played a role in his disappearance, and he strongly suspected Gennady would blame him somehow. "He was absolutely distressed after Guyana," Paige recalls. "But his Marine training kicked in," and Cowboy concentrated his energies on constructive pursuits, things he could control. "I really think his Marine training stopped him from drinking. All that discipline."

In 1988, Dion Rankin was transferred to Houston's FBI office, but the two American Musketeers stayed in close touch. Both men gamed out Gennady's disappearance. They had never, in fact, recorded their discussions with their Russian friend, nor had they gilded the lily in any of the reports they had filed. Cowboy and Dion came to consider the possibility that there was a double agent somewhere in the US intelligence establishment who had fingered

Gennady. This traitor would have to be a special kind of son of a bitch, because not only was he capable of an act of treachery against his own country; he also was willing to finger a completely innocent man to appease his Soviet client.

Cowboy considered his own nature. He was no longer under the thumb of alcohol, but the bottle perpetually beckoned, as it had for his beloved father and mentally ill mother. Why did people drink? Cowboy wondered, *Is nobody responsible for their actions anymore?*

Since Gennady's disappearance, however, something else had taken the place of Cowboy's addiction, and to his surprise, he felt no shame for this dark impulse. It was the Texan pull toward frontier justice. Cowboy Jack Platt was going to personally hunt down whoever was responsible for Gennady's disappearance, and when he found him, he was going to light the bastard up.

— 10 —

AN OLD ENEMY

Guess who's alive?

September 2005
Krasnaya Presnya Transit Prison

The next ring of hell for Gennady was the Russian mythic prison known as "Gulag Junction," the hub from which all prisoners would eventually be transferred to work camps spread out across the country. Krasnaya Presnya was an overcrowded, overheated, rat-infested hole, infamous for its wrongful 1940s imprisonment of dissident Russian novelist Aleksandr Solzhenitsyn, who later exposed the gulag system to the world.

Gennady joined the ranks of the wrongfully imprisoned still wearing Dion's bloody FBI Academy sweatshirt. He was ushered into an interrogation room, seated on a metal chair, legs shackled and hands bound behind his back, and sat there for what seemed an eternity with a high-wattage bulb in his face. Then he walked in, the man behind it all: Sasha Zhomov, the obsessive Russian mole hunter whose investigation had broadened in 2001. Since the breakup of the Soviet Union, when the KGB split into domestic counterintelligence (FSB) and foreign spying operations (SVR), Sasha had been tapped to run the North America division of the FSB.

With Sasha involved, it was clear to Gennady that his latest false imprisonment had nothing to do with a weapons charge. In truth, his country suspected him of either being a traitor or selling one out.

At first, mole-hunter Sasha played a Russian version of "good cop." He creepily told Gennady, "I'm putting you in prison to protect you." When that had no impact on the prisoner, Sasha reverted to his true form and a menacing tone. "These FBI men were trying to buy the file on our source. They approached many FSB, GRU, and ex-KGB until they got it. And they were there with you, in America, again."

Gennady protested his innocence. Begged for water. "Can I just call Masha to tell her I'm alive?"

"And then there's these…" Sasha flung onto the table intelligence reports of Gennady with Dion in Macon and Atlanta. He showed Gennady grainy photos—taken from Gennady's now ransacked apartment—of him with Rochford, Dion, and Cowboy, even their families. "Now, here's what I don't understand: you lost your pension, yet you are able to support two wives and two housefuls of kids—that we know of—a nice dacha in the country, and vacations in America, and right after someone sold our most precious files to the main enemy." He paused. "You're wearing the fucking FBI shirt he gave you! Do you think I'm a fool?" He slapped Gennady twice, and hard.

"I worked hard for my money. I sold no files! How would I even get such a file? I had been in fucking Guyana for four years before you threw me out of the service."

Summer-Fall 1989

One year removed from his Lefortovo ordeal, Gennady struggled to pick up the pieces of his life; Cowboy Jack—his perceived betrayer—was dead to him. After initial, albeit fruitless, attempts at the import-export game (vodka, food, clothing—anything), Gennady found his salvation in the form of tremendously good timing.

Help for Gennady's plight arrived courtesy of new Party chairman

Mikhail Gorbachev and perestroika. In June 1987, at Gorby's urging, the Kremlin passed the Soviet Joint Venture Law, which allowed and encouraged Soviet citizens to partner with Western businesses. In practice, the Soviet partner would supply labor, infrastructure, and connections to a potentially large domestic market while the foreign partner supplied capital, technology, entrepreneurial expertise, and, in many cases, products and services of world-competitive quality. Soon the Americans signaled their interest in the idea.

In December 1987, while Gennady had been enjoying his last month of freedom in Guyana, Ronald Reagan had met with Gorbachev in Washington for a continuation of their ongoing summit. In a joint statement released after the meeting, one sentence played a major role in Gennady's fortunes after his 1988 release: "[Reagan and Gorbachev] agreed that commercially viable joint ventures complying with the laws and regulations of both countries could play a role in the further development of commercial relations." It was the first Moscow-Washington "reset."

Almost overnight, some five hundred startups took out business licenses, although few would actually see a profit. One such company, conceived by an ex-KGB and volleyball friend of Gennady's named Alexey Morozov (KGB Department 19), was formed in 1988 with a California entrepreneur named Martin Lopata. It was called Sovaminco, which stood for SOViet AMerican INternational COmpany. Not only was Morozov involved, but also one of the senior executives was Elena Cherkashin, wife of Gennady's former DC *rezident*, Victor Cherkashin. The company hired Gennady to head up security.

Sovaminco's business plan started out with the idea of supplying photocopying services to Soviet citizens at public kiosks—until this point, all photocopiers, duplicating machines, and printing presses had been owned by the state. Consequently, Sovaminco was one of the first companies to facilitate printing for the average Soviet, with facilities also located at hotel gift shops in Moscow and Leningrad designed specifically for Western visitors. Larger commercial jobs were shipped to a central printing plant for overnight service. The company, which is still in existence, branched out into printing (T-shirts, business cards, and bumper stickers), publishing, and distribution, reaching a deal with *USA Today* to distribute the newspaper in Moscow and Leningrad on the same day of publication. As the company expanded, so did its need for security, and Gennady was just the person to oversee it.

Back in McLean, Virginia, Jack ran his company HTG and assumed that Gennady was *actually* dead, having likely suffered a terrible execution in Lefortovo. It had now been over a year since Jack had had any contact with his former friend in 1987, and he was plagued with guilt.

The CIA and FBI had been hard at work attempting to comprehend the leaks that had led to so many tragic losses over the past decade. They were in it for the long haul. Locating possible KGB surveillance of Agency communications or, worse, finding a double agent (or agents) inside US intelligence is painstaking, and often fruitless, work. Both John Walker Jr. and Edward Lee Howard had been uncovered in 1985, but their level of knowledge couldn't account for all the losses, especially those of Motorin and Martynov.

The investigative units went back at least to 1986, when the CIA's Hathaway had assembled the mole-hunting task force. By now, team member Jeanne Vertefeuille was facing a forced retirement, but she asked to stay on because she felt guilty about her lack of success so far. "She wanted one more shot at it before retiring," Grimes recalls. As for Sandy Grimes, she had been distraught since the loss of her Moscow asset Dmitri Polyakov. Of course, one of the reasons the investigation had dragged on for so long without success was that the Americans had been hoodwinked for years by Sasha's campaign of misdirection.

It finally dawned on FBI supervisor Bob Wade that the KGB

historically had one huge advantage in the game of spy wars: money. Yurchenko had told the Bureau that the KGB had long ago determined that bribery was the easiest way to obtain intel. Wade concluded that it was time to compete on an even playing field and just buy the damn information. Thus in 1987, Wade created the appropriately named BUCKLURE program, wherein the US made it known that it would pay $1 million for any evidence showing how US intelligence had been compromised. The CIA, thanks to senior counterintelligence officer Paul Redmond, teamed up with Wade and agreed to split the cost of any future payout.

FBI supervisors Jim Holt—who, like Grimes, hoped to avenge the loss of his asset Martynov—Jim Milburn, and R. Patrick Watson played key roles in creating lists of targets, KGB agents who might have access to the precious knowledge. One list, called the "Pennywise" (pound foolish) list started at 198 suspects, including 60 to 70 KGB officers. Jack, who maintained regular contact with his FBI and CIA colleagues, if only to facilitate his security consulting business, was most concerned with the one loss that did not involve betrayal: Gennady.

One afternoon in 1990, Jack received an unexpected phone call at the HTG office from Ukrainian George Powstenko, the man who had been like a father figure to Gennady. The first three words out of "the Ukee's" mouth, Jack later said, almost brought the Marine hardass to tears.

"Guess who's alive?" asked Powstenko rhetorically.

"How do you know?"

"How the fuck do you think I know? He called me," came the answer.

Jack persuaded Powstenko to hand over Gennady's new Moscow phone number and considered how to proceed.

"I think he's still pissed at you, and you can't blame him," said the Ukrainian. "They roughed him up pretty bad at Lefortovo, then threw him out on the street." Powstenko explained that the KGB bosses had been overwhelmed by support from Gennady's colleagues and underwhelmed by the lack of real evidence.*

Jack recalled, "It occurred to me to call an old friend, Luigi Cohanek, an attaché I worked with in Vienna and who now was in Moscow." When he did, he asked him, "Would you call Genya and ask him if he would talk to an old enemy?" Cohanek agreed and then got back to Jack with the go-ahead to call.

Jack took a deep breath and punched in Gennady's number. After a haunting silence came the familiar accented voice, but this time not as exuberant as before: "Chris, I've been expecting your call." Another pause. "Perhaps I will see you when I come to America on business." Gennady agreed to stay in touch with Jack. "I wanted to know the truth," Gennady says. "That's why I took the call. I was looking forward to grabbing him by the throat. I had lost everything, and I wanted to find out why he did it."

Eventually, Gennady concocted a plan to confront Jack in the US. He wrestled with alternative approaches. He could be confrontational, get in Jack's face and exploit his height to bear down on the smaller man. But what would this accomplish? While Jack would deny his complicity regardless, provoking a KGB versus CIA showdown would only bring out the Marine in Jack. Alternatively, Gennady could exploit Jack's conscience, which he knew ran deep. For now, Gennady decided to simply contact his old friend George Powstenko to let him know he might try to come to the US soon. Powstenko could inform Jack if he so chose, which he surely would.

In late 1988, after his release from prison, an unemployed Gennady was traveling through Poland by train to visit a friend in Warsaw and perhaps secretly boarding a flight to visit *another* old friend some

---

* The colorful Powstenko died shortly after this call was made, at age sixty-four, of sepsis.

4,500 miles away, Cowboy Jack. Somewhere in the wilderness near Brest, Belarus, the train stopped for no apparent reason. KGB agents climbed aboard and coldly told Gennady that he had a telephone call waiting for him. Gennady glanced out the train window and saw only forests and fields. *A phone call. Right.* They took him off the train and made him stand beside the tracks. The KGB men boarded the train again and Gennady waited for them to return. He was disabused of that notion when the train began to chug away, leaving Gennady stranded.

They will never stop screwing with me, Gennady said to himself as he contemplated being alone in nature. He suspected—rightly, it turned out—his old *rezident* comrade Victor Cherkashin. *To hell with them.* He reasoned, he had survived his childhood in the raw wilderness and he had survived prison. Tossing him off a train in the middle of nowhere was all they could think of to confound him? He could find his way out of the countryside with his eyes closed. Which he did, although he cannot remember precisely how he made his way to Warsaw.

In Warsaw, he showed his passport to Soviet guards, who said he had to come with them. "You have to go back to work," the guards said vaguely. Clearly, the KGB had sent down orders to keep inconveniencing Gennady in any way they could think of. So the guards sent him back to Moscow.

"Cherkashin sold me out," Gennady concludes. "He was still at the First Directorate. He was just doing his job. But I had had enough, so I quit the joint venture and started a new company called Bullit." The idea stemmed from the fact that the most successful of the new Soviet startups were in the corporate security and consulting arenas. Since government (including KGB) wages were so low (equivalent to two hundred dollars per month), tens of thousands of KGB officers had taken early retirement to improve their lot in what one such retiree labeled "free enterprise espionage." KGB recruitments had fallen off a cliff, and many of those who still enlisted saw Yasenevo as nothing more than a training ground for cushy private-sector jobs, and they retired immediately after the mandatory five-year stint was up. These *nouveau* capitalist operations offered electronic bug detection, intelligence gathering, bodyguards, and armored limousines to foreign businessmen looking to cash in on glasnost. Others merely convinced the CIA to pay for their defection to the West.

While Gennady considered other opportunities to travel to the US, the mole hunt was escalating. The FBI's operation was based out of the Washington Field Office. Over at Bureau headquarters, James "Tim" Caruso, who had earlier initiated a six-man team, was called back into mole-hunting service.

Also in the WFO, Musketeer Dion Rankin was back on the scene, brought up from Macon, Georgia, to assist in the hunt for traitors. He rented an apartment and for the next fourteen months commuted back to Macon on weekends. Working with about ten others under supervisor Bob "Bear" Bryant, he traveled across the country, interviewing persons of interest, and even journeyed to Moscow to retrace the steps of compromised officers like Marti Peterson and Paul "Skip" Stombaugh. "We put a microscope on every compromise," Dion remembers. "We found evidence of poor tradecraft. I was beginning to think that the mole idea was mistaken."

Dion wasn't the only friend of Cowboy Jack enlisted. The Russian-speaking FBI man who had acted as a driver for the Musketeers in 1979, Mike Rochford, was also brought in to head up still another offshoot of the mole hunt. "In 1992, I was asked to return from Nashville to look for the mole," says Rochford. "Now we were working out of headquarters, not the WFO." Roch tore into the "Pennywise" list with abandon, ready to jump on a plane at a moment's notice in order to make a furtive rendezvous anywhere in the world with a Russian source who might exchange the prize for a cool million and a new life with the "main enemy." One of Roch's key areas of interest was a micro study of the movements of Gennady's old boss Victor Cherkashin. Of course, both Dion and Roch maintained an open channel to their semiretired pal Cowboy Jack.

While Dion, Roch, and their colleagues made fruitless attempts to seduce ex-KGB men, one was about to show up voluntarily, and his trip from Moscow would set off a bizarre chain of events that led to the roll-up of the long-sought double agent, no lists or bank records needed. His name: Gennady Vasilenko.

— 11 —

A SECOND REUNION

Why did you sell me out?

Gennady finally obtained his own passport and US travel visa and journeyed to Washington in the summer of 1992. Jack and Dion had been counting the days with a not small dose of trepidation.

"Jack and I met Gennady at Dulles and went back to Jack's house," remembers Dion. "We all stayed there for a few days." Gennady had been cordial at the airport but uncharacteristically cool, far from the quick-to-hug friend they were accustomed to. It was clear he was seething inside.

Indeed he was. Gennady wanted badly to confront Jack about his ordeal, but he knew he couldn't do it at the airport. Part of him felt as if he might explode, and the airport was no place for such antics. In the car, his head was a confusion of nerves and acute emotions. What words would he choose to confront Jack with, and how could he expect to get answers if the only words he could think of were curses? But despite his rage, Gennady also felt something else: a visceral sense of joy and comfort in seeing his old friend. His own brain no longer made any sense to him.

"That night we were in the kitchen with Genya, talking about it, trying to figure out just how he had been compromised," says Dion. "It got tense."

"Why did you sell me out? Was that the plan from the beginning?" Gennady implored. He wasn't yelling, but his voice broke. More than a quarter century later, Gennady's eyes well up as he recounts this showdown.

Jack was wounded but not shocked. He had had an agitated sense that this confrontation would come. And he didn't blame Gennady in the least, given what he had been through. "What would I gain from hurting you?" Jack shot back. "Since when did I cultivate a taste for helping the KGB? Semper fi, baby. I'm a fucking Marine, and I love my country, just like you love yours."

"Were you recording me?" Gennady asked.

"Of course not," Jack answered firmly. "You know how I feel about having my fieldwork second-guessed by a seventh-floor suit."

"Did you say you recruited me?" Gennady asked. Jack said that he hadn't. That Gennady wasn't yelling made Jack feel worse, guiltier as opposed to instinctively defensive. Gennady's tone was more akin to an injured brother than a sworn ideological enemy. For his part, Gennady had never seen Jack this way—distressed, not his usual irreverent self. Jack explained that he had never claimed either verbally or in his reports that Gennady had been a recruit; he simply had reported that they met on occasion and Gennady was a *contact*, not a spy. There was a fundamental difference, as Gennady well knew. Jack could only wonder if the KGB had some other reason for wanting to scapegoat his Russian friend.

Jack completely dropped any remaining Marine exterior as tears welled up in earnest. "Jesus Christ, Genya, you're the brother I never had. I would never, could never…"

Suddenly, Gennady hugged his old friend like he had before he was arrested. Jack was crying and Gennady and Dion were close to it.

"I missed you guys so much," the Russian said as all three men seemed to exhale simultaneously.

As the week came to a close, Dion drove Gennady down to Macon for the weekend before his return to Russia. Before leaving, Gennady gave Jack a copy of his prison release document as a gift. It was his certification to Jack that he didn't believe Jack had betrayed him, a sacrament of forgiveness.

Gennady had many mouths to feed and a new career he was creating out of thin air. Coincidentally, Cowboy Jack was in a similar, if not as immediate, quandary. He had retired too young and still needed to contribute to his and Paige's expenses. By this time, the girls were grown and on their own, but their college loans remained. In one of their phone calls, Gennady explained to Jack how the joint-venture business was exploding in Moscow. It occurred to Jack that, with their combined contacts in the ex-spy world, they should be able to create a thriving enterprise. Jack's partners at HTG agreed and soon a joint venture between Bullit and HTG was born.

One of the new company's selling points was that, through Gennady's old KGB network, it had easy access to FSB men who facilitated the granting of passports. HTG could now expedite travel for potential Russian business partners. More importantly, HTG was able to vet Russian partners for wary American investors. As Harry Gossett points out, "Russia didn't exactly have a Better Business Bureau whose files you could check."

In 1993, Jack made his first of five trips to Moscow, and Gennady continued coming to the US at least once a year. On Jack's first trip, Gennady met him at Moscow's Sheremetyevo International Airport and immediately noticed Jack's apprehension. "I never wanted to come to Moscow," Jack said. "I wanted to start a second life. Been there, done that. But when I saw, through Gennady, the opportunity through business to come to Moscow, I came. It's very sad. It's the only country that's had five hundred years of bad luck." Jack was also well aware that the FSB had to have a thick file on him. "I was fully prepared to be arrested," Jack recalled. He told a chortling Gennady, "If I'm arrested, I'll never speak to you again." After a few days of Gennady watching his fellow Musketeer look over his shoulder, he pulled the car off to the side of the road and told his nervous friend, "Stop looking for it. It's not there."

Gennady also maintained frequent phone contact with Dion, back in Washington and Macon. When Gennady mentioned to Dion that his cash flow was still insufficient to provide for all his children, Dion drove to Atlanta to help him import high-quality cotton towels. Although hundreds of towels were sent over to Moscow, the gambit foundered quickly.

Also in 1993, Jack reconnected with journalist-publisher Joe Albright at their thirty-fifth Williams College reunion. Joe was the nephew of diplomat-philanthropist Harry Guggenheim, heir to the Guggenheim mining dynasty, and from one of the richest families in the world. The ex-husband of the first female secretary of state, Madeleine Albright, Joe was himself heir to a publishing empire that included the *Chicago Tribune*, *Newsday*, and the *New York Daily News*. He was now reporting from the Moscow branch of the Cox News Service, Jack well remembered.

Ever industrious, Jack prevailed upon Joe to write for Cox a profile of his and Gennady's new joint venture. Working with his new wife, journalist Marcia Kunstel, Joe set to the task. How could he turn down such a fascinating story? Jack and Gennady's unlikely friendship was made public for the first time when the story went to print in November 1993.

"The Cold War is truly done," wrote Albright and Kunstel. "Their whole relationship is hard to imagine, even less easy to understand— how two men standing on opposite sides of the world's most deadly geopolitical chasm could become chums, at the same time each was trying to lure the other to jump across." Jack and Gennady had merely redirected their immense skill sets to "the battleground of international capitalism."

The pair was most impressed with Gennady's manifest charisma, writing, "The tall and graceful Russian, whose Harris tweeds and soft-spoken manner give him a professional air..." But they acknowledged that Jack had come up with the idea for the joint venture. Speaking of himself and Ben, Jack told them, "We'd done our homework. We knew what was there—minerals, resources. We knew Gennady had contacts." Albright's piece described the duo's original meeting and the unlikelihood of their friendship and business partnership. However, Jack and Gennady weren't ready as yet to divulge the details of their espionage work.

While the joint venture expanded its network of ex-spies, current spy Sandy Grimes, who along with Jeanne Vertefeuille headed up the CIA's mole-hunting team, was zeroing in on Jack's old colleague in SE, Aldrich "Rick" Ames. In the SE Division, Jack had worked with Ames, whom Jack had seen as more of a "street" operative, like himself; his oddball personality certainly wasn't winning over many people at Langley. Jack had once assigned Ames a sensitive "handover," a Yugoslav source in New York, and Ames had handled the assignment perfectly—Ames had seemed to be a part of the team.

However, the analyses of Grimes, Payne, and Worthen said otherwise. Worthen, who drove by the Ames house every day on the way to work, happened to notice expensive curtains going up in every window of the house. That seemingly minor observation led to a thorough investigation of Ames's finances. Everything began to come into focus when the results pointed to big bank deposits ($15,000, $20,000, etc.) in the early 1980s on the very days—Grimes determined—when Ames officially had met KGB contacts from the Soviet Embassy, their names originally provided to the CIA by Gennady's colleagues Motorin and Martynov. Although these contacts had been sanctioned as legitimate attempts by Ames to penetrate the embassy, in fact, he had used his work role as a cover for other—private—business that obviously paid extremely well. Additionally, bank records showed that Ames, who used to carpool to work with Grimes, acquired a new habit of making extremely large cash purchases, unbefitting the GS-14 paycheck of a CIA case officer (at that time $70,000): the cash purchase of a $540,000 house, the purchase of a new Jaguar sports car priced at $43,000, among others.

Nonetheless, CIA superiors of Grimes and Vertefeuille said they needed harder proof, noting that Rick had told his colleagues he had come into a large inheritance from the family of his Colombian wife, Rosario—an excuse that was impossible to verify or disprove. Some on the team concluded that Ames's troubles all stemmed from the fact that he was trying to accommodate his wife's lavish tastes. But Grimes and Vertefeuille weren't buying either hypothesis.

Per regulation, the team's conclusion had to be shared with the Bureau, which would write the report. When the report was issued in March 1993, Team Jeanne and Sandy had assumed it would name Ames as the prime suspect. When it named him only as being on a short list, they were crestfallen; they had wanted the Bureau to focus all its energy on Ames before he could flee the country. "When I read that report, it was one of the worst days of my life," Sandy says.

Some in the CIA believed internal FBI politics, and perhaps no small measure of ego, led to the drafting of the ineffectual document. However, the team's morale improved not long after the report was issued, when the CIA obtained new evidence that the Bureau couldn't dismiss so easily. On page 144 of Grimes and Vertefeuille's memoir about the Ames affair, *Circle of Treason*, an oblique passage refers to something clearly too secret to amplify upon: "Luckily in 1993, additional information became available." That's it. Whatever it was, it "added to the comfort level of those who had not already been convinced." In a recent presentation at Washington's International Spy

Museum, Grimes used the same phrase, almost verbatim. No one in the audience asked for an elucidation during the Q&A. In a recent conversation, Grimes expanded, if only slightly. It wasn't just that the new evidence *pointed* to Ames; "It left no question that it was Ames."

Perhaps something can be gleaned from the 2014 ABC series *The Assets*, which was based, albeit loosely, on *Circle of Treason*. In episode 8, "Avenger," Grimes's character is seen taking a meeting with a KGB source in Berlin called "Avenger," who pointed the finger squarely at Ames, though without mentioning his name. Grimes recently denied any trips to Europe on the case but conceded that a critical new source did become available to the team. The AVENGER source was said to have been paid $2 million for the information. Most interestingly, one entire chapter of Grimes and Vertefeuille's book was deleted by the Agency. It is known that it concerned Gennady Vasilenko. Gennady wasn't AVENGER, although Gennady had known AVENGER since the mid-1970s, when both men worked at Yasenevo. Despite Grimes and her team knowing his name, the public's answer to the AVENGER riddle, including his identity, would come in 2010.

When the damning information was shared with the FBI, they moved quickly to set up a full-bore investigation of Ames, called NIGHTMOVER, headed by supervisor Les Wiser Jr. Thanks to agents like Dion Rankin, Ames was already on the Bureau's short list.*

Rick Ames and his wife, Rosario, were arrested on February 21, 1994. The newspapers and many forthcoming books would anoint the FBI's

---

* After the case had been closed out successfully, FBI director Louis Freeh once again recognized Dion, among others, with an incentive award for his role in pruning the list, saying in part, "Through your intense examination of numerous files, you were able to refine the list of suspects and identify six individuals whose activities warranted further probing. You exhibited a tremendous amount of expertise and patience while painstakingly collecting and piecing together details, and your sheer determination and keen awareness were vital to the establishment of credible evidence. The closure of this significant investigation was undeniably achieved as a result of your hard work, and I want to extend to you my deepest thanks for your invaluable contributions."

Les Wiser as "the man who caught Aldrich Ames" when, in fact, Jeanne and Sandy's team had had to lead the FBI by the nose to him. Ames cooperated and received a life sentence, but he was able to plea bargain a five-year sentence for his wife.

It was soon deter-
mined that Ames had
started his spree in 1985
by selling out Gennady's
pals Motorin and Mar-
tynov for $25,000 each,
and he continued sell-
ing secrets for the next
nine years, amassing
$4.2 million in total. In
an interview with Tim

Aldrich Ames's arrest, February 21, 1994.
(FBI photo)

Weiner of the *New York Times* soon after his arrest, Ames admitted that the main motive for his betrayal was money. But interestingly, he also faulted a culture flaw at the CIA that had similarly dogged Cowboy Jack. "I have had a kind of on-again, off-again binge drinking problem that occasionally reached the edge of scandal but never quite fell off," Ames said. "I usually had several drinks before a meeting [with the Soviets]. I would drink during a meeting." Each encounter saw the better part of a bottle of vodka disappear.

The CIA was less concerned with motive than with assessing the massive damage Ames had inflicted. In 1995, CIA director John Deutch summarized the harm caused by the turncoat:

- In June 1985, he disclosed the identity of numerous US clandestine agents in the Soviet Union, at least nine of whom were executed. These agents were at the heart of our effort to collect intelligence and counterintelligence against the Soviet Union. As a result, we lost opportunities to better understand what was going on in the Soviet Union at a crucial time in history.

- He disclosed, over the next decade, the identity of many US agents run against the Soviets, and later the Russians.
- He disclosed the techniques and methods of double agent operations, details of our clandestine tradecraft, communication techniques, and agent validation methods. He went to extraordinary lengths to learn about US double agent operations and pass information on them to the Soviets.
- He disclosed details about US counterintelligence activities that not only devastated our efforts at the time but also made us more vulnerable to KGB operations against us.
- He identified CIA and other intelligence community personnel. (Ames contends that he disclosed personal information on, or the identities of, only a few American intelligence officials.) We do not believe that assertion.
- He provided details of US intelligence technical collection activities and analytic techniques.
- He provided finished intelligence reports, current intelligence reporting, arms control papers, and selected Department of State and Department of Defense cables. For example, during one assignment, he gave the KGB a stack of documents estimated to be fifteen to twenty feet high.

Cowboy Jack, predictably, cut to the chase: "Ames single-handedly wiped out twenty years' worth of work. The combined efforts of people to develop the nine people he got killed in just seven pounds of paper."

Whatever the root causes of Ames's treachery, the effect was a staggering amount of damage. His capture raised the spirits of the entire US intelligence apparatus, though the feeling didn't endure.

By sheer coincidence, Ames was arrested while Gennady was

visiting Jack and Dion in Virginia, and the trio stayed glued to CNN's coverage. Dion and Gennady recall Jack's face going white at the news.

"Christ, Rick Ames! He worked for me as a case officer!" Jack exclaimed. "He was Hav Smith's guy, turned into a typical CIA drunk…" He paused. "I should talk. But at least I got clean. And I was never a first-class asshole, like Rick. I don't think he had a friend in the division. Now that I think about it, I'm not really surprised."

When the newsman mentioned Ames dropping off an envelope at the Soviet Embassy in Washington, that's when it hit Gennady: just a few feet away in Jack's guest bedroom was something he had brought for his friends to see. From his suitcase, he retrieved his own secret manila envelope and tossed it onto the table in front of the other Musketeers.

"I worried about bringing this the last time," Gennady said. "But they didn't search my bag then, so I brought it now. Maybe this Ames guy fucked up my life?" As Dion recalls it, "Gennady had brought nine legal pages of notes he kept from his interrogation, written in English. As he was reading them, they rang a bell for Jack and I." There were references to Pelton, Motorin, Martynov, his pharmacist friend, and even little Sherry, the bank teller in Guyana. "It sounded just like the memo we wrote from Guyana. So I went to Buzzard Point and retrieved our original. I came back to Jack's house and we laid the original memo side by side with Gennady's notes. They were like Xerox copies. That nailed it. A light bulb went off. Jack and I looked at each other, and we were thinking the same thing." Now Gennady could at last see physical proof that there was nothing incriminating in Jack's original memo, but every detail matched his interrogation. Gennady could also see that it wasn't just he who had been compromised but all three Musketeers. "If he had any lingering doubts, by now he knew for certain it wasn't us," recalls Dion.

"What did you write about us in your memo to the Center?" Jack asked.

"I never wrote one. I was forbidden from seeing you," Gennady answered.

"Well, fuck, if they had our memo and none from you, you can see why they were suspicious, like you were hiding something," Jack said.

"Jack then did some digging at CIA and determined that there was no way Ames could have had access to our Guyana memo," Dion recalls. "He was in Rome at the time. Plus we knew there were no tradecraft errors in Guyana. If anybody knew how to spot surveillance it was Cowboy. And thanks to Jack's IOC, I never made those kinds of mistakes. Now we all knew there was another mole besides Ames."

"We're still bleeding somewhere," Jack said.

Jack and Dion discussed the memo with other members of the joint CIA and FBI mole-hunting team, which included former Musketeer driver Mike Rochford, who had just met Gennady for the first time. Roch was struck by the Russian's charisma and fun-loving manner: "I immediately saw what Cowboy and Dion saw in him."

Mike Rochford catching up with Gennady and Jack in 2016.

The US intelligence community had breathed a collective, albeit premature, sigh of relief after the Ames roll-up, thinking the leak had been plugged. But to their dismay, they soon learned—courtesy of the Musketeers and other ongoing calculations—there was someone else at large in the warrens of the American spy apparatus, a traitor who had orchestrated what the Department of Justice would later call "the worst intelligence disaster in US history." As hard as it would be to comprehend, the at-large traitor was far worse than Ames.

The CIA and the FBI both came to agree with the obvious awful conclusion that Ames couldn't have been responsible for all the damage because things like Jack and Dion's memo, which had gotten back to the Russians, hadn't been under Ames's purview. Ames's treachery had led to the deaths of many US assets. This other bastard was also responsible for betraying intelligence valued in the billions of dollars. He, or she, was also the one who put Gennady in Lefortovo.

The mole hunt understandably escalated after the realizations of 1994.

Even Congress got involved, as the chairman of the Senate Select Committee on Intelligence, Dennis DeConcini, not only held hearings on the subject that year but personally interviewed Ames in his prison cell. The evidence was as clear to DeConcini as it had been to Jack and Dion. "There has to be another," DeConcini remarked, echoing the Musketeers' conclusions.

Mole-hunting units were expanded from Langley to FBI HQ to the Buzzard Point and New York City field offices.* Multiple lists were drawn up, again, with one list including three hundred CIA officers who had had questionable polygraph results and another containing the names of two hundred KGB agents who were in a position to know something. When a listed KGB man was tracked down, Rochford jumped on a plane to a far-flung region of the planet to offer him the million-dollar bounty. He counted twenty-eight pitches he made personally to try to solve the riddle.

---

* One new mole hunt at Langley was headed by Ed Curran of the FBI. His Special Investigative Unit (SIU) comprised seven CIA and four FBI agents. Elsewhere, the CIA's Mary Sommer and the FBI's Jim Milburn coordinated an investigation. Fifty FBI agents toiled at Buzzard Point, while Bob Wade, Tom Pickard, and Tim Caruso held court in New York and FBI headquarters. Others of note were Sheila Horan, Neil Gallagher, and Timothy Bereznay.

Bob Wade and Rochford also made a dozen trips to London to trawl through KGB files smuggled out of Moscow in 1992 by former KGB archivist Vasili Mitrokhin. When Yasenevo was constructed in the early 1970s, Mitrokhin had been in charge of transferring the KGB's records from the old Lubyanka facility. But secretly he made meticulous copies of many of the secret documents, and hid them in the floorboards of his dacha. By 1992, he had amassed twenty-five thousand pages, which he brought to Britain's MI6 when he defected to London that year. By the time Rochford and Wade showed up, the files had unmasked seven KGB spies and moles. It made sense to assume the new US source might be disclosed in Mitrokhin's cache. But he wasn't.

In 1994, Gennady's spying skills were pushed to their limits—but on the home front. Schooled in stealth by the best, he had always been good at hiding the details of his dalliances from Irina, who of course knew what was happening but tolerated it as a Russian way of life. Her one demand was that Gennady's infidelities remain discrete from their family's world. The challenge now was his attraction to Masha, a beautiful Muscovite twenty-five years his junior. When asked how the affair started, Gennady gives his typical response to thorny questions: "Shit happens, especially when I'm around women." Normally, Gennady had no problem navigating the treacherous shoals of adultery, but this was a special circumstance: Masha had been his daughter Julia's childhood playmate and remained one of her best friends.

Incredibly, Gennady was able to walk this tightrope for over a decade, even as Masha bore him more children and lived at an apartment Gennady kept for her in town. The insouciant Gennady would say today that he loves both his families and didn't want to hurt anyone. "It's just what it is," he says calmly. Consequently, he had no intention of getting divorced and was perfectly happy with how things were going with the family that bore the Vasilenko name as well as his secret second family. What added to the logistical strain for Gennady was the finances of it all: he had to support two families without Irina noticing the missing income.

In 1994, Gennady closed down Bullit when an old KGB friend offered him a VP position in a larger enterprise. The new multinational company, Securitar, run by ex-KGB officer Viktor Popov, was but one facet of Popov's new private-sector security empire. He also ran Oskord Security Group with eighty ex-KGB staff and a thousand total employees. "Here we carry out the same tasks we did for the state," Popov said in an interview. Securitar's brochure advertised personal bodyguards, business security guards, installation of security equipment, and consulting services. "We took the best of what existed at the KGB and set it up here."

Thanks to Jack's Williams College pal Dave Cook, who was now chief of security for the International Monetary Fund, Securitar quickly landed a major contract, providing security for the IMF's Moscow office. Gennady got to meet former president George H. W. Bush when he provided security for the opening of the Moscow office of Goldman Sachs in 1994. On that occasion, Gennady chided Bush, telling him, "I was spying against the CIA when you were running it in the  seventies." Despite the jab, Bush posed for a picture with his former adversary.

Securitar also signed a contract with a US medical supply company that was losing millions of dollars in drugs that simply disappeared after being shipped to Moscow, only to resurface back in the US on the cheaper "gray market" to compete with the original manufacturer. Gennady and Jack continued with their own business partnership, too, now renamed FKCFO (Former KGB, CIA, and FBI Officers).

Ironically, the joint venture spree engendered by the US-Russian reset almost derailed that very reset and fired up the '80s spy wars that had just recently calmed down. At the center of the storm was a dear friend of Gennady's, ex-KGB agent Vladimir Galkin, and the man in the shadows who helped extinguish the flare-up was another close friend, Cowboy Jack. The origins of the misstep were the hackneyed misunderstandings between those bureaucratic rivals, the FBI and the CIA. And who better to mediate what amounted to a dustup than a man respected by both?

Gennady's friendship with Galkin began when they attended the Andropov Institute together for three years in the early '70s. Galkin went on to become a senior officer in the First Directorate's Line X, where he was tasked with stealing scientific and technical secrets from the West. During his seventeen-year career, he had many successes, including the penetration of France's nuclear program. By 1996, fifty-year-old Vlad, who had retired from the KGB after the USSR's dissolution in 1991, had started his own Russia-US joint venture called Knowledge Express, and he had come to the US to buy surveillance equipment at a New Jersey trade show. Instead, the FBI arrested him on arrival at JFK Airport on October 29, 1996.

Galkin honestly identified himself to the FBI as a former intelligence officer, as so stated on his visa application, calling attention to an unwritten agreement between the CIA and Russian intelligence not to go after retired case officers. In custody, the FBI presented him with an ultimatum: cooperate on other outstanding espionage cases or face up to thirty years in prison. If he cooperated, however, he could be released to live in the United States, with a fat payday to boot.

Instead, Galkin demanded a phone, called his wife, Svetlana, in Moscow, and told her to inform Russian intelligence of what had happened. One of the next calls she received was from Gennady. "I heard the news on television in Moscow and immediately called Svetlana. Then I called Jack and asked him to alert his friends and the whole CIA retired community to do something to free Galkin; otherwise, there would be retaliation against CIA guys like Jack doing business here in Russia. Jack did it. He made a lot of noise in the US, calling all his CIA friends at AFIO [Association of Former Intelligence Officers]. We made a lot of noise in Russia as well."

The "noise" was heard, and the CIA ruminated over damage control while the arrest made headlines around the world. Galkin was hauled off to courts and jails in Brooklyn and Boston, and finally to the federal district court in Worcester, forty miles west of Boston. The Soviet Embassy hired New York defense attorney Jerry Bernstein (a former member of the Organized Crime Strike Force, which famously flipped goodfella Henry Hill) to represent Galkin, whom Bernstein recently recalled as being "a lovely man, charming—just a nice guy." The attorney remembers the judge glaring at the US attorneys, intoning, "You'd better not be starting World War III!" When Bernstein arranged what he thought was a nice bail package, allowing Galkin to stay in the Soviet Embassy, the KGB would hear nothing of it. "They wanted him completely exonerated and released or else they wanted him in jail where they could create an international incident over it," Bernstein remembers.

Behind the scenes, CIA Director John Deutch bickered with the FBI over who was at fault, with the Bureau claiming that it had notified the CIA of its plans to arrest the Russian, while Deutch stated that no such notification had ever occurred.

The tension reached a boil when, on November 15, Russia's prime minister, Viktor S. Chernomyrdin, called Vice President Al Gore to personally complain. With Gore's assent, Deutch convinced the DOJ to just drop the case. In court, as Bernstein remembers, "a motion to dismiss on the grounds of national security was introduced." Galkin was released after seventeen days in custody, and he immediately flew home to Svetlana. Before departing, the FBI apologized and gave him an FBI coffee mug. He and Gennady have maintained regular contact to this day, and Gennady has no doubt that Jack's intercession played a key role in getting the ball rolling on bringing the case to its climax.

With guarantees of safety for KGB capitalists now de facto codified, Gennady felt comfortable bringing his other ex-KGB colleagues, including his boss Popov, with him to the US to meet Jack and Dion and pursue mutual business opportunities in the security field. Before the first arrival in the US of Gennady's spook friends, Jack had told Gennady that he would be passing their names pro forma over to Roch and Dion, who would want to interview them. Jack embodied not only the loyal patriotic Marine but also the CIA man who never really retires, setting up the stereotypical consulting firm that keeps a cozy relationship with Langley—exactly how ex-KGB officers' consulting companies worked with Yasenevo. Jack told Gennady that Rochford was particularly interested in talking to Victor Cherkashin, now himself in the private security game, and asked if Gennady would invite him over for a future conference on the topic.

Jack assured Gennady that little would come of the referrals, since Gennady's friends likely knew nothing of interest and, especially Cherkashin, were all financially comfortable, with no need to sell out their country (Cherkashin by this time headed a private security company called Alpha-Puma, with dozens of big contracts with major corporations and with more than a hundred employees). It was just a way of keeping everybody happy. With no special enthusiasm, Gennady agreed to pass on the invitation. Jack had told his friend the truth; however, he lied to the visiting Russians when he assured them they wouldn't be pitched.

Alan Kohler was a young FBI man newly assigned to the Washington

Field Office's counterintelligence squad and obviously knowledgeable of the ongoing attempts to ferret out the second traitor. Soon after he landed at the WFO, he also became aware of Cowboy Jack and his revered reputation before even meeting him. "I knew of Jack as a legend," Kohler says. "All of the veterans talked about him." Kohler is very clear about what the retired CIA man could bring to the mole hunt years after his retirement: "Part of Jack's relevance was his ability to reach out to Russians."

As he had in the past, Jack turned to his family for assistance. Michelle, at that point thirty years old and with the nickname "Moxie," remembers, "My job was to babysit the KGB guys when they were between meetings in Washington. I'd take them shopping, to museums, whatever." But just like with the IOC training, Michelle/Moxie was also functioning as an operative for her dad. "I would be told which ones to distract so the FBI could target other ones. It was the same at parties. Dad would give me a look, and I knew to start engaging someone so Dad could have a private conversation with an asset or target."

In February 1997, the HTG-Securitar joint venture indeed brought retired KGB men Victor Cherkashin, Alexander Pavlovskij, and Viktor Popov to Georgetown University in order to attend a conference on nuclear waste disposal security. During that event, Jack and Gennady submitted a bid for the disposal on a Pacific atoll of spent nuclear fuel from many countries (the state of Colorado ultimately won the bid). When Cherkashin met Rochford and Dion's new WFO counterintelligence chief Ray Mislock at the conference, he was certain what was coming next, even though Jack again reassured him that no pitches were forthcoming.

During a break in the conference, the group had what would prove to be a fortuitous brunch in Alexandria with some of Jack's connected friends, investigative author Dan Moldea, espionage expert and documentary producer Jeff Goldberg, and former top Senate investigator, now private security consultant Phil Manuel.

Manuel, whose early origins were in military counterintelligence, had recently partnered with the HTG-Securitar venture and would travel to Russia twice with Jack. Since Jack and his HTG partner Ben Wickham were business novices—Ben the investigator, Jack the trainer—Manuel became the company's unofficial business advisor, helping to handle clients, primarily US firms that wanted to do business in Russia but were concerned about who they might end up dealing with as well as how to navigate the expanding oligarch corruption. An astute observer of human nature, Manuel liked watching Jack interact with people like Cherkashin, and he learned why the Agency put such faith in his training skills. "He was interrogating you, but you never *knew* he was interrogating you. He was looking for the slightest insight, a 'tell.'"

In Manuel's mind, Jack's "Cowboy" persona was disarming, and even Jack's coarse language could throw people off the scent—Manuel suspected Jack was always looking for traitors. "He would only tell you what he wanted you to know." Manuel's bond with Jack was intellectual; he knew the "serious Jack Platt." Jack enjoyed the Cowboy facade, but that guarded the man who knew Russian history and was a fervent anti-Communist—the last true anti-Communist warrior who had fought in the shadows but who didn't hate Russians, just their system, which he thought was dangerous. Manuel and Jack spent hours talking about how Soviet intelligence operated, with Jack turning Manuel on to the Russian political newspaper *Iskra* (*The Spark*), how Lenin felt revolutions got started, and the role of propaganda. "Jack was steeped in this stuff and felt it explained what the Russians were up to."

Moldea, who had recently been appointed to HTG's board of directors, had met Jack in 1994, introduced, like Manuel, by a mutual friend: DC Metro Police detective Carl Shoffler, famous for having arrested the Watergate burglars in June 1972. Other attendees at the quarterly Shoffler Brunch included ex-CIA officer Ben Wickham, ex-FBI agent Harry Gossett, and ex–New York mob guy turned FBI consultant Ron Fino. The group was a heady mix of Washington investigative insiders, and in years to come, these new associations would prove a valuable support system for Jack and Gennady. For a time, Jeff Goldberg, who became very close to Jack, considered writing a book about Jack's life, but for many of the reasons some books don't get written, it never made it out of the starting gate.*

Of course, in all matters concerning Jack and Gennady, comic relief and one-upsmanship were never off the radar. Harry Gossett recalls that he once accompanied the Musketeers to lunch at Evans Farm Inn, a favorite CIA watering hole in McLean. Jack's choice of venue, however, had nothing to do with the menu, as Gennady would soon discover. At one point in the conversation, Gennady bragged *sotto voce* that this had been one of his favorite drop sites when he was stationed in DC. "I knew that you guys would never suspect a dead drop so close to your own headquarters," Gennady proudly chided.

"You mean under a rock like that?" Jack said as he pointed to a roadside rock about the size of a basketball. Gennady nodded. With that, Jack motioned Gennady and Harry over to the rock. "I wonder if anyone still does that," Jack said. "Let's see." Harry noticed the smile on Gennady's face dimming as Jack asked him to roll the rock away. After he had done so, a folded piece of paper was revealed on the ground.

"I'll be damned," exclaimed Jack. "I wonder what it says."

Gennady picked it up and read it to himself.

"You son of a bitch!" Gennady said to Jack.

According to Harry, the note read: *We knew about this drop site all along. Love, Cowboy.*

In the absence of his IOC course, Jack's love of instructing young people found alternative forms of expression. Pat, the wife of his old

---

* The informal Shoffler Brunch continues to this day, in honor of its namesake, who passed away in 1996 at the untimely age of fifty-one.

Marine buddy Matty Caulfield, worked in the House of Representative's Page School in the 1990s and invited Jack to speak to the students. When Caulfield asked her how the session went, she said, "Great, and the students really liked his friend."

"What friend?"

"His friend in the KGB. He is the most handsome guy." Matty couldn't believe that Jack had snuck a former KGB agent into the House of Representatives.

In 1998, a one year after the Georgetown conference the Russians returned to the US, where Jack put up his former adversaries Gennady and Cherkashin at his Great Falls house. Harry Gossett has vivid memories of a large group of Russian KGB retirees drunk on vodka on Jack's front lawn. The ostensible reason for this trip was a police symposium on organized crime, to be held at the Espionage Research Institute in Virginia Beach, but Cherkashin had made the trip in part to visit his daughter, who was studying in California. Jack's FBI friend Courtney West, who used to be a car salesman, remembers that Cherkashin approached him about possibly starting an auto import-export business. "He said that the nouveau riche Russian capitalists loved to drive around in big old Buicks and Pontiacs," recalls West. "But just not as old as those in Cuba."

The group drove to Virginia Beach, where the Russians made presentations on tactics used to combat the Russian Mafia and agreed to furnish the Americans with whatever intel they needed. Cowboy Jack made a presentation on the American Mafia. While at Virginia Beach, Cherkashin felt a searing pain in his right side, and Cowboy drove him to a local hospital. After an injection, Cherkashin had an unpleasant taste in his mouth and suspected that the syringe contained a truth serum, in advance of a pitch from US intelligence. He was wrong about the serum but right about the pitch.

As he recovered on the beach, Cherkashin was approached by a dark-haired man, who walked right up to his canopied beach chair. As recounted in Cherkashin's autobiography, *Spy Handler*, the exchange went something like this:

"Victor Cherkashin?"

"Yes."

"My name is Michael Rochford."

After a little chitchat about the conference, Roch got to the point, admitting he was FBI.

"I work casing the Russian Embassy, and I know a lot of people posted there over the years. I want to talk to you about your time in the United States."

"I don't think I can be of much help to you," Cherkashin responded, adding that he'd been retired for seven years, and lying that all he knew about Aldrich Ames was what he'd read in the papers. Roch told the KGB man that he was looking for a different source, someone who knew about the executions of Motorin and others. Then possibly bluffing, or thinking of a CIA analyst wrongly under suspicion at the time, Roch said that an arrest was imminent; the Bureau just wanted corroboration. He added that he knew Cherkashin had met with the source, which was another bluff—and untrue. In fact, no one in the KGB knew the source's real identity, only that he went by the name of "Ramon Garcia."* In fact, just like the Americans, the Russians didn't know which agency "Garcia" worked for.

"The FBI is ready to pay you one million dollars," said Rochford.

Cherkashin wrote that he didn't have to think for a second about his response: "A million dollars is worth little compared to my honor." He added that he had enough money anyway. Cherkashin excused himself, only to be approached a few more times by Rochford during the conference. The Russian became so rattled that he left early for Moscow, without even seeing his daughter. But the Bureau was

---

* According to Jack Clarke of Chicago Police Department's C-5 anticorruption spy unit of the 1970s, where the mole worked previously, the mole knew of an agent code-named "Ramon" who spied on the Mexican Mafia. Even then, the mole was suspected of being a "counterspy," so Clarke "kept him on a short leash."

still not finished pitching the KGB's former DC counterintelligence chief, and Rochford was dogged in his hopes of turning him.

Jack and Gennady's next adventure was completely unforeseeable. When American TV networks were gearing up to produce special broadcasts to celebrate the CIA's fiftieth anniversary, the greatest American actor of his generation simultaneously thought to commemorate the occasion with a feature film. CBS, the Discovery Channel, and Robert De Niro all needed experts, especially colorful, telegenic ones. The two cowboys were ready for prime time.

— 12 —

GOING PUBLIC

You have to be a mother and a father to your agent…
You have to be ready to marry him!

As the search for the second double agent proceeded in the shadows, mass media outlets were loading up on espionage content, much of it inspired by the looming anniversary of the CIA's founding in 1947.

First up was Cowboy Jack's friend, and Shoffler Bruncher, Jeff Goldberg. From 1996 to 1997 Goldberg was in the midst of co-producing a three-hour documentary for the BBC and the Discovery Channel entitled *CIA: America's Secret Warriors*, to be broadcast on March 31, 1997. For the in-depth, Agency-approved show—which went on to receive the prestigious DuPont-Columbia Journalism Silver Baton Award for broadcast journalism—Goldberg brought on board Jack, Jack's former colleague Milt Bearden, and many other spooks of note. It was Cowboy Jack Platt's first media appearance. "I had to teach him how to handle interviews with the media," Goldberg recalls. "It was his first time in the glare." But Jack, ever the cowboy, would only absorb so much coaching. In fact, anyone viewing those first interviews would see that Jack brought his own unvarnished persona to the camera. They were the same traits that endeared him to his family and army of friends around the world—CIA brass notwithstanding.

Next to come calling was Milt Bearden, who approached all

three Musketeers about a job that came with some genuine glitz and glam: acting icon Robert De Niro was looking for technical advisors for his forthcoming true spy saga *The Good Shepherd*, which he would both act in and direct. Since his retirement in 1994, Bearden had carved out a new career for himself as the go-to ex-CIA media consultant. Some of his colleagues began referring to him as "Hollywood" Bearden. In 1997, De Niro was trying to develop a film about the CIA during the early '60s, but that project hadn't jelled. Then the *Shepherd* film, about the origins of the CIA, was brought to him. "I had always been interested in the Cold War," De Niro said at the time. "I was raised in the Cold War. All of the intelligence stuff was interesting to me."

The movie had been mired in a classic case of Hollywood development hell, having started out in 1994 as a script written by Eric Roth for Francis Ford Coppola and Columbia Pictures, before moving over to director John Frankenheimer at MGM, before pivoting to Robert De Niro and first Universal, then Morgan Creek Pictures.

When De Niro took over the project in the late '90s, the actor-director asked his good friend and fellow Manhattanite, legendary US diplomat Richard Holbrooke for ideas about consultants. Among his many postings, Holbrooke had served as the US ambassador to Germany in the early '90s. While working out of Berlin, Holbrooke had developed a good professional friendship with the CIA's then Chief of Station in Bonn, none other than Jack's former SE colleague Milt Bearden.

"It started out almost like a spy operation," Bearden recalls. "Bob [De Niro] said he wanted to do a spy thriller, and Holbrooke turned over a cocktail napkin and wrote my number on it."* De Niro proceeded to call Bearden at his home in New Hampshire. The former

---

* That same year, Bearden wrote some dialogue for De Niro when he shot *Ronin* (1998). De Niro and Bearden worked together on *Meet the Parents* (2000), too, in which De Niro played a retired CIA agent. Bearden was also a consultant on *Charlie Wilson's War* (2007).

spy initially didn't believe who was on the other end of the line. "Yeah, right," he said to the man who claimed to be Robert De Niro.

With his legendary attention to detail, De Niro told Bearden that he was especially interested in "street men" with a working knowledge not only of tradecraft but also of the KGB. "Bob was going to Moscow and asked if I knew any KGB guys," Bearden says. "That part was easy." Bearden knew that nobody understood fieldwork like former IOC director Cowboy Jack Platt, and nobody could open KGB doors like Jack's pal Gennady, who was loved by everyone save the KGB brass. Jack and De Niro were already aware of each other through Jack's sister. "Polly sent me a draft of the script of *The Good Shepherd* two years before I met De Niro," Jack recalled. "I said, 'It's a piece of shit.'"

Nonetheless, the Musketeers—along with Roch—enlisted in the project and, over the next few years as the movie was being developed and revised, helped Bearden school De Niro in spy tradecraft as well as introduced him to spies in both the US and Moscow. In the summer of 1997, Bearden accompanied De Niro to the Moscow International Film Festival, where the actor was to receive a lifetime achievement award. But De Niro used the festival as his "operational cover," from which he could slip away and meet with Gennady and his KGB pals, which included counterintelligence chief Leonid Shebarshin. Of course, the sojourn was also beneficial for Gennady and his joint venture with Jack since being seen with De Niro could only elevate their standing as players. According to both Bearden and Rochford, Jack was able to open doors in Russia by dropping De Niro's name because the KGB guys all wanted to meet the star.

As soon as De Niro could sneak away from the festival, he met up with Gennady, who introduced him to KGB friend Viktor Badonov, and the group took a tour of the KGB Museum, located in the old Lubyanka headquarters. At some point Gennady decided it was time to introduce the actor to a little Russian R and R. "We took Bob to a town where there was a lot of industrial storage," Gennady recalls.

"The town's mayor [had] built a huge sauna with a waterfall, and we all went into the sauna." Bearden has a strong memory of what happened next. "The KGB guys all wore felt hats in the sauna, while this huge guy with tattoos of Russian tanks on his arms would brush us with birch branches." Bearden recalls De Niro being whipped by "a nine-foot-tall masseur with a tank tattoo. He'd say to De Niro, 'Do you love me?' Bob didn't."

At the KGB Museum in Lubyanka: (l. to r.) Victor Badenov (KGB), Gennady, Robert De Niro, Barry Primus (actor), unidentified cameraman, Milt Bearden.

The Moscow trip included a visit to a stadium that housed a boxing training facility, and as if cued from a cliché movie scene, one of the local tough guys, who recognized the *Raging Bull* star, insisted that they go a couple of rounds in the ring. "De Niro was game for anything," Bearden says, "but he kept looking at me, as if to say, 'I sure hope Bearden isn't going to get me killed.' One of the other agents asked me what I thought would happen. And I said that Bob would have the guy down by three [rounds], and that's what happened."

Capping off the Moscow whirlwind, the group visited the Gromov Flight Research Institute southeast of Moscow, where De Niro met with a cosmonaut and suited up in a pressurized flight suit. But neither cosmonauts nor birch-branch-wielding Cossacks made as lasting an impression on De Niro as the Russian Cowboy, Gennady Vasilenko. The two men shared a similar joie de vivre, coupled with an unyielding work ethic. Both Bearden and De Niro were taken with not only Gennady's affable personality but also his telegenic charisma. "He is right out of Central Casting," says Bearden.

"I wanted him for the lead KGB role [Ulysses], but it didn't happen," De Niro recalls. By the time cameras finally began rolling for *Shepherd* in 2005, Gennady had fallen off the face of the earth once again.

De Niro learned not only the practical side of tradecraft from the Musketeers but also the human side. "Like anything, relationships are the whole thing," he said. "A person puts their life in the handler's hands. So the handler has to have the ability to make the asset feel comfortable…the KGB and CIA guys were brothers under the skin."

Recently, the actor seemed to echo what Cowboy Jack often said he'd learned from the Great Game: that spies have to be great actors. "I was putting on a performance twenty-four hours a day in case I was being watched," Jack said. "I'm on a stage, but the job can be fun." De Niro agreed: "You're not who you say you are. It forces you to make other people believe you. As I became friendly with people in intelligence, I learned how smart and charming they are. They're human, not sinister." Jack concluded about the actor, "He would have been a hell of a case officer."

Throughout the years of *Shepherd* development, De Niro met with more than forty CIA officers and more than twenty KGB. But his lasting relationships would be those with Bearden, Jack, and Gennady. For the Musketeers, it was a friendship that would soon have dramatic repercussions.

Intertwined with movie consulting was Jack and Gennady's ongoing security enterprise partnership. More and more, Gennady took his business trips to the US as an opportunity to experience the beautiful diversity of North America. On one occasion, he visited Dallas with his ex-KGB pal Mikhail Abramov, and State Senator Gonzalo Barrientos personally escorted them to the Mesquite Rodeo and other Lone Star State attractions. Later that year, Gennady brought his son Ilya over for an idyllic hunting and fishing trip in Bozeman,

Montana, and to see Yellowstone National Park, where they stayed with Jack's friend Nathan Adams. As Gennady became more and more enamored with America's natural wonders, Jack wondered how many KGB men might have been persuaded to defect had the CIA just shown them Paradise Valley.

If there were a metaphorical opposite to Montana's Big Sky Country, it was the claustrophobic crevasses of the Moscow espionage world, where Milt Bearden and journalist James Risen found themselves during this period while researching their book *The Main Enemy*. "I called my old KGB liaison," Bearden says, "which we referred to as 'the Gavrilov Channel' [named after a nineteenth-century Russian poet], and asked if he could arrange an interview for me with Sasha Zhomov. We had been conducting a sort of Kabuki dance with each other for years. I figured it was high time we had a face-to-face." The meeting was arranged at a posh Moscow hotel, where Sasha parked in a forbidden spot right at the entrance. Bearden watched as a concierge attempted to shoo Sasha away, whereupon the stone-faced KGB mole hunter showed his identification, causing the poor young man to turn pale and scurry off.

After some small talk about their shared history in the spy trenches, Bearden attempted a personal question. "How long do you intend to stay on the job?"

"Until I catch the bastard that betrayed us," Sasha answered, adding after a pause, "We know what you're doing with Vasilenko and Platt."

Bearden deftly switched topics, assuming that Sasha was referring to a campaign by the CIA to turn Gennady. He was not about to share with the enemy his own reservations about the perilous friendship.

In parting, Bearden said, "I'll let you know when I come back to Moscow."

"Ha! Don't bother. We'll know."

When he returned to the US, Bearden confronted Jack: "I tried to warn Jack that his closeness with Gennady could get his friend killed. I told him, 'Zhomov is watching!' But Jack wouldn't listen. They were playing a dangerous game. Jack was blinded by his love for Gennady. We always tried to warn our officers not to get too close because someone could die. It's one of the occupational hazards, because in order to get someone to betray their country, you have to establish a strong emotional bond—and it can become too strong, like it did with Jack and Gennady."

In the *Los Angeles Times* in 1998, Bearden's co-author, James Risen, wrote up the strange-but-true friendship of Jack and Gennady. This time the pair was willing to go deeper into their world than they had for the earlier Albright interview, including Gennady's wrongful imprisonment after Guyana. Seemingly unfazed by Bearden's warnings, and having become entranced by Hollywood, Jack and Gennady were testing the waters for a movie or book based on their lives. According to Matty Caulfield, "Polly wanted to make a movie of Jack and Gennady. They came to California for meetings in the late nineties, but it never happened."

One reader of the 1998 *Los Angeles Times* article was Phil Shimkin of CBS News, who was inspired to produce a *60 Minutes II* episode about them with correspondents Dan Rather and Scott Pelley. The episode featured Jack, Gennady, and a number of Gennady's KGB colleagues. Among the spy friends Gennady brought to the project were Leonid Shebarshin (former First Directorate chief), Colonel Viktor Popov (senior counterintelligence officer), Mikhail Abramov (expelled from Canada), Vladimir Galkin (mistakenly arrested by the US in 1996, long after his retirement), Evgeniy Karpov (who had worked in the Soviet UN office), and Vitaly Teperin (Gennady's classmate at the Andropov Institute).*

---

* When the *60 Minutes II* episode finally aired in 2001, the topic had been shifted to cover the recent arrest of the mole. The episode title was "The Heart of Darkness."

The documentary's interviews with Jack and Gennady serve as a primer on their spying philosophies, not to mention their innermost observations of each other. Gennady said that spies are motivated by "dissatisfaction with their bosses, with their life, with their wives." Jack firmly defined his job: "I'm not a spy. My job is to find people who'll spy. I can't get into the Kremlin!" Gennady summarized his spy handling technique: "You have to be a mother and a father to your agent… You have to be ready to marry him!" Jack took a "marital" view, admitting that he had been hoping all along to exploit Gennady's relative youth: "We have a whole lifetime together if this works out right." *Softly, softly, catchee monkey.*

Jack further conceded that despite their agreement to be just friends, there were moments when he nevertheless would suspend their covenant and try to pitch Gennady, summarizing, "It may not be what friends do, but it may be what good intelligence officers do." This powerfully suggests that whatever his genuine capacity for friendship, his patriotism ran even deeper.

While two of the Musketeers were warming to the media, their former colleagues were still toiling in the trenches to unearth the second Russian asset. One of those trenches was located on a beautiful Mediterranean island. In July 1999, when Gennady's old DC boss Victor Cherkashin was taking a vacation in Cyprus, who should show up at his hotel room again but the indefatigable FBI man Mike Rochford. According to Cherkashin, the retired KGB officer consented to drive Roch around the island nation and listen to his renewed pitch. Again the $1 million was offered. Again, no deal.

Finally, a relieved Cherkashin was certain that he had seen the last of Rochford. But to his utter amazement, when Cherkashin was attending his daughter Alyona's California wedding two months later, Roch showed up, this time at Alyona's apartment. Cherkashin cursed him under his breath for picking such an inappropriate time for conducting spy business. However, this time there was no pitch forthcoming. According to Cherkashin, Roch merely wanted an assurance that Cherkashin wouldn't recruit Alyona's new American husband into Russian intelligence. Cherkashin told him that it wouldn't happen. He never saw Rochford again.

Rochford was getting exhausted from the repeated failures. But neither he nor the traitor he was hunting could know that a Rube Goldberg–like cascade of events was about to set the turncoat's downfall in motion. Gennady would become the linchpin in the takedown, and in a stroke of poetic justice, the traitor would turn out to be precisely the man who had helped wrongfully imprison him in Lefortovo.

A HEAVY BOX OF CAVIAR

I'd say from now on your wife should never start the car.

It all began as a minor Securitar office nuisance involving Lt. Col. Anatoly Stepanov, the B. B. King–loving KGB agent who had been posted with Gennady years before in Washington. Since those days in the seventies, Stepanov had risen to the position of deputy chief of Department S, which handled the Illegals (*see Chs. Fourteen & Seventeen*). But all the while, he coveted the top spot, and the rank of General, neither of which he was granted. After the KGB disbanded, Stepanov became involved, like so many of his peers, in the security consulting game, albeit with a singular lack of success. He also dabbled, again like many other peers, in the import-export trade.

"I ran into Stepanov at the annual meeting of retired officers," remembered Gennady. The year was 1999. When asked how he was doing, Stepanov responded, "I don't have a job." Gennady's former colleague added that he was also recently divorced and that his son was having behavior problems.

"Come on, stop by our office," offered Gennady.

"Securitar had a very large office, and many of our former colleagues stopped by often to use our space," Gennady recalls. "The next week he stopped by Securitar and we said he could use a table and a phone."

At Securitar, Stepanov proved to be ineffectual, and a bit of a sad sack to boot. Someone in the office secretarial pool nicknamed him "the Snake." Gennady describes him as "a pain in the ass," and he had quickly rung up a four-hundred-dollar bill at the office. The "pain in the ass" soon shared a tale of woe: in a frantic effort to make ends meet, he had recently gotten jammed up with Russian mobsters on a convoluted caviar import deal and wanted to travel to the United States to see if he could make a score in order to clear his marker with the mafia.

Stepanov told Gennady that he could help secure a 20 percent commission for Securitar if they sent him to New York, where the firm could collect a finder's fee on a one-million-dollar shipment of caviar. That is, *if* he could convince the Russian hoodlums to not whack him in the interim. Cowboy and Gennady talked about it and mutually decided to assist Stepanov. Both Cowboy and Gennady have stated unequivocally that they had no idea the Snake's desire to go to the US had to do with more than gangsters and caviar—but it was about espionage of the highest order.

Gennady told Cowboy that he wanted to help Stepanov if for no other reason than to bounce his old, annoying comrade from his office. Cowboy was sympathetic. He hardly knew Stepanov and already wanted to strangle the guy.

"I'll try to bring him to New York. Does he have a passport?" Cowboy asked.

"No, but I can take care of that if you can arrange a visa," Gennady said. Stepanov had misplaced his passport years earlier. In those days, a Russian citizen could get a foreign passport issued by the Ministry of Internal Affairs or the Ministry of Foreign Affairs, where Gennady had many friends. "Since I knew all the guys working undercover at the foreign ministry," Gennady explains, "I got a contract that gave me permission to sign verification documents for passports. I had already made dozens of passports for employees, family, et cetera. It took about three or four months to get [Stepanov]'s passport, but I got it." Of course, visas were another matter.

On his next joint-venture trip to Moscow, Cowboy met with Stepanov, alone, in the Securitar office.

"Since you know Gennady, I can trust you," Stepanov said, then added, "Perhaps we can make a separate deal."

Cowboy held his gaze for a moment. He had an instinctively negative feeling toward the guy, but truth be told, Stepanov had never given Cowboy cause to dislike him. Until now. Cowboy thought he knew what Stepanov meant: trading intelligence for profit. He sensed that Stepanov might betray some relatively inconsequential Soviet information if he was safely in the US. After all, a lot of ex-KGB guys were now approaching the West, hoping to grab some quick cash.

Instead, Stepanov explained that in addition to the caviar caper, he wanted to sell some items in the US markets, specifically Russian matryoshka dolls. *Fine, whatever,* Cowboy thought.

Cowboy, for his part, was hell-bent on nailing whoever had sold out Gennady in Havana, but in the absence of knowing who that was, he wanted to help his associates in the FBI and the CIA in their never-ending campaign to hunt down traitors. He would therefore attempt to introduce Stepanov to the FBI's mole-hunting team if the man indeed came to the US, just as Cowboy had done with many of Gennady's colleagues. Gennady was aware he was doing it but thought nothing of it; none of his colleagues knew anything about moles and double agents.

"I didn't want any FBI salary," Cowboy said. "I just did it to find out who killed Gennady's friends and sent him to Lefortovo. Eighty percent of my motivation was to find out who killed them and who almost killed my friend Genya." Cowboy also knew about the Bureau's "Pennywise" list of the Russians who could, at least in theory, have information about who American traitors might be.

Soon after his discussions with Stepanov began, Cowboy alerted Mike Rochford in Washington. Roch realized instantly that Stepanov was, unbeknownst to Cowboy and Gennady, near the top of the "Pennywise" list. Roch had, in fact, had a few exploratory meetings with Stepanov in Europe but never got very far with him, in large measure because Stepanov didn't feel safe, and wouldn't until he was in the United States. At the time, Roch had been searching for information about CIA officer Brian Kelley, who was wrongly suspected for some time of being the traitor. Perhaps some seemingly innocuous piece of information Stepanov possessed might get the Bureau one puzzle piece closer to closing the book on Kelley, or whoever the bastard was. By this point, every scrap of information, no matter how small, was precious.

Cowboy kept his old colleagues at the CIA informed about what was going on on his end, but they treated him like a nuisance, convinced he was simply trying to prove that he had been right all along about the Americans' investment in Gennady, which in fact he was.

Now the challenge was how to get Stepanov to New York to meet with Rochford in a way that would make him feel comfortable and wouldn't raise the hackles of Russian intelligence. Gennady, who was facilitating the passport application, obviously couldn't write "Seeking to collect for the Russian Mafia fee owed by applicant for stolen caviar." Furthermore, Cowboy and Roch couldn't make the whole effort seem too urgent or Gennady would perceive risk and shut the entire passport process down. So Cowboy and Roch had to find a suitable business partner for Stepanov's Russian doll deal.

Cowboy orchestrated the charade beautifully. The FBI had a contact who had become an art curator at the prestigious Frick Collection in New York. According to sources, Edgar Munhall, who was openly gay, had attempted to join the FBI as a young man but was put off by its intolerant culture. Nevertheless, he had maintained

Jack surprises Genya
at the Pegasus in
Georgetown, Guyana,
February 1985.
(*Courtesy of
Dion Rankin*)

Genya, "The Russian Cowboy," in
Bozeman, Montana, in 1997.

Genya and Robert
De Niro.

The Shoffler Brunch Group: (l. to r.) Jack, Dan Moldea, Jeff Goldberg, Genya, Ben Wickham, Harry Gossett, Phil Manuel. *(Courtesy of Dan Moldea)*

Genya brings ex-KGB officers-turned-entrepreneurs to the United States in 1997. (l. to r.) Phil Manuel, Victor Popov, Genya, Jack, Dan Moldea, Victor Cherkashin, Aleksandr Pavlovsky. *(Courtesy of Dan Moldea)*

Aleksandr "Sasha" Zhomov and friend. *(Courtesy of Milt Bearden)*

Cowboy Jack with Anatoly Stepanov in Moscow. *(Photo courtesy of Michelle Platt)*

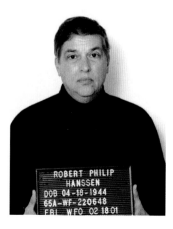

Robert Hanssen, traitor. *(FBI photo)*

Ron Fino with Gennady and Jack in December 2013.

Тамбиев Хусейн Закриевич, прож. МО, Химки, ул. Пандимова, 14-38, соучредитель ранее упоминавшегося ЧОП Секьюритар, по имеющейся информации активный участник т.н. Ингушской ОПГ, ранее проживал в Грозном ЧИАССР, также изображен на фото 15.

Шапкин, бывший высокопоставленный сотрудник СВР.

Джек Плат, бывший сотрудник США, в настоящее время состоит в Разведывательного Управления США.

его дочь – Мишель Плат

Приложение: копии фотографий на __8__ листах, оригиналы фотографий на __25__ листах.

Начальник 6 отдела
майор милиции   Б.С.Михайлов

Вл. Реляков К.Г.
тел. 200-85-63.

KGB-seized "evidence" document used against Gennady at his trial in 2006 (note Jack's photo, center).

Aleksandr Zaporozhsky (r.) with his lawyer at his sentencing in Moscow in 2003. *(Yuri Mashkov/ITAR-TASS/ Getty Images.)*

Genya's new passport, issued before his 2010 release.

Genya in 2016, with the T-shirt he wore on the flight from Vienna.

Genya's flight touches down at Dulles Airport on June 9, 2010. By sheer happenstance, freelance photographer Jim Lo Scalzo captured Jack's image as he watched Gennady's plane touch down at Dulles. (*Jim Lo Scalzo/EPA/Shutterstock*)

Reunited at The Old Brogue.

Two Cowboys attend a friend's 70th birthday bash in New York, August 2013.

Gennady wearing a tux? His cameo in the 2012 film *Silver Linings Playbook*.

contacts with the Bureau and indicated that he would be pleased to introduce Stepanov to some art dealers who might be in the market to buy precious Russian dolls.

Cowboy had a few preliminary meetings with Munhall, who had no idea of the role he was playing in the big picture, and who constantly addressed Cowboy as "Hey, Handsome!" Cowboy growled at him and contemplated how he, a Marine from Texas, could be involved with the whole New York art scene. Cowboy ultimately concluded that if *he* could barely tolerate it, the homophobic Russian intelligence services would surely not suspect that a counterintelligence operation was under way.

In Moscow, Gennady countersigned the paperwork for Stepanov at the KGB's passport office. Gennady has always said that his only motive for arranging for the passport was "getting this asshole off my back about coming to the US to try to make a buck."

Cowboy reminded Gennady that he would introduce Stepanov to Rochford, as he had with all of Gennady's visiting ex-KGB pals. "You know and I know I'm helping the FBI," Cowboy said to his friend. "But not to worry, because this snake won't talk to them—and he probably doesn't have anything anyway."

In April 2000, Stepanov flew to New York. And Mike Rochford, with an FBI team in tow, was on his way, too. Cowboy traveled separately by bus. Before Stepanov's arrival, Cowboy and Rochford met at a hotel to plan out how they were going to manage the recruitment. "I'll meet him first, take him to the curator, and suss him out to see if he's approachable," Cowboy told Rochford.

After Stepanov arrived in Manhattan, Cowboy introduced him to Munhall at the Frick, who, true to his word, expressed curiosity about Stepanov's Russian dolls. Stepanov's eyes lit up at the prospect of making some money from the sale. Cowboy took note and asked himself, *What if the bastard is led to believe he'll lose the deal?*

During a lunch that followed, Stepanov told Cowboy that he

possessed "volume one of the case." Cowboy thought, *What the hell does that even mean?* But he really didn't want to know. However, Cowboy had never made a secret of how badly he wanted to nail whoever got Gennady nicked in Havana years before, so he wishfully assumed it might have something to do with the US traitor. Later, back at the hotel, Cowboy reported the "volume one" reference to Rochford and said that Roch should proceed with Stepanov. At that point, Cowboy's job was to make the Frick's curator unavailable to Stepanov for a while in order to buy time for Rochford to make his move.

One day, Stepanov emerged from a meeting onto a New York sidewalk and he "accidentally" ran into Mike Rochford, who said, "Hey, I'd like to talk to you." Stepanov looked at Roch like he was "crazy," Roch says, "and he should have. [He] tells me he doesn't talk to strangers, and I show him my business card, and we start chatting." Roch reminded him that they had met before, overseas.

Stepanov said, "Mike, I never trusted anybody who won't drink with me."

Roch quickly located a watering hole with a suitable private corner table.

When Stepanov wasn't meeting with Rochford, he was meeting his new friend Jack Platt, who in turn was reporting back to Rochford. By week two, the FBI man was ready to throw in the towel with this Stepanov character. That's when Jack gave Roch a pep talk, one that changed history.

In a later interview for Washington's International Spy Museum, Roch described, without naming Jack, how a "team member" kept "kicking me out the door. I didn't want to go." Jack recalled, "I told Roch, 'Whatever you're doing, keep on doing it, because he hasn't asked about you. He hasn't mentioned being interrogated. He'll meet with you again.'"

Jack had to massage Stepanov's psyche, edging him ever closer to betraying his country. At this stage, Jack had gone from being dismissive of "the Snake" to thinking this could actually be the real thing. Even the swashbuckler Jack was now nervous playing this game, employing all his countersurveillance skills as he feared for his own safety. Writing a brilliant script on the fly, Jack met with Stepanov and informed him that the Frick curator had changed his mind about the Russian dolls. Suddenly, Stepanov found himself stranded in New York without any money and with only one prospect: selling whatever "volume one of the case" was. Jack was now certain "the Snake" was primed to deal with Rochford.

With his job accomplished, Jack left the city, and Rochford and others on his team took over the operation. Jack was anxious to get back to his consulting work and didn't give the Snake or the curator another thought.

Back in the bars, Stepanov insisted that establishing trust with Roch was critical to moving the relationship to another level. Roch understood and agreed. So they drank, the Russian-speaking Rochford remembers. "Over two weeks, we bar hopped. When we drank Tullamore Dew [triple-distilled Irish whiskey] he loosened up. I wanted to rename the operation 'Tell Me More, Dude.'" After about the tenth day of speaking Russian and sniffing each other out, Rochford was again on the verge of writing off the feckless doll/caviar trader, when Stepanov offered to tell him about how the KGB came upon a "particular event" and its status. Author David Wise coaxed some of the ensuing conversation out of Rochford for his 2003 book *Spy.*

Rochford told his target that he didn't know what "particular event" he was talking about.

"I can tell you know what I'm talking about," Stepanov said. "You'll have to agree to sit down with me, and we'll write up a contract, and we'll set out how I will go about the business of trying to help you solve this matter."

"Well, that's worth my time. We'll get off the streets, we'll go up to the hotel, and we'll do this."

Stepanov pressed the FBI for money. The FBI's response was simple: "No dossier, no dough."

During the course of Rochford's discussions with Stepanov, the Russian informed him that he indeed possessed what the Americans were looking for: explosive information about the Russians' asset inside the US intelligence apparatus. Rochford, normally so skilled in maintaining a poker face, was stunned, and worried that he betrayed his surprise. This one sentence vindicated Rochford, the literally hundreds of mole-hunting staff, and the great expense that had been allocated to the operation for over a decade. Of course, one major detail nagged at the investigator: How on earth had a KGB snake like Stepanov come to possess the mother lode?

Interviews with well-placed sources, who understandably would rather go unnamed, assert the following series of events:

Nine years earlier

In August 1991, a cabal of Communist Party hard-liners decided they had had enough of President Mikhail Gorbachev's reforms and audaciously decided to stage a coup. Vice President Gennady Yanayev declared himself president and had Gorbachev "detained" at his Crimean summer home. The military, ostensibly under Yanayev's control, closed the Crimean airport so Gorbachev could not return to Moscow. Soviet states (now independent countries) condemned the coup, as did US president George H. W. Bush. Realizing their lack of support, within two days the coup leaders fled to the Crimea, and Gorbachev returned to power.

The swiftness of the coup's collapse masked the sheer uncertainty and terror being felt in the bowels of the Soviet government. On August 22, the blowback against the hard-liners reached its peak, with some twenty thousand protestors storming Dzerzhinsky Square, the fabled home of the KGB inside the Lubyanka building. After hours of toil, a government employee commandeered a massive German crane, from which a noose was placed around the neck of "Iron Felix"

Dzerzhinsky, the fifteen-ton, thirty-six-foot-high cast-iron statue of the KGB's founder. As the statue was being garroted for removal, inside Lubyanka, fears were mounting as to just how far the KGB-hating celebrants would take this catharsis.

The Soviets became panicked that their most sensitive and incriminating intelligence files would be exposed during the riots, confiscated by the ecstatic, yet unruly, hordes. Watching from his fifth-floor Lubyanka office, KGB chairman Leonid Shebarshin gave the order: "Close and block all doors and gates. Check the gratings."

After the Moscow riots, workers load the dismantled statue of Felix Dzerzhinsky on a flatbed truck, August 23, 1991.
(AP Photo: Alexander Zemlianichenko)

The last of the Soviets had reason to be terrified. And the coincidence of the German crane was not lost on any of them. Two years earlier, during the waning hours of the East German regime, officers in the headquarters of the once menacing Stasi, the Ministry for State Security, began frantically destroying files. They shredded some and burned others. Some of the Erfurt townspeople noticed that dark smoke was bellowing out of the chimneys. Realizing the building was heated by gas and that gas produced white smoke, a furious mob rightly assumed that something other than gas was being burned. They stormed and occupied the building on December 4, 1989. They alerted military prosecutors and, once inside headquarters, began tossing state files out the windows and into the streets. Prosecutors seized the files for immediate review. This phenomenon had been replicated in Stasi buildings all over East Germany.

While the word "paranoid" is often wrongly invoked to describe the sentiments of the mighty, paranoia is defined as an irrational fear. What the KGB was feeling as news of the Soviet coup spread was a completely rational fear of their secrets being exposed.

Mindful of the sheer terror East German officials had felt when the oppressed masses stormed their headquarters, the KGB began surrounding their own buildings with guards, especially Lubyanka and the Yasenevo headquarters. They proceeded to load their files onto trucks for transport to a temporary "safe" storage facility in Smolensk. There was little or no supervision, not to mention a complete absence of inventory. There were thousands of archival storage boxes of files being loaded into trucks, with hundreds of KGB officers involved in this frantic exercise.

One of the transporters at Yasenevo was Anatoly Stepanov, who felt there was a good reason why people hid things: because there were terrible things they did not want you to know!

At the time of the coup, Stepanov had a lot on his mind, one being the outrage of having been passed over for a recent promotion. He was also worried—not about the Russian mob, but about his future, as were most of the newly unemployed KGB agents he knew, who were scrambling to get out. All his comrades were now his competition. What would an erstwhile KGB officer do under a new regime? Be indicted? Executed? Flee the country for a new life someplace? And where would that someplace be? Perhaps someplace that wanted to better understand the inner workings of the KGB. Someplace like the United States.

Anatoly Stepanov needed an edge.

At the Yasenevo facility, Stepanov was one of many soon-to-be-former KGB officers moving files from storage vaults onto rolling carts, then down endless corridors to loading docks, and finally onto transport trucks. As he was loading one cart, his eyes caught a particular box of material labeled in Cyrillic, which translated to English as LINE KR/US TOP SECRET. *In the box were envelopes with US postmarks, smaller boxes containing floppy disks of US manufacture, a reel-to-reel tape box labeled* RAMON GARCIA, *and two dark green plastic trash bags of the type usually used for clandestine drop-offs. Whether it occurred to him in the moment or he had it planned all along, Stepanov decided that this particular box would stay with him for closer observation. It might hold valuable information that he could ransom off for a new life far away from the Russian Mafia and the disintegrating USSR. In the chaos, as he pushed the rolling cart slowly down the hall, he needed to come up with a plan.*

Perhaps he waited until he was alone in the hallway to quickly move the box into a janitorial closet for later removal, or he pretended it was part of his personal belongings, which he cleared out of his desk as many did that night. In any event, the treasure made its way into his car trunk before dawn and eventually to his vacation cabin in the country. When he had the box safely inside his dacha, Stepanov read the detailed letters and knew what he had, and the implications of it were consequential in the extreme.

Stepanov haul was the equivalent of winning the international espionage's lottery: the KGB's official file on their prized second traitor inside US intelligence. But wanting to sell off the incendiary material and doing it were two very different things—getting caught would likely mean a year of torture in the gulag, followed by a bullet to the skull in the basement of Lefortovo. And who knew what would happen to his wife and children?

*So Stepanov cogitated, and waited. For eight years. After almost a decade of keeping his treasure in storage, he put his Machiavellian scheme into high gear when he saw the relationship between Jack and Gennady, in late 1999, when Stepanov met Jack Platt in Moscow. Stepanov knew that in order to market his jackpot he would need to make his way to the United States to speak with the American authorities. He also knew that Cowboy Jack was just such an American authority.**

At the end of their two-week New York courtship in the spring of 2000, Rochford and Stepanov finally agreed on the terms of their deal. Rochford explained that he would need a signoff from the directors of the FBI and the CIA, and a legal contract would have to be drawn up for payment for Stepanov's services. While the terms have never been made public, and Rochford won't discuss

---

* There are differing theories about whether Stepanov had been looking for this particular box or just got amazingly lucky. Cowboy Jack thought that the odds were too enormous for the Snake to have just stumbled on the treasure, whereas ex-KGB men like Gennady tend to call him "the luckiest man in the history of the Soviet Union."

them, sources have said that Stepanov negotiated himself into a fat $7 million payday—much more than the ascribed $1 million bounty. He and his family also were to be relocated to the US and receive new identities.

Now the question was *How the hell would they get the material to the US?* Arrangements were made for Stepanov to return to Moscow, retrieve the goods (Cowboy theorized he had been keeping it in his dacha), and make a handoff in a neutral country. During this time, the CIA's Mike Sulick authorized a hefty deposit into Stepanov's new US bank account while other CIA case officers made plans to pick up the package in the neutral country and send it to a third country via diplomatic pouch, then on to the United States by chartered plane. Pulling off the delicate transmission would take months of planning and execution. In one heart-stopping instance, the CIA thought it had been the victim of another brilliant Russian con, when Stepanov failed to show for the exchange. The Bureau established a reconnection, likely with Jack's assistance, and the transmission was back on track.

In October 2000, while Rochford and his team set about having Stepanov's material arrive safely in the US, Jack made his last HTG trip to Moscow. While visiting Moscow's KGB Museum inside the Lubyanka, a young military type approached Jack, and Jack could tell right away he was FSB.

"I work for the Russian government," said the stranger.

"Cut the shit and save both our time," Jack responded in his best Cowboy mode. "Who do you really work for?"

Moscow Oct 2000

Jack's last visit to Moscow: (l. to r.) Vitaly Teperin (KGB), Gennady, Victor Popov (KGB), Jack.

The man then smiled knowingly, showed Jack his Ministry of Internal Affairs ID, and asked, "Can we talk?"

"Sure, but not here. Tomorrow at the Securitar office."

Later that night, Gennady took Jack on a sightseeing tour of Moscow. While Gennady wandered off, likely to flirt with an Intourist guide, Cowboy was taking photographs of Red Square when a group of thugs approached. Emboldened by the sight of an older man wearing cowboy boots, a Stetson, and a black vest, they pointed to his camera, expressing their annoyance of his clicking shutter noise. The Muscovites lumbered toward Cowboy, knives drawn. Cowboy hadn't lost his vanity, his self-perception that he was a Marine who could handle himself, and while he wasn't afraid, he was at a loss for tactics. What would he actually do, a sixty-one-year-old, against four twenty-something Neanderthals? One of them knocked the camera out of Cowboy's hand, and it fell to the ground, parts scattering. It was the only time in Cowboy's life when he wished he had carried his .357.

"I guess somebody's got a guilty conscience," Cowboy said. He didn't know why he had said it, but people seldom know why they do what they do under siege.

The assailants looked at one another in disbelief. A leather-clad unibrow reached to grab Cowboy by the collar with his free hand, but all the air retreated from Unibrow's lungs and he felt sharp spiderwebs of pain radiating from below his neck as if a missile had hit him high on his back. His knife fell to the ground. Unibrow staggered as the man to his right turned and found his chin briefly but decisively attached to the end of an implement that was not meant to intersect with a human jaw. This man was the second to be put out of commission by the primal, bat-wielding Gennady, firing Russian epithets from his mouth as if it were the barrel of one of his cherished guns.

The third goon stood in shock, seemingly more at the alien language than the prostrate condition of his cohorts, and Gennady banged him just hard enough on the mouth with the end of the bat to make him spit teeth onto the sidewalk. Meanwhile, the fourth man suddenly found himself a solo operator. "I think you are my favorite," Gennady told the terrified mook in accented English. "When you got up this morning, you didn't plan on being alone, did you? It's easy to have confidence when you have friends."

Gennady head-faked the last man a few times. After the fourth or fifth fake, a "Fuck this shit" expression fell across the man's face, and he tore away to parts unknown.

Gennady looked at a thunderstruck Jack Platt and pointed to his camera. "Get your camera, Jack. We go now."

They ran to their car and drove off.

"Genya, you saved my life."

Gennady was philosophical. "Okay, then. You will someday save mine."

Jack did not tell Gennady that he had once dreamed that all this would happen.

Back at Securitar the next day, the FSB man arrived on time, and he and Jack walked outside for a tête-à-tête.

"Okay, why are we here?" Jack asked.

"We're interested in you," the FSB agent responded. "We saw that mafia report you did in Virginia Beach. Why don't you make a contract with us, like you have with Gennady?"

The poor guy had no idea that he was dealing with one of the most patriotic Marines imaginable. Jack knew exactly what the agent was pitching.

"Take this back to your bosses," Jack said. "*Fuck no!* And I never got a contract with Gennady!"

The poor guy jumped, Jack later said.

As a result of these encounters, Jack decided never to return to Russia.

That same month, after some time away, Anatoly Stepanov stopped by the Securitar office and explained his absence to Gennady by saying that he had just been very busy. Gennady remembers that he then "just disappeared, for good."*

Soon after Jack's return from Moscow, Stepanov's box of material completed its circuitous route to FBI headquarters in Washington. At least one highly placed member of the FBI's mole-hunting team says that the "coincidence" of Jack's return and the appearance of the prized file was anything but. "Jack and an FBI agent went to Vienna to retrieve the cache," says the source, who requested anonymity. It would make sense that the Bureau would want the master of surveillance avoidance to retrieve the precious bounty. Also, Jack had been stationed in Vienna, so he was familiar with the city's best handoff and dead-drop locations. It is also a reasonable assumption that Jack made the Vienna side trip after his Moscow excursion. Or perhaps the Moscow trip had been an elaborate cover for the real reason for Jack's overseas travel. If Jack indeed acted as courier for the coveted mole file, it would add weight to his reason for never wanting to return to Russia, where the vindictive Sasha Zhomov might see to it that the next group of thugs was much more adept than the ones Jack had recently encountered.

Whatever the details about the handoff, the cache arrived safely and FBI analysts got to work. Included among the paperwork and floppy disks were two of the traitor's plastic dead-drop bags, which, after being powdered, revealed two telltale prints. There was also a taped conversation between the traitor, who used the pseudonym "Ramon Garcia," and his KGB handler. What the analysts heard stunned them. They had been expecting to hear the voice of the CIA's Brian Kelley. But instead they heard the voice of one of their own, FBI agent Robert Hanssen. When the prints were analyzed, they also belonged to Hanssen.

---

* One would think that the new millionaire would tip his facilitators for their role in the acquisition of the largesse, but the Snake disappeared without so much as a thank-you.

There was a war going on inside Mike Rochford's gut. *They got him!* But "he" was an FBI man. Nobody had thought the bastard would be FBI, let alone the straitlaced, low-key Bob Hanssen. Hanssen was no Rick Ames, he of the newly capped teeth, young wife, shiny Jaguar, and cash-paid suburban house with the fancy curtains.

On his birthday, February 18, 2001, Jack received a call from someone at the Bureau whom he later would only identify as a friend. "Listen to the news tonight. Happy birthday."

Jack tuned in the evening news and learned that Hanssen had been arrested in Northern Virginia. It was soon determined that he had sold out not only the United States' most hard-won spies but also its billion-dollar tunnel underneath the DC *rezidentura*. As a result, the Russians had been feeding disinformation into the tunnel for years. The tunnel had been the penetration that Stepanov had alluded to during his negotiations with Rochford, the one that had knocked him off-balance.

To say that Robert Hanssen was an odd duck would be an understatement. He surely was no exotic "Ramon Garcia," the name he gave his Soviet handlers. The son of an overbearing Chicago policeman who reminded young Bob of his inadequacy at every turn, Hanssen was, on the surface, a convert to Catholicism who lived with his wife and four children in suburban Virginia. Some described Hanssen as a dour and pale office dweller with a gloomy appearance. These colleagues referred to him behind his back as "the Mortician." Indeed, in his mug-shot photo, a black-clad Hanssen resembles the cadaverous Lurch in the television serious *The Addams Family*.

This portrayal, however, may be driven too much by hindsight and the self-serving human instinct to proclaim, "I knew it!" Other coworkers thought of Hanssen as a shy but pleasant intellectual who enjoyed engaging with others with whom he was comfortable. His arrest, in fact, struck younger colleagues with horror, as they had come to think of him as a mentor. If *they* had failed to flag Hanssen as a traitor, what other fundamentals about their universe were they getting wrong? This was a question that pierced the vanity of the FBI as an institution. There was a reason Hanssen was such a devastating spy: *he was very, very good at fooling the best of the best.*

Hanssen was a member of Opus Dei, a cultlike offshoot of Catholicism that demanded extraordinary and even self-punishing ritual demands of its practitioners. In his soul, he was the mirror image of what he projected to the world. He visited strip clubs and secretly—and routinely—videotaped himself with his wife, Bonnie, having sex. He even alerted at least one friend to his amorous schedule so that the friend could observe the Hanssens in bed from a perch outside their window.

Genuinely smart, Hanssen saw himself as being intellectually superior to his FBI colleagues. Still, he was careful not to inflict his brain on others. But there was a confection of arrogance and insecurity baking deep—very deep—beneath the surface. He surely thought that never meeting his Soviet handlers face-to-face was a stroke of brilliance that would insulate him from capture, and for a long time he was right. Scholars of the case suspect that, in addition to the $1.4 million he received for his services, his grandiose and unrequited sense of destiny drove him voluntarily into the arms of the Soviets not long after joining the FBI. After all, the Soviets hadn't seduced Hanssen: *he had gone after them.* No, the genius Hanssen had been too gifted to rise slowly through the ranks like the dullards around him. He had made his financial and psychic fortune on the side, undermining his employer and his country at every step—facilitating murder if he must—all the while living in a rich interior realm where he alone was king.

When Gennady heard the news about Hanssen's arrest so soon after he had signed Stepanov's passport application, he had a sickening feeling that Cowboy had possibly jeopardized him yet again. The Russians already thought Gennady was too tight with the Americans. And Sasha was still lurking somewhere in the FSB shadows.

When Gennady spoke to Cowboy, he was furious. He shouted, "You used me, you son of a bitch! I could have been killed."

Cowboy explained, "I handed him over, but no one really thought he had anything. I sure as hell didn't think it would be Hanssen. He was the bastard that dropped the dime on you in Havana! The one who put you in Lefortovo!"

"And you're the one who might get me a bullet in the head! Why didn't you tell me what you were after?" Gennady pressed. "I thought it was about caviar and some matryoshka doll bullshit!"

"I didn't know what we were gonna get, Gennady. And in the long shot that we'd get something big, I didn't want to put you in jeopardy. But this is my country. I didn't take yours away from you. Don't take mine away from me! I'm an American; you're a Russian."

"They're going to think I knew!"

"Nobody knew!" Cowboy said. "All you did was sign a passport application. A million things had to happen totally out of your reach, out of your knowledge, and out of your control."

"You know the CIA, but I know the KGB," replied Gennady. "Here, evidence isn't even needed for an execution."

Gennady might have made his worst ever mistake. But what could he do? He knew what he had done and what he hadn't done. He saw no action for himself other than to hope that his old nemesis Sasha Zhomov would never differentiate between the passport application Gennady had signed for Stepanov and the scores of others he had routinely signed. No, all he could do was hold his breath.

Ben Wickham says that both Cowboy and Gennady had had no idea they were getting the double agent by signing off for Stepanov. For Gennady it had been just a way to get the Snake out of his hair; for Cowboy it had been the longest of long shots. "It wasn't terribly unusual to get a visa for someone," Wickham explains. "Cowboy was almost [as] surprised as Genya when he heard that [Stepanov] actually had *the* file."

Both double agents had finally been taken down—Hanssen's

twenty-two-year traitorous career had cost not only lives but also over a billion dollars of electronic, computer, and spy-satellite information, while Ames's nineteen years of espionage had killed at least nine CIA assets.

Asked if he ever thought about getting Ames or Hanssen in a room, Cowboy said, "I think about it a lot…I'd say, 'From now on your wife should never start the car. Look who you've put in jeopardy. Fuck you!'" Indeed, Matty Caulfield says, "The only times I saw Jack insanely mad was over the Ames and Hanssen betrayals."

The takedown of Robert Hanssen was an intersection of extreme patience, good luck, firewalls, and operatives—witting and unwitting—bumping into one another and exploiting one another as circumstances arose. Nobody fully knew what they had until Hanssen was arrested, not even Stepanov.

The Hanssen takedown also prompts a few questions:

Is it possible that Gennady truly knew nothing about what the endgame of the caviar caper had been? The short answer is that everyone involved with the operation insists Gennady was kept in the dark about its objective. This is supported by the claims of the players that no one—not even Stepanov—was fully aware of what was in those pilfered files. To believe that Gennady knew he was conspiring to take down the prized Russian asset is to accept that the multiple players in the enterprise knew from the beginning, in linear fashion, precisely what the payoff would be.

Might Gennady have suspected at the very least that he was helping in some kind of counterespionage operation without knowing its details? Perhaps, but the kind of opportunistic deals that were presenting themselves in the business and intelligence communities after the collapse of the Soviet Union were commonplace. It is reasonable to assume Gennady signed off on Stepanov's passport application, as he did with others, without differentiating it from the numerous other inquiries that crossed his desk. To this day, Gennady categorically states that he had no idea he was doing anything to help nail Hanssen.

Another question is why would Jack Platt manipulate his friend Gennady in a manner that would get him in trouble, all the while claiming that his true objective was to get the man who had set up Gennady's capture, torture, and imprisonment years earlier? There are a few possibilities. The first, of course, is that Jack, too, was operating in the dark. This is hard to believe because, by his own admission, he wanted to capture the man who turned out to be Hanssen. Jack also worked actively with the FBI. One cannot both be part of a top-flight team to take down one of the greatest traitors of the twentieth century *and* be a babe in the woods.

Far more plausible is that Jack wanted to help roll up a big traitor *and* didn't really know where the whole program would lead. We can also look again to his own words when he was asked during the *60 Minutes* interview if true friends put each other in peril: "It may not be what friends do, but it may be what good intelligence officers do." Indeed, while Jack's friendship with Gennady mattered enormously to him, his commitment to his duty mattered more. Semper fi.

Years after Hanssen's takedown, Rochford said,* "[Stepanov] is really somewhat of a hero to the US government…I'll always be thankful to him for what he's done." Rochford has no idea where Stepanov is today, though. "He was ready to talk and to cooperate. The government was ready to write the check and support him in ways that he needed, and so we came to a good understanding. We were flexible, and he was flexible at a tough time in his life, so I think that's what it takes. You have to realize that it's a relationship, and these things aren't just 'Slam, bam, thank you, ma'am, we're done.' These things are ongoing."

Other heroes in this episode were Musketeers Jack Platt and Dion Rankin, who concluded that had they not been patient with Gennady for two decades, against CIA wishes, Stepanov would never

---

* Rochford never divulged or corroborated Stepanov's name to the authors. His identity was learned from a number of other sources.

have met Cowboy Jack, who then turned him over to Rochford, all leading to the unmasking of Robert Hanssen. It was these two Musketeers all along who had pleaded with their respective bosses to take things slow with Gennady. They knew that if their investment was to pay off, it would pay off in the distant future, even if no one envisioned precisely how—and no one could have. It had been, in the meantime, *softly, softly, catchee monkey.*

The Hanssen roll-up was not the only spy drama that played out in 2001, in what turned out to be a big year in espionage. And these other events would have grave implications for Gennady in the years to come.

Stepanov, of course, never collected the $1 million caviar payment because there never was any caviar, or matryoshka dolls, for that matter; the whole escapade had been a ruse. He collected many times that amount for nailing Hanssen. And Gennady, having unwittingly taken the second biggest risk of all, was left with a security job and the nagging fear that somewhere out there Sasha Zhomov would be looking for somebody to pay the invoice for Robert Hanssen. Anybody.

— 14 —

затишье перед бурей

(CALM BEFORE THE STORM)

Shortly after Jack's birthday present of Hanssen-on-a-stick, Gennady's old friend, the source known as AVENGER,* who may have provided the final nail in the coffin of Jack's SE colleague Rick Ames and who had been living temporarily in the US, was arrested in Moscow. Said to have been paid $2 million by the US for the Ames information, the fifty-year-old AVENGER and his wife had lived for a while in Haymarket, Virginia, then in Cockeysville, Maryland, where, sources say, the CIA had bought them a house for $980,000, then another for $400,000, in 2001. In Maryland, AVENGER ran a company called East-West International Business Consulting from his home. Although he said he was a consultant, some perceptive neighbors thought he was a spy (or at least he was suspicious), while one thought he was a pornographer.

AVENGER had been lured back to Moscow in 2001 for what his wife said he thought was a KGB reunion. Before leaving the US, he met with Mike Rochford and another agent for lunch in Virginia. Both agents tried to warn the asset, saying that his identity was

---

* In some references, the source is also code-named SCYTHIAN by the CIA. Scythians were Eurasian nomads whose culture flourished from around 900 BC to around 200 BC. They were known for their barbarism.

included in one of the files given to the Russians by Hanssen just a year earlier. "He refused to believe us and returned anyway," Rochford says. AVENGER was arrested on arrival at the Moscow airport.

"The evidence was so well documented," the Moscow *Gazeta* reported of AVENGER's subsequent 2003 trial, "that judges sentenced the traitor to two years longer than the prosecution demanded," for a total of eighteen years. It was not the last the world would hear of AVENGER. Seven years later, in 2010, his actual name would surface and be forever linked to Gennady Vasilenko, when one man's disclosures would play a critical role in the fates of both AVENGER and Gennady. In fact, they would inadvertently save Gennady's life.

Following the United States' Stepanov success and the AVENGER loss, another former KGB officer made himself—and his files—available to US intelligence. According to both Russian and US sources, that officer was forty-nine-year-old Minsk native Aleksandr Nikolayevich Poteyev. Having risen up through the KGB ranks, Poteyev went on to serve in Russia's new SVR, the Foreign Intelligence Service, where he was assigned to New York in the early 1990s. It was during his New York stint that he is believed to have been recruited by the CIA. After he rotated back to the Yasenevo Center, he was eventually promoted to the post of deputy director of the SVR's Department S, which runs spying operations in the United States. There at the Center, like Stepanov and so many other Russian spies who feared a looming nationwide economic depression under Putin and the oligarchs, Poteyev stashed away his own espionage nest egg.

Sometime in 2001, Poteyev cashed in, allegedly to the tune of between $2 and $5 million, when he tipped the Americans to ten of his US-based Russian agents living deep undercover with false identities, at least two of whom had maintained their "legends" for sixteen years by that point. Known as "Illegals" in Russian espionage parlance, these sorts of deep-cover agents, who blend in seamlessly with the target country's citizenry, are a Soviet/Russian trademark. They are considered "illegal" because they are unregistered with the host country's state department or interior ministry, which is the agreed-upon rule among hostile intelligence services. The Illegals program was initiated after the 1917 Russian Revolution, when the new Soviet Union was not formally recognized by other nations, and thus had no diplomatic cover available. The few trainees accepted into the program, culled through many hundreds of aspirants, were subjected to what the *New York Times* described as "grueling training, psychological screening for a life of isolation and stress." Soviet Party Chairman Leonid Brezhnev pointed out that only the most stoic, brave, strong people, without any weaknesses or defects, served in the program. In 2015, Lieutenant General Vadim Alekseevich Kirpichenko, who headed the program during the 1970s, described the pressures on the Illegals to the Espionage History Archive, saying, "It's one thing to become someone else for an evening or a theatrical season. And it's something totally different to turn into someone who once lived or a specially 'constructed' person, to think and dream in another language and not think of oneself in the real dimension. Therefore we often joke that an illegal going out into the operational arena could already be given the rank of people's artist." In the Russians' scheme, Illegals, who were never allowed to meet one another, would only activate in the event of war or a pre-war crisis, when diplomatic ties are severed and the "legal" Russian *rezident* spies from diplomatic missions are forced to leave. In that eventuality, the Illegals would handle the local contacts normally handled by the *rezident* spies; otherwise, they remained in deep hibernation, specifically ordered to refrain from recruiting assets or any other spying activities that could blow their cover. If a crisis never occurred, the Illegals could live their entire lives without taking on an assignment.*

---

*Perhaps the most famous Russian Illegal was Rudolf Abel (see the 2015 movie *Bridge of Spies*). His legend was so perfect that, after a decade spying under many aliases taken from deceased individuals, when he was tried and convicted by the US in 1957, even the prosecutors were fooled: they believed his real name was Rudolf Abel. However, in 1972 American journalists visited "Abel's" grave in Moscow and learned his actual birth name from the tombstone:

In 2001, there was no indication that these Illegals had been activated in any meaningful way, so US authorities decided to monitor them, in hopes of penetrating Russia's sources and techniques (such as determining their sophisticated electronic methods of communicating with one another and Moscow).

Ex-KGB agents were making money deals left and right with the "main enemy," while in Moscow, Sasha Zhomov was seething. And he now had one more traitor to track down. When—not if—he collared the offenders, Sasha vowed to make an example of them.

Everything in 2001 changed in the time it took two hijacked commercial planes to crash into two New York City skyscrapers. Unsurprisingly, security firms like Jack's HTG saw their phones light up on a nonstop basis after the attacks. Around the same time, Harry Gossett notes, there were also a number of terrorist train attacks overseas. Consequently, HTG was enlisted to conduct weeklong training exercises designed to recognize terrorist methods of casing public transportation installations for eventual destruction. Training was undertaken at most of Amtrak's large stations, from New York to Los Angeles.

Jack's daughter Michelle remembers accompanying her father and other HTG supervisors, like Gossett, to New York for some of these exercises, where the group spent after-hours penthouse time with De Niro and his downstairs neighbor and frequent co-star Harvey Keitel at their 110 Hudson Street address.

Jack, Harvey Keitel, Michelle Platt, Robert De Niro, and Gennady. (l. to r.)

William August Fisher. He had actually been born in the UK to Russian émigré parents. However, Fisher's great lifelong sacrifice achieved nothing of real significance. During his years as an illegal resident he appears not to have recruited, or even identified, a single potential agent.

De Niro, still researching his *The Good Shepherd* project with the help of Bearden and the Musketeers, watched the staged interrogations of the agents portraying the terrorists. He also learned about some of Hav "The Illusionist" Smith's best spy magic.

"One day on the set I showed Bob the accordion fold," Milt Bearden recalls, "which is folding a piece of paper, standing it on end, then lighting it at the creases until it disappears. There's no smoke. When the ashes floated to the ceiling it was coincidentally reminiscent of *Shepherd* screenwriter [Eric] Roth's feather scene in *Forrest Gump*, so it was a keeper."

Jack recalled one humorous incident that played out during the still-ongoing De Niro consulting gig: the actor wanted to be taught Haviland Smith's "brush pass" technique in a crowded environment. With Amtrak's permission, Jack took a bespectacled, hat-covered De Niro into Penn Station for the exercise. However, even with a porkpie hat pulled down over his brow, the actor was constantly recognized. What kind of spy gets asked for autographs in the middle of an operation? Jack laughed and called the whole thing off with two words De Niro had likely never heard before: "You're fired!"

"The serious part," remembers Gossett, "was that our trainees eventually rolled up a number of terrorists who were casing the stations."

Back in Russia, the business world—and life in general—was in a different kind of turmoil. The old hard-liners, embodied in the nascent strongman presidency of former KGB colonel Vladimir Putin, now shared power with the oligarchs, Russia's version of the United States' robber barons. The Russian variants of the Vanderbilts, Rockefellers, and Morgans had names like Abramovich, Berezovsky, and Prokhorov. The oligarchs had come to power under former president Boris Yeltsin, and his successor, Putin, was purging those who did not take a vow of loyalty to his new regime. The remaining oligarchs were wealthy businessmen who offered their support for Putin in exchange for the right to continue secretly buying off—at fire-sale prices—many of the country's most valuable assets and natural resources.* As author and Russia expert Gregory Feifer explains, "Putin and the oligarchs narrowed the space for competition, boosted the role of law enforcement, brought in a measure of suspicion and fear, which surely caused some former intel officers to think about lying low, and oversaw an explosion of corruption that enabled the Kremlin, and otherwise well-connected businesses, to snap up others." For small operations, the joint-venture honeymoon was over almost as fast as it had begun.†

Ben Wickham, HTG's CEO, recently reviewed the company's books during the post-honeymoon period. "Much of the inquiries we made through Gennady and others in Russia fell off during that period," Ben reports. "We had one major client whose interest in Russia in terms of due diligence declined, probably due to a number of factors: (a) [the] Russian bank collapse [in] 1998 and (b) the increase in Putin's power and fear by American banks and investment firms of a nationalization of Russian companies involved particularly in the oil and gas sectors."

For Gennady, this reversal meant reprioritizing his business career, especially after the denial of his 2002 passport request to come to the US and jump-start the joint venture. He now desperately needed one of the few well-paying, full-time jobs available in Russia. In 2003, Gennady, as was typical of him, landed on his feet at one of the snapped-up enterprises, NTV Plus,‡ where he was named deputy chief of security. Once again, Gennady's old-boy KGB network had come to his aid, this time in the form of his new boss, ex-KGB man Igor Filin, who had been a colleague—and fellow DC *rezidentura*

---

* A recent study concluded that the top 1 percent of Russians controlled 74 percent of the nation's wealth, despite Putin's "reforms."

† During the period from 1992 to 1995, 18,000 foreign joint ventures had been formed, involving $10 billion in private foreign direct investment (FDI), with the number of Americans involved rising from 625 at the beginning of 1992 to 2,800 by the end of 1993.

‡ Putin had recently purged the company of its Putin-critical owner, Vladimir Gusinsky, forcing him to sell off the company to Kremlin-controlled Gazprom-Media.

volleyballer—in the 1970s. This new, highly compensated job was a great financial boost for the extended Vasilenko family, as juggernaut NTV Plus was the first digital satellite channel in Russia, a division of the analog NTV channel, which was available to 70 percent of the Russian people. At the time, NTV was the only statewide independent TV channel in Russia. (Today, NTV Plus boasts 240 channels in its service.)

In late 2004, Milt Bearden wrote Gennady at his NTV office on De Niro's behalf, reminding him that he would soon be meeting with casting agents to read for his role in *The Good Shepherd*, which after almost a decade of germination was finally set to begin filming in August 2005. "I auditioned with other actors, but I was so nervous," Gennady recalls. "So I drank before the audition and didn't think I did so great because reading English is not easy for me—especially when I'm drunk." He was told that the studio would make a decision later that summer.

On March 28, 2005, after finally securing a passport and visa, Gennady arrived in New York with Igor Filin for meetings with their counterparts at Time Warner and HBO, as large corporations shared security strategies in the wake of the 2001 terror attacks. On his personal time, Gennady caught up with Robert De Niro, their discussions revolving around Gennady's potential casting in the role of "Ulysses." Gennady then traveled down to Washington to visit with his fellow Musketeers.

By this time, the friendly spies had concluded that all the drama in their lives was finally over. Gennady had been imprisoned and exonerated, and he and Jack had become successful businessmen who traveled often to see each other's families. Despite the oligarchs' thievery, life for Gennady was good; he had great friends all over the world, a lucrative job that allowed him to travel (a luxury for Russians), a country dacha, and an extended family he doted on—*and* he was about to become a movie star. His fellow spy pals in the US, the Musketeers, also seemed content in semiretirement, finally able to spend quality time with their families. Dion Rankin was living the good life in Macon, Georgia, while doing occasional contract work for the Bureau. Cowboy Jack was in Great Falls, running training sessions for HTG by day and, as a borderline insomniac, re-watching tapes of his favorite movies, the spy-themed *Hopscotch* and *Live and Let Die*, by night. Walter Matthau's *Hopscotch* was especially poignant for the Platt family: the plot centered on an authority-detesting CIA officer who has been assigned to a desk job.

Jack also finally had more time to devote on his sole grandson, Diana's son, Cody. Years later, Cody recounted taking Jack to his elementary school's Career Day: Before the class, students were asked to write down what they'd like to do for a living when they grew up. "When Jack walked in, in his tattered cowboy gear, they thought I [had] brought in a homeless person," Cody remembers. "Then he told them that he was a spy hunter, and I saw my classmates furiously erasing what they had written down for career choices. I felt bad—they had been hearing from lawyers, firemen, whatever, then I bring in fucking James Bond."

For Gennady, an enjoyable 2005 summer of hunting and fishing would culminate on his daughter Julia's thirty-ninth birthday on August 25, which would coincide with Moscow Days which Gennady, Masha, and his second family would be observing at the dacha.

Meanwhile, in Yasenevo, Sasha Zhomov had Gennady Vasilenko squarely in his crosshairs.

YOU DON'T KNOW ME

Everybody is bent–it depends how much.

August 25, 2005

As he drifted in and out of consciousness on the jail floor, deliriously recalling the commandos that had just tackled him in front of his family, Gennady strained to understand why the FSB was demanding that he confess to the Hanssen betrayal. Could it be that Zhomov just needed a scapegoat? Were they still holding a grudge regarding their inability to make the case against him stick in 1988? Was it the passport he signed off on for Stepanov, "the Snake" who sold the Hanssen file? Or was it another misinterpreted cable, like the one Cowboy had written and Hanssen had furnished to the KGB in 1988?

Years later, it would hit him that it might even have been a misinterpreted book. There is no way to know if Gennady's misinterpretation theory is correct, but it is certainly a possibility. In 2002, award-winning espionage author David Wise published his volume on the Hanssen saga, *Spy: The Inside Story of How the FBI's Robert Hanssen Betrayed America*. When the book finally made its way to the North America section at Yasenevo, the translators' eyes lit up when they read three unfortunately worded sentences on page 220 of the paperback edition. Regarding the FBI's quest to find someone to sell them the KGB's file on the second traitor (Hanssen), Wise wrote:

The FBI counterspies began to focus more and more on one former KGB officer. When he was stationed in Washington, he had been of interest to the FBI. The Russian had gone into private business after he retired from intelligence work and was living in Moscow.

Of course, that description fits the real traitor, Anatoly Stepanov, to a T, but it coincidentally fits Gennady Vasilenko even better: the former Washington-based KGB officer who was so close to the traitor Motorin; the Muscovite friend and private business partner of Jack Platt; the Line KR officer of such unending interest to FBI man Dion Rankin; the third Musketeer now convulsing on a concrete jail cell floor.*

How else, his tormentors must have wondered, could this outcast, stripped of his pension, have prospered so well that he could afford two families, a half-dozen children at least, a business office in the US, and a dacha in the countryside? What other gifts had the CIA or the FBI given him? While his main tormentor was the FSB's obsessive mole hunter Sasha Zhomov, elsewhere in Moscow, Sasha's minions destroyed the Vasilenko apartment, just as they had his dacha. They were busy looking for—and planting—evidence of betrayal.

Gennady lay in agony on the floor of his prison cell—wearing the

---

*The KGB had begun trolling Western spy books in earnest for such clues after some KGB colonels saw the 1975 movie *Three Days of the Condor,* based on the 1974 CIA thriller written by James Grady, who would go on to become, ironically, one of Gennady's many American friends linked to the Shoffler Brunch crew. *Condor's* main character works in the CIA's book analysis department. After the movie's release, the KGB established the Scientific Research Institute of Intelligence Problems (NIIRP), which employed thousands of book/magazine/newspaper reader-analysts. Coincidentally, Grady's book drew heavily on none other than David Wise's seminal 1964 nonfiction book on espionage, *The Invisible Government.*

FBI sweatshirt Ilya had brought for him after being told the clothes he had been wearing during his arrest had been soaked with blood. As he anticipated his next beating, a different kind of torture was unfolding in an area of the prison that was meant to be more civilized. In the waiting room, Masha was seated at a stark table, desperately trying to occupy her two young sons, Ivan, ten, and Alex, seven. The boys were grabbing at her, grabbing at each other, crying. There wasn't a couch to lie down on, a television set, a magazine, or even a pencil and paper for the boys to draw on. Didn't any of these police people have children of their own? Did they know what it was like to try to distract small children even when you had rudimentary entertainment at your disposal? They not only had been terrified by the violent Spetsnaz raid on the Vasilenko dacha but also had no idea what was coming next. Besides, they were hungry, having been pointedly deprived of food and water. The authorities had told them that they must wait, but for what? As the hours passed, the three were miserable. When Masha inquired, she was told to wait. Wait. Wait. As if they had something very special in store for her.

And they did.

A few hours later, another family was escorted into the waiting room. It was Gennady's wife, Irina, along with Ilya. They recognized one another immediately; after all, Masha had been a close friend of both Julia and Ilya, Gennady and Irina's children. So, Irina thought, what was Masha doing in the waiting room of a prison with two small boys who bore more than a passing resemblance to Gennady? Ilya found himself gazing into the eyes of his younger selves, a betrayal he would come to not easily forgive. His father's ordeal would give him additional reasons to be angry in the years ahead.

It didn't take a graduate degree in genetics or psychology from Moscow State for Irina to figure out what was going on here—what *had been* going on for a long time, evidently; Masha's facial expression was not exactly that of a seasoned spy. It was one thing to know her husband was a serial philanderer, which Irina had come to terms with years ago, but his supporting a second, secret family was more than any wife should be asked to accept.

A sniggering guard closed the door to the waiting room, and no one else was allowed to enter the seething human cauldron.

Gennady never found out precisely what words were exchanged during the kind of reunion only Sasha Zhomov and the FSB could coordinate, but the showdown was so terrible that virtually no one who was present will talk about it, even years later. As Gennady lay writhing on a concrete floor, an FSB operative paid him a visit to let him know the wonderful news: there had been a family reunion only a matter of yards away. He was left in isolation to imagine what had taken place.

Gennady's mind bounced between three things: the raw, physical throb of his injuries; the horror of what might await him now that the FSB firmly believed he had given up Hanssen (not to mention having been accused of terrorism); and what would become of his two families. How would he continue to support Irina, let alone look her in the eye? How would he face his older children, whose childhood friend had borne him two children? How would he take care of Masha and the boys?

Even in the throes of unimaginable adversity, Gennady maintained a childlike capacity for fantasy and wishful thinking. He had always figured he could pull off his two-family caper. Why would it be that difficult? He and Irina hadn't had any connection for years. Gennady loved his children, but what they didn't know wouldn't hurt them. He had always taken his pleasures as he found them. Was that so wrong given all he had been through in his life? Besides, he was a spy. Spies were stealthy and clever. If he could tiptoe in the shadows on behalf of a superpower, why couldn't a superspy keep his other family a secret? "Shit happens" is still how Gennady answers these questions today, without a modicum of reflection. But in that moment, since he didn't know what his future held, he knew that his marriage to Irina was over.

*   *   *

Sasha Zhomov personally interrogated Gennady during his early imprisonments in and around Moscow. "I'll keep you in prison in order to protect you until I find [the traitor]," Sasha vowed. He was very aggressive and went nose-to-nose with his captive but left the actual physical work to others. People lower down on the FSB food chain roughed up Gennady out of Sasha's earshot. Gennady, of course, never passed up an opportunity to goad Sasha by wearing either the FBI sweatjacket given to him by Dion Rankin or his YOU DON'T KNOW ME/WITNESS PROTECTION T-shirt, depending on the weather. When Sasha harassed Gennady about his inflammatory sartorial choices, Gennady earnestly told him, "It's comfortable and warm. If you bring me a comfortable FSB shirt, I'll wear it if it would make you happy." *Would a genuine Russian traitor be so brazen as to wear FBI gear?* Sasha must have asked himself. *Or was it that he just didn't care?*

After five days in the police jail, the FSB made a point of humiliating Gennady by moving him from one awful prison to another—first, a week at the Solntzevo police prison, followed by two months in the infamous Krasnaya Presnya, "Gulag Junction." In the five years ahead, he would find himself in a blur of more than a dozen prisons and detention colonies—sometimes doing multiple stints in the same hellhole. Given that Gennady was tortured, often mentally and physically unwell, and disoriented from being held in occasional solitary confinement, it is challenging to say precisely what happened where, when, and how. The authors have attempted to reconstruct and streamline, with Gennady's input and scattershot documentation, the highlights and lowlights of his incarceration between 2005 and 2010.

The impromptu transfers from prison to prison were conducted in the hope that incarcerated criminals would torture the new guy, the worst of turncoats, until he couldn't take it anymore. But Gennady possessed the superbly toned physique of the elite athlete he was, and he hoped it would help him survive. The irony wasn't lost on him that it was his facility in sports that had brought him, three decades prior, to the attention of Cowboy Jack, the man whose friendship had again landed Gennady in this position.

Back in New York in 2005, Robert De Niro, not knowing of Gennady's arrest, was ready to turn the charismatic Russian into a movie star. In the very month that Gennady was taken into custody, principal photography began, after years of delays, on De Niro's *The Good Shepherd*. Apparently, Gennady had passed his audition. "I wanted Gennady to play Ulysses," De Niro recently said. "But we couldn't find him." (The part ultimately went to Ukrainian actor Oleg Shtefanko.)*

In Virginia, Jack was in distress. He had quickly located articles about Gennady's arrest on the Internet. He felt responsible for putting his friend in harm's way, and now he could only imagine the horrors Sasha was inflicting on him in Russia's torture-chamber prisons.

More than once, Jack pulled his inscribed copy of Jacques Rossi's chilling memoir, *The Gulag Handbook*, off the shelf. The book Jack had convinced Rossi to write decades ago now replaced the Walter Matthau comedy *Hopscotch* as evening diversion. With his friend Gennady in mind, Jack read about the grim, overcrowded, and unsanitary dungeons—what Rossi called his "intimate nightmares." Included among those nightmares were tales of a prisoner roasted alive on a red-hot sheet of metal and a young escapee slaughtered in the snow, who then became the only food for prisoners trying to run away across the tundra. The thought of similar punishments being inflicted on Jack's charismatic, happy-go-lucky best friend was unbearable.

---

* The movie finally premiered on December 22, 2006, to mixed reviews. It ultimately earned approximately $100 million at the box office. Cowboy Jack had "mixed feelings" about the final result, especially the typical filmic exaggerations that are a necessity in most docudramas.

Ira Silverman, the dean of network TV investigative producers, was a friend of Jack's and recalls many an evening spent commiserating at Jack's Great Falls hangout, the Old Brogue Irish Pub—where Jack kept himself regimented to near beers and soft drinks. "Jack talked about it every day," Silverman remembers. "He couldn't forgive himself. He was desperate to help Genya and was asking everybody for advice." Likewise, Harry Gossett remembers Jack asking everyone, anyone, "What else can we do to help Genya?" Gossett says that Jack was in regular contact with Ilya and passed on Ilya's awful updates to the Brogue gang. "I remember once Jack said that Genya had a vascular problem in his leg," Gossett says. "He thought his friend was dying."

Immediately after Genya's arrest, Cowboy began sending him messages of support, via Ilya. But his imprisoned friend did not—most likely could not—respond. Cowboy's frustration and anger only intensified, and he would repeat the refrain to anyone who would listen: "Genya's arrest was pure damage control. They needed someone to arrest in response to Hanssen."

REPLY: MOI BRATI

AS YOU SEE, I GOT THE MESSAGE. VERY HAPPY TO HEAR FROM YOU. UNDERSTAND THE HIGH DEGREE OF FRUSTRATION BECAUSE OF INJUSTICE ALL WHO KNOW YOU, YOUR CAREER, YOUR TEMPERAMENT. KNOW THAT THIS WAS A "TRAP" -- G A V N O...

FOR NOW, THE FOLLOWING FRIENDS HAVE DEMANDED THAT THE FIRST MESSAGE TO YOU MUST CONTAIN THEIR FOND GREETINGS TO YOU-- THAT YOU ARE N O T FORGOTTEN-- THAT SOME PEOPLE ARE TRYING THEIR BEST FOR AN EARLY RELEASE FROM THE PRESENT SMOLENSK LOCATION.

JACK AND PAIGE, FATHER-OF-2 AND JENNIFER, BEN AND JULIE, BOB &TONI, DEE AND CODY AND BOB AND MISH, THE GODFATHER AND TONY OF FBI FAME, MAD DOG AND MIKE THE COUNTERSPY, ALL THE GUYS FROM SHOFFLER BRUNCH (DANNY, PHIL, HARRY, JEFF, TOMMY THE COP, KARL THE COP, IRA AND HIS TV FRIENDS), VAL AND IRENE, KARL SEGER AND FAMILY, MANU FROM TEL AVIV, THE DESK GUYS AND STACEY AT THE VIRGINIA BEACH HOTEL, POLICE CAPT BILLY DEANES, PHIL PARKER, AND LANE'S WIFE MARY ELLEN, AISLING FROM "ROCCO'S".

FINALLY, ILYA KNOWS YOU GOT A CARD (CHRISTMAS) FROM DE NIRO. THE DATES ARE NOT FIXED YET BUT WHEN BOBBY D VISITS MOSCOW (TO MAKE THE MOVIE) HE WILL ASK TO VISIT YOU WHEREVER YOU ARE.

CHEERS,
SAD BUT SMILING MUSKETEER

By the spring of 2006, Jack's concerns had reached a breaking point, and he decided it was time for action. As a seventy-year-old retired CIA officer, he was well aware that he would need help from younger men still in the game. But by this time, Jack was so disgusted with the CIA and its nonresponse to Gennady's predicament, that route wasn't even an option. Thus the best conglomeration of the needed skills clearly resided in the members of the Shoffler Brunch, with its diverse attendees, which included CIA officers, FBI agents,

DC police, congressional investigators, mob informants, and private investigators. This crew either knew how to tackle the most sensitive operations or knew someone who could.

One Shoffler mainstay was fifty-six-year-old investigator-author Dan Moldea. The Akron, Ohio, native and former president of the Washington Independent Writers association has a storied and respected history of taking on some of the most powerful people (the mafia, corrupt teamsters, President Ronald Reagan) and institutions (the NFL, MCA, the *New York Times*) in America. His prodigious and indefatigable investigative skills, combined with his congenial and scrupulously loyal manner, have made him arguably the most connected insider in the nation's capital. For over thirty years he has coordinated the DC Authors Dinner, which twice yearly brings more than one hundred of the country's best writers to Georgetown for an informal networking bash. Jack, who had been introduced to Moldea a dozen years earlier by the eponymous Carl Shoffler, sought his advice regarding Gennady's predicament.

"After Gennady disappeared again, Jack called me," Moldea says, remembering that Jack's usual jovial voice sounded uncharacteristically somber. Moldea had met Gennady twice before at Shoffler Brunches in 1997, when Gennady and his ex-KGB pals like Cherkashin had been visiting Jack on HTG business.

"Meet me ASAP," Jack said. The next day, at the Marriott Hotel restaurant in Rosslyn, he pleaded with Moldea. "Can you help Gennady?" He told Dan that Gennady's situation stemmed from how Gennady had assisted the FBI with a huge security problem. "Without even knowing it, he led the FBI to Hanssen," Jack whispered.

"I had never heard of Vasilenko's role in this matter before," Moldea says. "In effect, I considered it my patriotic duty to help free him." After a nanosecond of consideration, Moldea replied, "I think I got a guy."

Moldea's recommendation was his longtime friend and source Ron Fino, a former officer in a mobbed-up union in Buffalo, New

York, who had secretly worked as an undercover consultant for the FBI and the CIA for many years, helping put scores of major mafia figures in prison. Fino would eventually work in Russia, importing vodka into the United States while developing information about Russian mobsters, among many others, for US intelligence and law-enforcement agencies.

The next day, Moldea approached Fino. "During this meeting, Fino and I discussed the Vasilenko situation," says Moldea. "He suggested that we raise the necessary money to bribe a Russian government official who might be able to get Vasilenko out of prison." Jack remembered Fino from years earlier, but only by his code name, GORKY, from when the two of them had helped legendary CIA officer Dick Stolz on arms-smuggling investigations. Jack recalled the reintroduction years later: "Moldea introduced me to Fino because his wife's family, which owns a meat-packing factory in Belarus, are in contact with Russian mobsters who might be able to help."

According to Michelle Platt, Jack made some kind of deal with Fino, the upshot of which was that Fino's wife's family would get their meat supplied at half price if, and only if, they could keep Gennady from getting killed in prison. (Either no one knows the particulars or they know and don't want to elaborate.) Fino then supplied Jack with the names of major Russian mob figures; Jack, in turn, passed those contacts along to Gennady's son Ilya and suggested Ilya make contact.

One of the mobsters whose name Ilya received was a fearsome character based in Moscow's Luberetskiy district known only as Slava. Slava got word back to Fino that he would help Gennady for $10,000. Ilya came up with the money, ostensibly from his family's savings, and reached out to Slava's minions. Meanwhile, Gennady was freezing in his prison cell. Notes made in his diary from around this time read, "Still no heat in sell [*sic*]. We are freezing."*

---

* Genya wrote the diary in English so as to keep as many prying eyes from reading it as possible.

Recent interviews suggest that the next act played out something like this:

Thirty-five-year-old Ilya tracked down Slava's boys in the back of a run-down store. Ilya entered with a mix of terror and hope. *Terror* because he would be dealing with murderers. *Hope* because these murderers might be in a unique position to get his father freed, or at least treated humanely. *One can't expect the kind of men who can get big things done to be sweethearts,* he reasoned.

The store was one of those stores that didn't sell anything. He had heard about places like these and seen them in movies about the mafia, where a vague sign out front masks the kind of activities taking place inside. He wondered if the Russians had borrowed this shtick from American cinema or if criminals all over the world had a viral understanding that this was how things were done.

A young tattooed punk stood against a doorway and eyed Ilya up and down, sniffing as if he were unimpressed. Indeed, Ilya—lean, baby-faced, and looking like a university student—was visibly out of his depth, and the punk let him know it without saying a word. He just crossed his arms and smirked at Ilya, who supposed that non-verbal humiliation was what counted for amusement in the criminal underworld.

Ilya explained that Slava had sent him. Tattoos wasn't impressed. He gave Ilya a look as if to say, "Big man knows Slava. Please don't hurt me, big man."

Ilya swallowed hard and pressed, emphasizing that he was here to help his father. *As if this hoodlum has any empathy for a son trying to help his imperiled old man.*

Tattoos turned and went into a back room. He emerged in a few minutes and waved Ilya back. Ilya moved cautiously into the dark, concrete-floored room. There he encountered two stocky, unshaven men sitting at two corners of a cheap table, as if they had been playing a game or counting money, but there was nothing on the table now.

The older of the two men spoke. "You are Ilya?"

"Yes."

"Ilya Vasilenko?"

"Yes."

The gangster said with a smirk something about Ilya being the son of the famous superspy.

Ilya said nothing. The lead gangster—we'll call him Dr. No—didn't ask Ilya to sit, and Ilya was not inclined to make the request. His instinct was to get the hell out of there, and fast. But he couldn't run now. Between these two goons at the table and Tattoos on the other side of the doorway, Ilya didn't see a viable way out. And assuming he could escape, the gangsters knew who he was and who his father was, and they could surely get to them. Having no good options, he had to stay and try to survive the encounter.

Since passivity was getting him nowhere, Ilya decided to assert himself, at least a little. After all, he wouldn't have been there if he didn't know some interesting characters himself, men with their own unique capabilities.

"I was told that Slava could help my father and was given this address to come to."

"How were you told Slava could help?" Dr. No asked.

"My father is in prison. He was charged with terrorism, something he did not do—"

"I was told he was a traitor," Dr. No said.

Ilya explained that Gennady was not a traitor, that he had been framed. Dr. No reasoned the situation out differently, expressing that if Gennady had been framed, then perhaps important people wanted it that way. Who was he to judge their motives and get mixed up with their plans?

Dr. No asked again how Ilya was told that Slava could help. Ilya stated that the objective was very simple: given that Gennady had been wrongly imprisoned, his family wanted the court to understand that he was innocent and release him.

Dr. No reasoned that this was the job of a lawyer.

Ilya shifted on his feet as the two hoods sat comfortably at the table. He expressed doubt that a judge would listen. He had been under the impression that Slava knew someone in a position of authority who might understand that his father had been framed.

The gangster feigned shock. Was Ilya suggesting Dr. No would bribe a public servant? Why, heaven forbid! He would never do such a thing here in Russia! After all, bribes were illegal. Who did Ilya think they were?

Ilya soldiered on, stressing that he had been led to believe that Slava could speak—or have someone speak—to the appropriate authorities to help his father get out of prison, or at least be treated better while he was in prison, to be protected.

Dr. No asked if Ilya had the money. Ilya said that he did, removing the equivalent of $10,000 from his coat pocket, and set it down on the table. The junior gangster took the envelope and looked inside. He nodded as if he was pleased with its contents.

"Will you help?" Ilya asked.

"Yes, of course," Dr. No responded.

"What will you do?"

"Let's see, what will I do…?" Dr. No then outlined his horrifying proposal: He would leave Ilya alive, period. And he would do nothing for Gennady. Nothing. If, in fact, the FSB wanted him to rot, why shouldn't Dr. No enforce their will? Who was he to tangle with the FSB? Ilya was instructed to tell whatever clown had told him to use Slava's name that he met with a fine gentleman who vowed to do all he could to help his traitor father—even though he would get nothing from Dr. No. Ilya would say nothing else because if he did, Dr. No would find him, kill him, and mail pieces of him to his father. And then he would kill Gennady, too.

"Do you understand?" Dr. No asked, unconcerned with the answer.

Ilya felt his body go numb and break into a sweat. Did he just hear what he thought he heard? These animals would take his money and not raise a finger to help Genya. He looked at the two men as they sat passively at the table. He waited for a smile or a hearty Russian laugh along with an exclamation such as "We were kidding! Of course we'll help you, silly boy!"

But there was no reassurance, only the black eyes of a shark that would devour its prey as a matter of remorseless biology. Why did moviemakers feel the impulse to make these animals into Shakespearean kings, full of complexity and operatic pretentions, when they were nothing more than cockroaches?

Ilya knew there was no arguing at this point. The affair had been adjudicated. He left the back room, a journey of only a few steps that felt like a long climb to the summit of Mount Everest. As he passed into the store, he thought that the tattooed punk from earlier might jump out and knife him. He had no knife, but his mocking words cut deeply as Ilya opened the front door to leave.

A voice mocked him from the shadows: "Say hello to Slava for us."

Ilya proceeded down the dark Moscow street, his head aflame with betrayal and despair. Cowboy and his fabled connections had come up woefully short. Even Cowboy, with all his shadowy associates, was capable of getting scammed in the new Russia. What would he do now? What would become of his father given the kinds of beasts that inhabited this world? Was his father getting his just deserts for something he had done in the world of espionage, or even in the karmic sense because of how he had treated his family? Ilya wasn't sure where he would even go now. He didn't know how he could tell his family about what had just happened, but he would have to tell them *something*. Things couldn't get much worse, could they? Yes, they could, he decided. They could kill his father. They could kill his family. Still, Ilya was filled with such rage now, he decided he would tell his family, and Cowboy and his father's friends, exactly what had taken place.

As he made what he thought was a life-or-death decision, Ilya was overcome by terrifying possibilities: What if his ordeal had nothing to do with freeing Gennady at all? What if it had been nothing more than an opportunistic *mafiya* scam to shake down a vulnerable family for cash? What if his father's fabled spy friends were no better connected than the old woman standing on the corner in a babushka with a sack of spoiled groceries. *Hell,* Ilya thought, *there probably had never been a Slava at all.*

Back in Virginia, Ron Fino was likewise stunned when Cowboy told him what had happened to Ilya in Moscow during the Slava caper. He assured Cowboy that he had been in touch with serious players and vowed to find out what had gone down. Fino, however, wondered why the CIA wasn't doing more, asking, "Why do you want to do this on your own?"

"Because," Cowboy answered, "my own fucking company is a coward."

Meanwhile, Cowboy, Fino, and the Shoffler Brunch boys dug in, and Ron Fino took Ilya's rip-off so personally that he made a partial reimbursement out of his own savings.

— 16 —

THE GULAG REDUX

C'mon, Jack. Don't forget me. I once saved your life.
Now you can save mine.

Gennady's first trial finally took place in May and June of 2006 in the Golovinskiy district court of Moscow. The initial charges were for terrorism, given the explosives and firearms "found" at his dacha. Gennady was certain that the terrorism charges were psychological warfare and that they wouldn't actually bring such a thing into open court—but they did. Moreover, the prosecutor was asking for nineteen years, essentially a death sentence, with a little torture thrown in. Gennady couldn't believe it and was sure a jury wouldn't either when they saw the evidence. His attorneys requested a jury trial, but the judge denied the motion. No, a judge—one judge—would decide his case. Gennady knew what that meant: an *operative* in the pocket of the FSB.

Gennady was hospitalized at least once before his trial began, other than for the injuries sustained during his arrest, but Ilya arranged through his father's friends for the medical leave as a reprieve from prison. The FSB, of course, made sure that Gennady was held in a hospital within the walls of the notorious Matrosskaya Tishina (Sailor's Silence), where some of the plotters in the 1991 Soviet coup had been held. The message was clear: this was a prison for traitors. "I was chained to a bed like a dog for two weeks," Gennady recalls.

As the case against him unfolded, Gennady's diary notes betray abject desperation. "Reading the case! Something unbelievable!!! Liers!!! [*sic*] Savage!" The witnesses brought against Gennady were straight out of a Kafka story. Some of them were actually his fellow prisoners, who were given the same baggy suit to wear as they testified against him in exchange for shorter sentences. Gennady recognized them from around the jailhouse. *These* were the witnesses against him? Yes, Gennady had admitted his terrorist plots to them, they said. He wanted to blow up the Kremlin. Lenin's tomb, too. Did he want to blow up the Black Sea? Oh, yes, he certainly wanted to blow that up. There were no monuments or natural resources inherent to the Russian identity that Gennady wasn't plotting to immolate.

At one point a witness was asked to identify Gennady in a photo lineup with two other men: Motorin and Martynov. This lineup was submitted into evidence. Of all the photographs the witness could have been shown, the other two chosen for the lineup were the two notorious Soviet turncoat friends of Gennady's. Really? The prosecutor asked the witness "which spy" did he speak to, just to send a message to Gennady that the FSB was screwing with him because he was a traitor.

Prison authorities testified against him, too. They alleged that Gennady had smuggled weapons into the prison and had been violent. "Same shit!" is a repeated entry in his diary. Gennady's lawyers investigated the witnesses in order to prepare their cross-examinations, but the witnesses were either inmates who had been coached in their testimonies beforehand or, worse, ciphers who didn't appear to exist at all.

Team Gennady knew things weren't going well—and how committed the FSB was to nailing him—when they found out they had also stocked his garage, located a few miles from his dacha, with explosives. Gennady had a relative who used that garage for a car repair business, and he had visited the guy in the weeks before his bust. Apparently, the FSB had been following him and tapping his phones to make sure all their bases were covered. They wanted to be able to show that Gennady was so devious that he used an off-site garage for his terrorism business. To mimic telltale forensics, they laced his car's steering wheel and door handles with the same kind of residue that was in the garage where the explosives were found, to create a link between the two locations. Gennady theorized that the FSB noticed he had bought paint for his dacha and had been cleaning his hands with kerosene. Fearing he might wash off any explosives residue, they had probably waited to apply a fresh smattering of residue in strategic locations immediately before his arrest just to be on the safe side.

Gennady's lawyers were frustrated and embarrassed that they could do nothing to stop the morbidly cartoonish prosecution. He had hired about a half-dozen attorneys since his arrest. Ilya had had to sell his father's car in order to pay Gennady's counsel, the very one that had been laced with explosives residue. Each of the attorneys came into the case ambitious and fresh eyed but left despondent when they realized what they were up against. Eventually, Gennady sensed that even his own lawyers were afraid to press things too hard lest they become enemies of Russian intelligence services. He was well aware that Russia doesn't believe in a vigorous and adversarial defense, or even codified law, the way the US does, and lawyers are considered prudent to be mindful of this convention. "It's not like in the US, where they have to prove a crime. If FSB says it's a crime, it's a crime." Gennady eventually instructed Ilya to "stop spending money on lawyers. It's decided."

While Gennady's trial received scant media attention, journalists who paid attention to the case thought something didn't seem kosher. Indeed, author and Russia expert Gregory Feifer, who witnessed the trial, recalls there was a theory floating around that Gennady had been arrested as part of a power play related to a security job he had held at his media company, NTV Plus. The story was that a Kremlin big shot wanted to take over the network and Gennady's boss was resisting—it was all about dueling oligarchs. Gennady's arrest, according to this theory, was a message: if the boss didn't accede to the takeover, he might suffer a similar fate. Regardless of the seriousness of this account—and Feifer acknowledges it was just loose gossip—the words that crop up to describe the circumstances of Gennady's arrest in news reports include "murky" and "unclear."

Then there came a sliver of light. Two KGB colonels and friends of Gennady testified that he had never even learned how to deal with explosives and that such weapons had played no role in his education. Gennady sensed at this point that even the judge became worried that the frame-up was too outrageous. Watching the surprise testimony, Gennady's mind spun with the possibility that perhaps Jack had worked his magic after all.

Gennady's lawyers saw an opening and they took it. They sensed the judge's trepidation. It was one thing to preside over a conspiracy but another to preside over a farce. Conspiracies were respected in Russia; farces were problematic because they created political risk. The charade of jurisprudence was central to the illusion of a modern and progressive Russia. The lawyers positioned the judge's newfound willingness to consider new evidence, however limited, to their client as a victory, and perhaps, on some level, it was. They aggressively pressed the court about the ends to which Gennady was involved with terrorism and argued that the prosecution hadn't produced a single witness to link him to a particular event or political cause. If Gennady was a terrorist, what was the target of his hatred? Who exactly were his associates? What exactly had he intended to blow up besides, well, everything?

After the pushback on the allegations, the court lowered the charges against Gennady from terrorism to possession of explosives. The judge convicted him and sentenced him to three years in a low-security prison (which actually turned out to be a series of prisons). Gennady was too miserable to see this as a victory despite it being far better than the initial nineteen-year request from the prosecution. After all, he was getting three years for doing nothing. Nothing at all.

Gennady hadn't been wrong to wonder whether the judge's newfound flexibility hadn't been due a little help from his friends. Indeed, Ron Fino had been doubling down on his contacts in Russia and likely got to the son of either a judge or someone in a position to influence the court. In other words, there was a distinct possibility that Gennady's somewhat improved fate had been due to something other than shrewd lawyering. Moldea says, "Although there were complications with our mission, I later learned that the payoff to the Russian official was made and that, although he was not released, Vasilenko received a significantly reduced prison sentence."

But the hard work was just beginning. Gennady was still extremely vulnerable in the Russian prison system, and something bad could happen to him at any time. In Russia, you were only as good as your last payoff, not to mention your last blessing from someone powerful, or very, very scary. Fino was able to reach out through intermediaries, including a notorious arms smuggler, to the elusive Slava, who was furious to learn what had happened when Ilya had met the thugs to make a payoff for his father. The mobster who had pocketed Ilya's money, a man known as "Timor," soon found himself on the receiving end of a "valuable life lesson," according to Cowboy, who wouldn't go into details about the punishment, save that it was gruesome. "It makes my lost finger seem like a splinter," he said. "Let's just say he will never live another minute on this planet without being acutely aware of his fucking mistake." With that, Cowboy made a gesture of zipping his lips. But he couldn't suppress a subtle grin, leaving the rest to the imagination.

Fino also worked other Russian contacts, including Alexander Orlov, a former Kremlin journalist who introduced him to Pyotr Aven, president of Alfa Bank. Through these contacts, Fino got word back to FSB operatives that Gennady had never given in to Cowboy's overtures and had not, in fact, betrayed his country. While skeptical of this report, Gennady was nevertheless transferred to a somewhat less brutal prison in Smolensk.

During his inexorable shuttling from prison to prison, Gennady was able to correspond with Cowboy a few times, including via email from a low-security *koloniya* (colony) in Desnogorsk, which is distinct from the harsh prison also located in that town. In Desnogorsk *prison* there were no toilets, just buckets. Also, in *koloniyas*, inmates can sleep; in prisons, they regularly cannot because they have to rotate on concrete, often urine-stained floors. Gennady never knew when he'd be in a prison or in a *koloniya*. Masha and the boys even visited Gennady at Desnogorsk *koloniya*, and the photos from that time depict a smiling, if gaunt, Gennady—and a very relieved-looking Masha.

Dion Rankin heard from Gennady only once during his imprisonment. Gennady called him from Desnogorsk in December of 2007, saying, "I'm okay, but I'm in the hospital. I needed a rest." Gennady said he had injured himself while working out. "We spoke for an hour. His spirits were pretty good. Then he got busted for having [an] illegal cell phone with an illegal SIM card," Dion says.

The backdrop to Gennady's imprisonment was his captors' unrelenting pursuit of a confession, and they had no intention of releasing their prize catch any time soon. How vindictive were Russian bureaucrats? On the eve of Gennady's long-scheduled 2008 release, they planted an illicit SIM card in the duffel bag in his prison cell.

The SIM card bust was no small deal. Initially, Gennady had been told that his stay at Desnogorsk would last three weeks, but then he got pinched and knew he was in big trouble. Gennady wrote in his diary: "The doom's day [*sic*]...I was set up. The authorities dropped SIM-card in my bag and [indecipherable] punishment, means official report and no release from prison!" The following day, Gennady added: "First thing in the morning I was officially punished…At 11 o'clock I have a heart attack—ambulance gave me a few shots and disappear. I feel terrible…I'm in their hands. They want my death… <u>Fuck them</u>!!!!"

It is unclear whether Gennady actually suffered a heart attack in the clinical sense, but there is some evidence of his suffering an acute cardiac event. In one diary entry, Gennady wrote: "Hell of a day! Blood pressure = 200 x 130!" Even if he didn't have a heart attack, one couldn't blame him for suffering a serious stress-related episode given the frame-up and what surely awaited him, which was another trial and extended prison stay, this time in Desnogorsk. He was charged with "severe rule breaking," and in addition to the SIM-card count, the prison accused him of illicitly using someone else's computer.

During a trial in November and December of 2007, Gennady's lawyers found an ally who would claim that he had accidentally put the SIM card in his bag. The ever-patient Sasha Zhomov was tiptoeing through the shadows and colluded with the judge in Gennady's case to make sure the ally's claim was soundly rejected. Moreover, when he returned to his cell, the ally found himself on the receiving end of a serious beating for abetting Gennady's defense. Gennady was convicted, which added a few more years to his sentence. This time, his ultimate destination was the dreaded prison in Bor.

But first, a few more stops.

The sudden-transfer scenario was becoming more familiar to Gennady: He would be adjusting to prison life when early one morning he would be kicked awake by a guard holding his duffel bag. "Time to move," the guard would say, and Gennady would be tossed into the back of a windowless van and transported to some other gulag-like abomination.

In one of his more flexible prison stays, Gennady was coaching volleyball and heard a voice coming from behind him. He had grown accustomed to voices so hostile that they sounded like weapons, thus he was surprised to hear one that was not only friendly but familiar: "Wouldn't it just be easier to bring in ringers?"

Gennady turned around and saw his old volleyball-playing friend from Yasenevo, Aleksandr Zaporozhsky.

Gennady hugged Zaporozhsky so hard he nearly knocked him over. "What is a nice guy like you doing in a dump like this?" Gennady asked affectionately, the first time he could recall being playful in a very long while.

"I figured you were dead by now," Zaporozhsky said, piquing Gennady's curiosity. *What exactly had he heard?*

Gennady cut his coaching short and sat with his old friend against a fence in the prison yard. Zaporozhsky told Gennady that he had likewise been tortured by order of Sasha Zhomov. Gennady asked him why he had been imprisoned.

"They found me guilty of helping the CIA," Zaporozhsky answered.

"Did you?"

Zaporozhsky offered an ambiguous expression and shrugged. "Who knows what to believe?"

"I wonder how much that cost the CIA," Gennady said.

"I'm guessing around two million dollars, but I'm just guessing. So why exactly are you here?"

"I kidnapped the Lindbergh baby. After I stabbed Julius Caesar to death."

"Seriously," Zaporozhsky pressed.

"Hanssen."

"You son of a bitch. How—?"

"But I didn't... It's complicated. I helped a guy get a passport. One thing triggered another..." Gennady tried to explain.

"And what did *you* get for it?"

Gennady looked around, gesturing to the prison. "You're looking at it."

"I was such an idiot to come back for that reunion." Zaporozhsky sighed, referring to the KGB old-boys gathering.

"In 2001? I was there, but I didn't see you."

"I didn't make it—Sasha grabbed me at the airport."

Ah, Sasha. "You're lucky," Gennady said. "At least he didn't torture you."

"Oh no?" Zaporozhsky lifted up his shirt, revealing a hopscotch of what appeared to be cigarette burns.

Gennady gasped. "Motherfucker."

It turned out that Zaporozhsky worked in the prison canteen, a fact that made the reunion extra special. "He smuggled out some decent food for me, vegetables," remembers Gennady. "It was the best present I got in prison." Pretty soon they would be back to playing volleyball together.

The two men sat and talked about their home lives and the state of their erstwhile country, which, as far as both men were concerned, didn't exist anymore. "Our country is past," they agreed, invoking a phrase Gennady uses often. Zaporozhsky didn't press Gennady on the intricacies of his two families, and Gennady didn't press his friend on the details surrounding the takedown of Jack's colleague Rick Ames. The last thing he needed was more information that could be beaten out of him by Sasha's jackals. Better to be bloody and ignorant, Gennady reasoned, than bloody and insightful.

Zaporozhsky said that he missed the US, specifically how much he had enjoyed living in Northern Virginia. On one hand, it was close to Washington. On the other, it was its own country. The US, Gennady thought, was actually many countries.

"I once knew someone who lives there." Gennady teared up, thinking of Jack Platt and their days roaming the Virginia woods, shooting guns at whatever seemed to scurry along the ground, and sometimes even things that didn't. "I miss him," Gennady said. "Our country is past, and some friends are past," he added, his eyes wandering from fence to fence, and wall to wall.

*   *   *

By 2008, Jack had heard nothing from Gennady for over a year. He approached his former CIA colleague and fellow De Niro consultant Milt Bearden for help in putting pressure on the Russians to treat Gennady gently. Jack's core argument was that Gennady should be freed since he had *never* been a traitor and had not knowingly given up Hanssen. According to Jack, Bearden turned him down, and Jack would never speak to him again. Bearden, however, explains that he wasn't being merely contrarian; De Niro's loyalty to his many friends can overwhelm him with favor requests, and Bearden was trying to shield him from getting involved in a murky situation. "What did he want Bob to do?" Bearden asked recently. "At the time, Jack didn't even know exactly why Gennady had been arrested. Yet he wanted Bob to make it 'a cause.'"

Bearden's observation came with an unspoken implication: even if Gennady hadn't actually become a traitor, his relationship with Jack had been insanely reckless and had provoked the Russians into taking an understandable, if draconian, retaliatory action. *Had these two espionage cowboys actually thought they could carry on the way they had and the vindictive Sasha Zhomov would do nothing?*

Jack's guilt was eating away at him; he knew he had put Gennady in a position where it appeared to the Russians that he had betrayed them. Consequently, Jack was determined to locate and help Gennady in any way possible—wherever he might be.

Around this time, Gennady got into trouble for having a cell phone and was transferred once more to a strict facility. Fino tried to help him again, but by this time fluctuating relations with the US were at a low point, and no one would assist.

Jack then concocted a backup plan to get a message to Gennady and, more importantly, his tormentors. He went around Bearden and paid a visit to De Niro in New York, and De Niro readily agreed to help by passing one of De Niro's annual Christmas cards to Gennady via De Niro's friend, revered Russian film director Nikita Mikhalkov.

The director, through his contacts in the Kremlin, should be able to determine what had become of Gennady and have the holiday card forwarded to him. Mikhalkov agreed that if he located Gennady, he would pass along De Niro's card to him. Since De Niro was (and still is) revered in Russia, the thinking was that both the inmates and the prison officials would never treat a friend of his badly.

A few weeks later, the famously laconic De Niro called Jack with good news in the form of just two words: "He's fine." De Niro's Christmas card—with a photo of him with Gennady—was his prison Teflon, not to mention the kind words passed down from the very real Slava, whose main contribution was permitting Gennady to invoke his name. From that point on, Gennady was treated humanely. Russian guards and inmates alike, all of whom respected tough guys, real and fictional, wanted a piece of the man who knew young Vito Corleone, Jimmy "the Gent" Conway, Al Capone, Paul Vitti, "Ace" Rothstein, "Noodles" Aronson, Travis Bickle, Jake LaMotta, and so many other characters De Niro had brought to life.

More protection came in the form of fellow prisoner Aleksandr Kuptsov, brother of famed composer Vladimir. Aleksandr successfully protected Gennady by telling him to mention that he was friendly with fearsome Moscow mob boss Slava, and he would be left alone. The ploy worked.

Now, at least, Jack could sleep at night. But how to get his friend's sentence commuted? Even De Niro couldn't help with that one.

As he tumbled through the kaleidoscope of prisons, Gennady scribbled furiously in his diary. Entries such as "There is no justice in this fucking country," "Black day of my life," "Nobody wants to take responsibility," and oblique references to Slava abound, but so does Gennady's more optimistic spirit with notes like "Let's celebrate another day of living" and "Happy Birthday little son!!! 9 years!!! Big Boy!!!"

But Sasha, unimpressed with Gennady's big Tinseltown connection, hadn't given up. He had his jailers tell Gennady that they had incarcerated Ilya, promising, "Your son will spend all his days and nights in Lefortovo until you confess to the Hanssen thing."

"I knew nothing about Hanssen!"

"Poor little naïve KGB officer," one interrogator told Gennady, patting his head like a schoolboy. "Just taken advantage of against his will. Hanging around with FBI agents and CIA officers—with no idea that they could possibly be up to something."

Gennady repeated that he had known nothing about the endgame of Hanssen's capture.

"Are you feeble-minded, Vasilenko?"

"Of course not."

"Then you're either a smart, seasoned KGB officer or an idiot," the interrogator told him. "You cannot be both! You expect us to believe that an elaborate operation by the Americans to expose and shut down one of the greatest assets we have ever had was one big comedy of errors?"

"All I know was that I played no role in the operation."

"But you signed the paperwork for the passport for [Stepanov]?"

"I signed lots of paperwork for lots of passports!"

"Then if you signed the paperwork," the interrogator said, "how can you claim you played 'no role'—your exact words—in the operation?"

"I didn't play any role *knowing* what they were doing," Gennady explained.

"Ah. And you think these men, Platt and Rochford, are your friends."

"Yes, they were my friends."

"*Are* or *were?*"

Gennady was devoid of words.

"Think about this, Vasilenko. First you say that you played no role. Then you say that you played no *knowing* role. You sound like an American lawyer, not like a KGB officer. Then you tell us you're not feeble-minded. Then you don't seem to be able to distinguish between whether men are friends or enemies. Or maybe you want to talk tricky like an American lawyer and say you were all the best of enemies. At worst, you are a traitor. At best you are a traitor who is also a fool—and because of your foolishness became a traitor. Men can be treacherous and men can be foolish. Either way, it ends up at the same place." The interrogator paused. "No matter: we have your son."

It was too much to bear—either to lie and say he was a traitor to his beloved Motherland or to know that his son was being tortured because of his choice. Whatever reprieve he had benefitted from during his imprisonment had now passed. And meanwhile, the men who had *actually* betrayed Russia were millionaires living in the US. That's when it occurred to sixty-six-year-old Gennady, wasting away inside the bowels of Russia's decrepit prison in Smolenskaya, that only his death could solve the conundrum.

Death might be a sweet escape for reasons other than Ilya's welfare. The prison floors in Smolenskaya were made of sticky, uncleanable asphalt covered with insects. Gennady and his fellow inmates had to sleep on these floors, in small cells where ten people had to take turns sleeping, sitting, and standing. Even when Gennady managed to fall asleep, he was perpetually anticipating when the next guy whose turn it was would kick him awake and tell him it was time to go and stand somewhere. He never knew what time of day or night it was.

Gennady may have been knocking on sixty-seven years of age, but he felt more like one hundred. How would he feel in a few short years? Certainly not better. Moreover, if he ever got out, he'd be an old, sick man who would feel like an ancient, dead man. Of what use would such a zombie be to his family, to the world? Never was there a more apt deployment of the cliché "better off dead."

Gennady considered how best to kill himself. His two best options were hanging himself with a bed sheet or using a metal rebar pole sticking out of a concrete pillar. He figured he could get a running start and impale his head on it. Perhaps he could line himself up so that the point of impact would be the soft gelatin of his eye; that way the spike could pierce his brain directly rather than have to penetrate his hard skull. Gennady bent down and lined himself up in a practice run at the rebar, but as his eye approached the spike he found that his instinct was to flinch as he got within a foot of it. He decided against the impaling because if one thing went wrong he could simply find himself alive and in a coma, which would give Sasha the opportunity to take a wait-and-see attitude toward Ilya's fate. No, there had to be a better way than spiking his skull on some wayward rebar.

Gennady sobbed as he stared at his left wrist. In his right hand, the one that had guided countless successful handoffs and dead drops with fellow spies, he held a razor blade that he'd had smuggled to him by his new prison friend Aleksandr. *If only I hadn't helped another KGB alumnus by countersigning his passport application eight years ago,* he thought.

Before he could do the deed, from the adjacent cell Aleksandr motioned for him to take a loaf of bread he was squeezing between the bars. "Eat the bread," Aleksandr whispered.

"I'm not hungry," Gennady said.

"Eat. The. Bread," Aleksandr repeated, giving a serious glance at the snack.

Gennady stared at his fellow inmate as he took the bread and tore it apart. There was a note inside. The terse missive contained just five words that changed everything: "Your son has been freed."

Gennady now knew that he could survive any trumped-up charges and sentencing extensions the authorities threw at him. His thoughts drifted to that night in 2000 in Moscow, when he had saved Jack from a group of Russian toughs.

C'mon, Jack. Don't forget me, he thought. *I once saved your life. Now you can save mine.*

When Gennady eventually found his way to the terrible prison in Bor, he was placed in quarantine for two weeks. That is, *after* rabid dogs barked and sniffed at him while he was in a barren room with one hundred other men and a single hole in the ground in which to urinate and defecate. The Bor authorities were given extensive background on the inmates before they came to the prison, largely because it was an institution specializing in military spies and traitors. Before prisoners could get settled, the guards demanded money from them in what amounted to be a massive enterprise. It was clear that these bosses hadn't gotten the memo about De Niro's good friend Gennady. Or, more likely, they didn't give a damn.

The Bor guards lived like kings, comparatively. They had televisions and refrigerators, all subsidized by powerless prisoners. If an inmate didn't pay, he was beaten. Gennady was told that any complaint about his beatings would fall on deaf ears, as investigating authorities would be told that he had simply stumbled and hit his head on rocks or loose boards. Given that these authorities were on the FSB payroll, they would be believed absolutely. If Gennady resisted paying a satisfactory amount, contraband would be planted in his cell—and he had already danced that polka. He was also told that if he became a smartass, he would be accused of assaulting inmates and guards. The worst offense would be if the guards should happen to find a weapon in his cell. And the guards kept plenty of knives around for precisely that purpose. They even showed him their impressive collection. *So many options.* "It was a hellhole," Gennady says. He describes this prison as the "worst of the worst."

Each prison had a boss, or *khozain* (host), who controlled everything. He was a criminal businessman, like a head mobster up to whom the money flowed. Some bosses could earn as much as a million rubles a day on the food concession alone. There were other rackets, such as medical care, movies, and sundries. If you wanted any goodies, you paid. Big.

At first, Gennady told his Bor persecutors that he didn't have money to pay them. He was lashed with a chain. Then, ever defiant, he said, "I told the guards they would be sorry if they beat me." That only made the guards get more specific. Gennady was told he needed to pay them between $5,000 and $10,000 or his stay in Bor would become very unpleasant. Eventually, broken, Gennady bought time by telling the prison bosses that while he didn't have any money, he would see what he could do.

As Gennady tried to figure out how he could come up with money, another inmate accused him of stealing his pen. Gennady remembered seeing a *Seinfeld* episode at Jack's house with a similar plot. That's what his life had become: a *Seinfeld* sketch written by Kafka. Prison snitches were no more beloved in Bor than they were in Sing Sing, so Gennady knew it was a scam perpetrated by the guards. He told the faux snitch during the inquisition that followed, "I have more good pens than your piece-of-shit pen!"

This went over poorly with the guards, who claimed to have more "witnesses," which surely they could conjure up. After this inquisition, the guards cozied up to Gennady and told him, as if they were on his side, that if he just paid them they could "get" the witnesses to recant—witnesses that didn't exist in the first place. They added that if he failed to pay, they would plant a knife on him and accuse him of attempted murder, and he would never get out of Bor.

A guard demanded of the inmate, "Did Vasilenko do anything else to you besides steal your pen?"

"Yes," the inmate said. "When I didn't give it to him, he beat me." Another lie.

Gennady observed that the FSB always seemed to level their charges against him when he was on the verge of being freed from prison, or at least being transferred to a friendlier *koloniya*. "My biggest mistake was my desire to go home," Gennady recalled years later. Not only did Sasha want him in jail; the guards had been holding out for a payday from this former KGB big shot. Neither the FSB nor the prison brass had any incentive to free Gennady. Quite the opposite: "Harassing prisoners is big business."

Finally, after the latest round of harassment, Gennady said he could probably get his hands on some money to bribe the guards. He once again convinced Ilya to bring money, and when Gennady tried to give it to the guards, he was arrested for bribery. Sasha and company found witnesses to attest to this, while the guards feigned shock at the corruption.

Gennady went on trial for the third time in 2009, in Bor, behind bars, on charges of bribery. He denied the charges but was predictably convicted anyway, attaching a couple of more years to his sentence.

The year 2010 began with a despondent Gennady having lost all hope. There had been no correlation between his good behavior and the length of his sentence. Sure, he had provoked Sasha and mouthed off to the authorities, but he had also complied with their financial demands and been punished for that, too. Gennady had never paid much attention to religion—he had seen too much hardship to ever believe what so many Americans did, the notion that if you did as God wished, you would be rewarded with his grace—but he recalled a televangelist prattling on about a long-suffering character called Job. And what was the lesson there? That sometimes God tormented a certain individual for reasons only he knew? That this person should, nevertheless, keep believing in the monster that had done this to him? And what, exactly, had a millennium of war done for the Russians? Had adversity made them stronger? Perhaps, but who cared? It was still more war, more misery. And that's what Gennady had in store for him.

While he didn't believe in a magical king in the sky, incredibly,

Gennady still believed he was lucky. He didn't know why he still believed this since the past few years had indicated only that he was, in fact, the unluckiest man on the planet. But somehow there remained a notion within Gennady that the past five years had been an aberration, that he was still the toddler who had been saved by a soldier from the bear drowning him in the Siberian River.

Where was his soldier now? His Marine? His Cowboy?

17

RESET: THE RED BUTTON

You were sent to USA for long-term service trip. Your education, bank accounts, car, house, etc.—all these serve one goal: fulfill your main mission, i.e., to search and develop ties in policymaking circles in US and send intelligence reports to the Center.

—Encrypted message sent to the Illegals from the Yasenevo
Center in 2009 (translated and decrypted by the FBI)

On March 6, 2009, in Geneva, US secretary of state Hillary Clinton presented a smiling Russian foreign minister Sergei Lavrov with a small yellow plastic box topped with a red button embossed with the English word "reset."* After ceremonially pressing the button, Lavrov accepted the gift, aimed at announcing a reset of the traditionally stormy US-Russian relationship.† Four months later, Russian Federation president Dmitry Medvedev, hopeful that the West would invite Russia into the World Trade Organization, and perhaps even NATO, announced that US armed forces supplies could pass through Russian airspace on their way to Afghanistan. Two months

---

* The button also contained the Roman alphabet transliteration of the Russian Cyrillic alphabet word "перегрузка" (*peregruzka*). Unfortunately, the best translation of that word is "overload," not "reset."

† The US has a habit of giving gifts to Lavrov. In May 2017, he would be treated to top secret terrorism intel as a parting gift inside the White House Oval Office, courtesy of President Trump.

after that, President Barack Obama stated that the United States would drop its plan—long seen by the Russians as provocative—for a missile defense shield in Eastern Europe, as proposed by the previous (Bush) administration.

The reset continued apace for the next year: in March 2010, the two former Cold War adversaries reduced their nuclear arsenals; two months later, they agreed on sanctions against Iran; and three days after that, Obama canceled sanctions against the Russian state arms export agency, which the US had initiated in response to the Russians' exporting arms to Iran.

The vibe flowed down through their respective intelligence services. CIA Director Leon Panetta wrote that he was in the midst of developing "a sound relationship" with his Russian counterpart, the Putin-appointed SVR chief Mikhail Fradkov. In his memoir, *Worthy Fights*, Panetta describes the "occasionally candid relationship" he developed with Fradkov, noting that Fradkov wanted "to share information and collaborate on some common operational activities." Panetta had hoped "perhaps naively, that we could look for ways to cooperate [with the Russians] in areas such as Chechen terrorism, where we had common enemies." All seemed right with the world. But some at the CIA weren't buying it.

By this time, one of Jack's former students in the IOC, Michael Sulick, had risen to the number-two post in the Agency, Deputy Director of Clandestine Services, otherwise known as the man who ran the nation's spies. Like Jack, Sulick was old-school and suspected a Kremlin setup with the alleged "reset." He knew Putin as a dyed-in-the-wool KGB man who wanted nothing less than to reconstitute the old USSR. As Panetta later wrote in his memoir, Sulick and those who shared his philosophy warned that "[t]he Russians would never share, and they'd use the whole thing to get close to our officers and try to recruit them as spies." But Panetta thought differently, and the administration was already committed to the reset.

Internal objections aside, in 2009 Panetta hosted Fradkov at the

CIA's Langley headquarters. Afterward, they had dinner at the acclaimed Embassy Row organic eatery Restaurant Nora, where Fradkov uttered an unending series of incoherent Soviet-style platitudes that left both Panetta and his chief of staff Jeremy Bash dumbstruck. "What the hell was that?" Panetta asked Bash later as they walked to their cars. In 2010, Fradkov reciprocated as host, showing Panetta and Bash around the Center at Yasenevo. Panetta then met his FSB counterpart at Lubyanka, where Jeremy Bash whispered to him, "I think I can still hear the screams from the basement." It was a reminder that the trip was taking place under extraordinary circumstances that only the Americans knew about. The Musketeers were also unaware of certain developments in the world of espionage and how they were fomenting a chain of events that would ideally lead to Gennady's freedom.

What was going on? Just prior to his Russian excursion, Panetta had received intel that threatened to upend whatever diplomatic progress had been made up to this point: in the ongoing nine-year FBI surveillance of the Illegals, called Operation Ghost Stories, things were heating up. The FBI had been quietly watching the Russian plants since Aleksandr Nikolayevich Poteyev had given them up in 2001, and in the spring of 2010, the Bureau learned that some of the Russian spies were planning to return to the Motherland. FBI sources add that there was more to the heat-up, but those details are still secret. However, it is widely believed that Russian intelligence had ordered the Illegals to escalate their espionage activities—with special attention to various federal institutions, like the CIA and the State Department—before returning to Moscow. The change in operational status became a political conundrum: Should the US allow the Illegals to leave and share all their intel and inside knowledge with their bosses, or arrest them and derail the reset?

Panetta briefed President Obama in February 2010 about the broad strokes of the Illegals story, triggering weeks of meetings at the White House about how to proceed. On June 11, Panetta again informed Obama and the National Security Council, convincing them that the arrests should be made and the reset would survive. Although the Obama administration worried that the much-hyped reset might be *re*-reset in the wake of the Illegals' arrests, they hoped such a reversal might be averted by instantly proposing a swap, in place of a scandalous trial that would embarrass the president's new best buddy, Medvedev, who would arrive in the US in a mere two weeks. The arrests had not been planned to facilitate a trade, but since the Bureau had concluded that the spies hadn't *yet* caused serious injury to US security, it was determined that Washington, and the reset, could benefit more from using them for barter than as prisoners to be locked up for years. Obama and Panetta agreed to the plan. Fortunately, the FBI's Alan Kohler, who had moved on from the Washington Field Office and was now chief of the Russia unit in the New York Field Office, had had a detailed swap contingency plan in the works as far back as 2004. Soon the Bureau and the CIA would learn whether the Russians would agree to the swap.

On June 24, after productive meetings on trade with US businessmen in California, Medvedev arrived in Washington and met with Obama.* "Russia belongs in the WTO," Obama said as the two leaders stood side by side in the East Room, smiling after several hours of meetings. Obama then took Medvedev and Vice President Joe Biden for hamburgers at one of the president's favorite burger joints, Ray's Hell Burger. Later that day, before returning to Moscow, Medvedev traveled to Toronto for a G20 Summit, content with the results of his

---

* Among other successes: a $4 billion deal was announced between Boeing and a Russian firm; Cisco Systems announced it was going to spend $1 billion in Russia, in part to develop a Moscow version of Silicon Valley; the Export-Import Bank of the United States announced a new deal to underwrite—with US taxpayer dollars—US business exports to Russia; lastly, Obama submitted a US-Russia nuclear cooperation agreement, backed by powerful business interests, to the US Congress.

US diplomacy. Yet those living in the shadow world made moves that would have removed any and all smiles from the faces of the Russian contingent.

On the very same day that Obama and Medvedev grabbed the headlines, SVR colonel Aleksandr Poteyev, the man who had betrayed the Illegals nine years earlier, was quietly exfiltrated to the US and resettled with a new identity. Leaving his wife, Mary, behind, the fifty-eight-year-old Poteyev fled through his native Belarus and was placed under the protection of US intelligence agents.

"Mary, try to take this calmly: I am leaving not for a short time but forever," Colonel Poteyev wrote in a text message sent to his wife as he fled Russia. "I did not want this but I had to. I am starting a new life. I shall try to help the children." It is known that one daughter, Marina, lived in the US. It was later learned that Poteyev had used a stolen Russian passport and identity ("Victor Dudochkin") to facilitate his travel to the US. The Russians located the real Victor Dudochkin, who explained that when he had previously applied for a US visa, he had turned over his passport to the US Embassy in Moscow while the visa was being processed. The Russians concluded that CIA agents stationed in the embassy had made a copy of Dudochkin's passport and given the forgery to Poteyev for his escape. It is believed that Poteyev was paid as much as $5 million in return for his files.

On June 27, 2010, within minutes of Medvedev's plane leaving Canadian airspace, and with Poteyev safely ensconced in the US, the FBI rounded up the Illegals. It was an anxious June 26 phone call, monitored by the FBI, between Illegal Anna Chapman and her KGB father that supposedly prompted such a quick seizure. In the call to Moscow, Chapman had voiced suspicions that she might have been "made." An FBI plant inside the Illegals' clique had requested a face-to-face meeting with Chapman earlier that day—it was something that was just never done; previously, all contact between Illegals and their controllers had been through encrypted private computer networks only. Gennady says the consensus today is that the Illegals should have known much earlier that they were being watched. "They were enjoying life in US too much and had lost their vigilance," he explains.

In the New York area, where many of the Illegals lived, the FBI's Alan Kohler helped coordinate the roundups. "The arrests were uneventful," Kohler recently said. "They knew their time was coming." Kohler added that the arrestees' only seeming concern was the welfare of their children, who had no idea that their "American" parents were even Russian, let alone Russian spies. But thanks to years of planning, the Bureau descended on the scene fully equipped with a battery of social workers and child therapists, who assured both parents and children that they would be together very soon.

The Bureau alerted the press, and the operation instantly became front-page news around the world, with the arrestees named:

- "Richard and Cynthia Murphy," real names Vladimir and Lidiya Guryev
- "Michael Zottoli" and "Patricia Mills," real names Mikhail Kutsik and Natalia Pereverzeva
- "Donald Howard Heathfield" and "Tracey Lee Ann Foley," real names Andrey Bezrukov and Elena Vavilova
- "Juan Lazaro," real name Mikhail Vasenkov, and Vicky Pelaez (her real name)
- "Anna Chapman," real name Anna Kushchenko (or "Irene Kutsov") and Mikhail Semenko (his real name)

But whom to swap for? After researching their SE files, the Agency could come up with only three apposite assets held by the Russians:

- **Aleksandr Zaporozhsky**—Gennady's friend since 1975, the former colonel in the Russian Foreign Intelligence Service

(SVR) had been charged with treason and sentenced in a secret 2003 trial to eighteen years of hard labor for espionage on behalf of the United States. Author Ronald Kessler wrote that, according to the Russians and a number of highly placed US intelligence sources, Zaporozhsky was indeed the man called AVENGER, the asset who had given Sandy Grimes's team the final piece of the Ames puzzle back in 1993, the piece that convinced the FBI to make the Ames collar. As noted, upon retirement in 1997, Zaporozhsky/AVENGER moved to the United States, where he was suspected to have shared more classified information with Western intelligence agencies. But Zaporozhsky was arrested upon returning to Russia in 2001 and was convicted in 2003.

- **Igor Sutyagin**—a forty-five-year-old arms researcher convicted of spying for the United States, sentenced to fifteen years in 2005. He had told relatives that he was loath to leave his homeland, but the deplorable Russian prison conditions and the possibility that he would prevent the release of others left him no choice but to go along with the swap.
- **Sergei Skripal**—a former colonel in Russian military intelligence who was found guilty of passing state secrets to Britain and sentenced to thirteen years in prison in 2006.

Mike Sulick says that there was a desire to even up the exchange a bit more, so the Agency pondered who else might be added to the US list. "We had ten of theirs. They really didn't have any of ours to swap for, but we wanted to balance out the trade," he recalls. "I suggested to Panetta that Gennady be placed on the swap list. I felt that [the] CIA bore some responsibility for his situation. It was a leaked CIA memo that was misinterpreted that put him under suspicion in the first place." When asked if Cowboy Jack had any input into this addition, Sulick replied, "This was a 'close hold' negotiation. Jack had no idea."

Relying on their "sound relationship," Panetta, surrounded by Sulick, Counterintelligence chief Lucinda "Cindy" Webb, and other Russia experts, placed a speakerphone call to Fradkov, which Panetta recounted in his memoir:

"Mikhail, we have arrested a number of people, as you saw in the press. Those people are yours."

"Yes, they are my people," Fradkov replied after a long pause. With just that utterance, Fradkov had made it possible to begin negotiations.

"We're going to prosecute them," Panetta threatened. "If we have to go through with trials, it is going to be very embarrassing for you."

After another long pause, caused in part by distance and translation delays, Fradkov asked, "What do you have in mind?"

"You have three or four people that I want. I propose a trade," Panetta offered. The Russians considered the swap idea for two days and then agreed to negotiate. According to one officer who was very close to Panetta, when Panetta suggested adding Gennady to the list, Fradkov, likely in a nod to Gennady's free-spirited lack of discipline, replied, "Be careful what you ask for."*

Over the next few days, Obama and Medvedev waited as their intelligence executives expedited an agreement, with Russia demanding signed confessions from their prisoners as a prerequisite to pardons from Medvedev. In the US, court appearances and similar plea deals were hastily arranged for the Illegals. The US required that no retaliatory steps be taken against Americans in Russia, that the Illegals agree never to return to the United States without permission from the attorney general, and that any money made from publication of

---

* Fradkov's name resurfaced recently. Reuters obtained two confidential documents from the Kremlin's Russian Institute for Strategic Studies think tank, which showed that the institute devised the initial cyber strategy to compromise the 2016 US presidential election. Fradkov was appointed by Putin to head the Institute in January 2017. Some believe it is gearing up to interfere in future US elections.

their stories would be forfeited to the US Treasury. The Illegals who owned property, including real estate, further agreed to forfeit those assets to the US.

Panetta and Fradkov sealed the deal on July 3. Three calls over the course of one week.

As these prisoner exchange details were being finalized in the last week of June 2010, Gennady was incarcerated in prison 1K-11, in the Nizhny Novgorod region. He had heard about the arrest of the ten Illegals but had no idea that he was part of any swap. On the Fourth of July, Gennady celebrated the US holiday alone with a strong cup of Russian chifir' tea (aka, prison tea) that he raised to silently toast his friend Cowboy Jack, who he knew was working on his behalf. It was his fifth year served of a three-year sentence.

The next day began normally with a 6 a.m. rise, followed by exercises, breakfast, and a return to the barracks until noon volleyball. Gennady's prison diary best describes what occurred next:[*]

> At about 1 o'clock, while on the volleyball court, I was given the order to pack my stuff within fifteen minutes and be ready for a transfer. It was a shock for me—I didn't expect any transfers, and besides, transfers happened once a week on a certain day, but not on this day and not this time of a day. I was told by the administration that it was unexpected even for them. Now I was nervous.
>
> So I packed my stuff, was put through the traditional humiliating strip-search, and was put in the prison's truck for the trip—to where, I had no idea. In about an hour and a half the truck entered the N. Novgorod prison, where I had spent more than a year, so I recognized it. I thought that I was brought over there for another round of interrogations, or for the court

---

[*] Grammar and spelling throughout the diary are faithful to the original.

to consider one of my complaints. But I wasn't moved into the prison. Instead I was told to move immediately to another car with all my things. In the prison yard, I noticed a lot of authority figures, and some of them were even taking pictures of me. It was strange and unusual.

The car I was put in was not standard for moving prisoners, it was brand new VW van, but unfortunately inside the van was a freshly painted, small cage made of solid steel. It was like a gas chamber, especially if you take into consideration that outside it was about 85 degrees and of course we had no air conditioning. I thought that I might be taken to the railroad station to be put on train for still another destination.

I was wrong. I knew that the travel time from the prison to the railway station took not more than thirty minutes, but we had already been traveling more than forty minutes. Perhaps the destination was Moscow? I hoped I would survive the heat. After about an hour inside this moving gas chamber with little oxygen I started melting and panting. I started making noise and complaining, asking to open the door or stop for fresh air. The guards told me that they were in the same situation and they were not allowed to stop. Besides that, they were receiving calls with orders to reach the destination as soon as possible. I told them if they have to deliver my dead body, it's OK, but if they have to bring me alive they have to give me a chance to get some fresh air. In about 30–40 minutes of bargaining the guards gave up and let me out of the car for a few minutes.

While outside, I noticed two more cars with guards, one car in front and one behind. The rest of the trip I survived easier, since it became cooler. At about 2 o'clock in the morning I found myself back in Lefortovo prison, a very familiar place for me.

For two hours I was put through the standard procedure: searches, fingerprinting, documentation, shower, and at 4 o'clock in the morning I was finally put in a cell. Of course I couldn't sleep. I was trying to understand what could be the reason to bring me here again. I already knew about the arrest of the Illegals in New York and the only reason I was taken to Lefortovo, I guessed, was so that I could be a witness for the conviction of [Stepanov], whom I had helped to get a passport and visa to go to the US. I thought maybe he was involved also with helping identify the Illegals. That must be the reason I was spending a 6th year in prison on a three-year sentence.

At 9 o'clock, on the morning of July 6th, I was taken to the office of the chief of the prison. When I entered the room I saw five people, two on one side of the table and three on the other. Three of the men looked like foreigners, and I thought they might be from some international human rights committee that received my complaints about unjustified conviction and humiliating treatment in prisons (beatings, provocations, blackmailing, etc.). One of the Russian representatives was Aleksandr "Sasha" Zhomov, from the FSB—the thug who had interrogated me on my first week in Krasnya Presnya prison in Moscow.

One of the foreigners started speaking in Russian, introducing himself as the CIA Chief of Station, and the others were from Department of State and from the Justice Department. When I heard that one of the visitors, Dan [Payne, formerly of Sandy Grimes's team], was the Chief of Station, I assumed that this is just another provocation, a ruse. I'd never read or heard of a CIA officer identifying himself, especially in front of an FSB representative. I was shocked, I even asked for their identifications. Then I realized that it was a stupid question: the FSB could make any kind of forged documents.

My conviction that it was a provocation became stronger after "Dan" read some items from "an agreement between the

Russian and American governments," according to which I have to sign a document admitting that I was working for the US government. I turned to Dan and told him that if he really represents the CIA, he should know that I never worked for any government besides the Russian one. Dan was trying to convince me that everything he told me was true, and not a provocation. It's just the conditions of an agreement. If I would sign the document, I would be freed and flown to the US the next day.

My head was breaking apart. I didn't know what to do. Dan told me that I had to make my decision immediately. My mind couldn't comprehend the situation. I'm in prison and I am told I can spend the rest of my life there unless I confess and admit that I'm a CIA spy...and the next second, somebody else is trying to convince me to sign a paper admitting that I'm a spy, but promising me freedom and life in US. And the time for making the decision is just a few seconds. Was this an elaborate FSB trick to make me confess in advance of my execution?

Dan told me one more time that everything was real—it's not a dream, and not a provocation. I had just to sign the document admitting that I was working for the US government, which I hadn't. I thought, I had nothing to lose, but if everything is really true, I will be free in a day. I decided I would sign the document and so told the officials. I don't remember how I ended up back in the cell. It was such a hurricane in my head. I regained consciousness when the guard knocked at the door and gave me a document to sign. It was an appeal to the president for a pardon. It meant I had to lie to the whole world, to my family and friends, telling that I'm a spy. The FSB was covering their ass with my name. It took me 3–4 hours before I signed the document and gave it to the authorities. That night passed without sleep. I was "running" in the cell like a crazy man. *My thoughts were about the situation, kids, mother, my future life...*

On the morning of July 7th the authorities informed me that I would be allowed to see some of my family, so I asked them to invite my son Ilya and Masha with the kids. The day passed in slow motion. I was too excited by the events—the possibility of freedom, transferring to US, seeing my kids that I hadn't seen for four years. I was like a wounded animal in the cage.

In the evening, about 7 o'clock, I saw Vanya [Ivan] and Masha. It's hard to find the proper words to express my feelings. I was in heaven. Vanya had grown up and looked like a man, smart and wise. When I told them that I will be released tomorrow and will be taken to America, they thought that I'd lost my mind, that I'm crazy. I was trying to explain the situation, but they couldn't believe it. I told them that they have to be ready to join me in the States and stay with me for good. For them it was a bomb, even harder to understand the situation than for me, and I realized it. Everything was like a fairytale. Later they told me that when discussing our meeting on the way home, they came to the conclusion that I had lost my mind and that's the reason the authorities arranged the meeting.

After the meeting with Masha and Vanya was over, I waited for the meeting with Ilya, but an authority told me that he would not come and he didn't explain the reason. For me it was another blow I couldn't understand. He was the only person with whom I wanted to discuss the situation and all the nuances for the future. I needed him badly. His disappearance tortured me until I had a chance to call him from the States a week later. Only then did I find out the reason he couldn't come to see me because his mother-in-law had died the same day.

Of course I didn't sleep the night. I was trying to find

the answers to too many questions—first of all why I was put in the list for the swap??? What's going to happened in the future with my mother, my kids, my wife, etc. Did I make the right decision to sign the papers? How I'm going to live in exile?

It so happened that the 8th of July was a holiday, "The Day of the Family." What a happy coincidence. I was going to be free today. It was too much, I still couldn't realize what was going on, and everything was not real, like a dream, a miracle... Today I'm going to be free and go to bed in America as a free man...

At about 10 o'clock I was escorted out of the cell to the reception room where already my bags were. I was allowed to put on my own clothes from what I had in my bag. It was my first step to the freedom and I was ready to make it, despite of heavy worries inside of me.

I make a coffee, packed 2 bags, one with documents and another with some personal staff. With impatience, I was waiting for the trip to the freedom. There were the most exiting hours. The time was passing, but no movement. I was still in prison. At 2 o'clock I was offered the lunch, but I couldn't eat, no appetite. I was shivering like in the cold. Each hour was like eternity... This situation continues till 6 o'clock. I started thinking that everything was a set up, it was a play, but I couldn't guess the aim of it. Only after 6 o'clock, I was told by an authority that there will be no action today; the flight had been postponed till next day, 9th of July. I was ordered to change my clothes back to the prison uniform and escorted back to the cell. Again I started thinking that everything was a game to kill me psychologically. All my dreams began vanishing, I was in frustration and depressed. In spite that I get used to a lot of different provocations in prison, this one wounded me badly; I even had to ask the authority for some medicine. It was *another sleepless night, the 3d one in a row. I tried to put myself together, accepted the reality and just wait…*

Unbeknownst to Gennady, a government-chartered Vision Airlines Boeing 767 jet had departed New York's LaGuardia Airport en route to Vienna. On that plane, a team of State Department officials, CIA officers, and FBI agents were escorting the ten Illegals to Vienna for the swap. The keys to Gennady's freedom, and likely his very life, were on their way without his knowledge. Alan Kohler, from the New York Field Office, led the Bureau's escort team. As Kohler recently described, the FBI agents sat in first class while CIA officers spoke quietly with the Illegals and their Russian minders in coach, surrounded eerily by hundreds of empty seats.

On the long flight, Kohler, who occasionally went back to the coach section, observed the curious dynamic. "It was like two opposing football teams," Kohler says. "The Americans versus the Russians—and they respected each other after a brutal three-hour game. No recriminations. Just cordial conversations." Kohler describes what appeared to be a strange sense of relief on the faces of the prisoners.

It was the first time most of the Illegals actually had met one another, so they introduced themselves. With eight hours to kill on the flight, they also read the news reports of their arrests, and one startled Russian spy exclaimed to Kohler, "Wow, you really had microphones in my house?"

Back in Russia, there was no sense of relief for Gennady, just apprehension. That morning, for good luck, he wore his YOU DON'T KNOW ME/WITNESS PROTECTION PROGRAM T-shirt—a gift from Cowboy.

Gennady's prison diary describes the scene in Lefortovo:

9th of July, 2010, Lefortovo prison

At 4 o'clock in the morning I was escorted back to the reception room and was allowed to change the clothes and make a coffee. Than I was given some papers to sign, which I did automatically and begin to believe that something is going to happen soon, maybe what I was told 2 days ago is still real. At about 6 o'clock I noticed some activity and in a few minutes I was told to take my bags and follow the guards. Soon I found myself in the prison's yard where I was ordered to sit in the standing van.

Before Gennady took a seat on the van's floor, he hadn't bothered to make eye contact with the other prisoners, a lesson he learned early in his ordeal. Eye contact tended to provoke unwanted hostilities, so he kept his head down. He sensed just a few others. After he sat, Gennady felt a presence behind him. And the presence had a voice. Alex Zaporozhsky said, "We've got to stop meeting like this!"

After few minutes the column of 5–6 cars started to move out of prison's yard. We had been under reinforced security not free. I understand that the swap exchange is a very serious operation. I'd been looking through the window hoping to see my home on the way to the Sheremetyevo airport, from where I thought the plane would fly to US. But soon, I realize that we were going to Domodedovo airport. When we reach the airport another group of special security forces join the column. All the cars came to the airfield. Then we had been given some papers about our release to sign, but nobody gave them to us. After that one by one under heavy guards we had been moved to the plane. I thought that we had been free…but I was wrong. We still had been surrounded by strong security. General Zhomov, who started my interrogation on my first week after arrest, was on the plane too.

When the plane carrying the prisoners took flight late that morning from Domodedovo, one of the US reps, possibly Dan Payne, passed the information up the chain of command, and within seconds, Panetta and the others at Langley were aware of the operational status. Someone quickly decided that a certain CIA retiree also needed to be updated.

A gaunt Gennady on the day of his release.

In her Virginia home, Jack's daughter Michelle was awoken at 4 a.m. by "a friend on the inside," who called to tell her that "someone named Vasilenko" was on the swap list. "Think it's your Gennady?" the friend asked. Michelle immediately called her father, also asleep, in Brooklyn, where he was visiting his beloved ailing younger sister, Polly (she would die a year later, at age seventy-two, of ALS). Michelle told him that she thought Gennady might be on the swap list. Jack was excited but also skeptical. He said he'd call back if he was able to confirm the news.

Gennady's diary continues:

> The flight to Vienna (as we understand the swap was going to happen there) was quiet and seemed short, since I was sitting with [fifty-nine-year-old] Alex Zaporozhsky and we talked all the way and didn't notice the time. But we still were not free; the guards accompany us even to the toilet. At about 1 pm [Moscow time, noon in Vienna] the plane landed in Vienna airport.

On their flight to freedom, Gennady and Zaporozhsky were caught in that soupy netherworld between existential bliss and practical reality.

"Can you believe it's real?" Gennady would say.

Zaporozhsky didn't need to be told what "it" was: freedom. "I think it may be real."

"Do you think it's a trick?"

Zaporozhsky gestured to the plane around them. "All this would be a mighty big trick."

The men would loll off for a time and then Zaporozhsky would say, "Genya, you think we'll make it to America, right?"

It was Gennady's turn to be optimistic. "Of course we will." Then he would turn to the workaday. "Where do you think we'll live?"

Zaporozhsky answered Northern Virginia. "I've lived there before. I like it there."

"Me too. I have friends there—very good friends," he said, thinking of Jack. "I'd like a house with land, where I can shoot. Schools in Virginia are very good, so near Washington."

"Besides, it's close to the CIA, so we can keep an eye on the enemy."

The Russian Yakovlev Yak-42 and the US Vision 767 arrived in Vienna within minutes of each other and parked nose to tail. Simultaneously, inside the cabins of both planes, the bartered spies rose and prepared to head out to a new and uncertain life. "In Vienna, the Illegals all thanked us for our professionalism, and for taking care of their kids, who arrived the next day," recalls the FBI's Kohler. "Interestingly, they never actually set foot in Vienna. At the bottom of the stairs they got onto a people mover, which carried them directly to the Russian plane."

Gennady stated in his diary:

> The walk from one plane to another went smoothly and quiet. We were going out of the plane and saw the group on the opposite side of the swap going out of another plane, which parked nearby. So, the two groups changed planes.

As he walked the tarmac to the US plane, Gennady came eye-to-eye with his nemesis, Sasha Zhomov, for whom he had only three parting words: "Nice try, motherfucker."

Gennady wrote:

When I put my step on the ladder of American plane I'd felt the real freedom, no guards, no motherfucker Zhomov. It's hard to explain the real feelings of freedom after almost 6 years of imprisonment under a 3 years sentence... I was in heaven, feeling as if I was intoxicated... It was hard to believe that 3 days ago I was in a strong security prison where I was told I would spend the rest of my life and now I'm in the plane which is taking me to freedom. Miracle...

"In Vienna it was a weird dynamic," Kohler recalls. "The Illegals were happy to leave the plane, while the four Russians were happy to be getting on it. Within minutes, the four Russians [had] arrived. Like clockwork. Not sure if they saw each other passing by, but they might have. Gennady wore this 'You Don't Know Me' T-shirt and stuck out. On the plane, doctors checked them out. They looked bad and smelled like they hadn't had showered in a month. They spoke to CIA people who were assigned to talk to them."

The entire swap operation, an homage to the reset's improved cooperation, went off seamlessly; the Russian plane took off at 12:38 p.m., while the Vision Airlines charter, heading first to London, was right behind them, wheels up at 12:45.

Again from Gennady's diary:

The flight from Vienna was joyful, we talk and laugh a lot, and it was fun. We even drink some champagne. The plane made another short stop in London where two guys from our group were taken by Great Britain authorities.

The plane landed at RAF Brize Norton in Oxfordshire, England, to drop off two of the exchanged Russian nationals, Igor Sutyagin and Sergei Skripal, then proceeded across the Atlantic to Washington's Dulles International Airport, while the Russian jet returned to Moscow's Domodedovo airport, where, after landing, the ten Illegals were kept away from local and international press. Gennady says his KGB contacts told him the reason for the isolation: "Putin wanted to arrest the Illegals when they got back—for ten years they did nothing but party." After consideration, Putin thought better of it.

Back in New York, at approximately the same time that Gennady's plane took off from Oxfordshire, Cowboy Jack's Trailways Express was pulling away from Penn Station, bound for Great Falls, Virginia. For three decades, Jack had been chasing his Russian friend. Now it was Gennady's turn to chase Jack, from thirty-seven thousand feet above. When Jack's bus exited the Holland Tunnel, he glimpsed Lady Liberty and hoped it was a sign that his friend had finally achieved his own freedom.

In the air over Oxfordshire, in the plane that could seat more than three hundred, Gennady and Aleksandr could finally exhale. "Someone broke open a bottle of scotch," Alan Kohler remembers. "It was very emotional." The FBI man chatted casually with both of his charges, but one exchange has stayed with him. "The most meaningful discussion I had on the flight was with Gennady. After we gassed up in England, it was clear that he was beat. We folded back two armrests between the seats so he could lie down. He put his head up on his elbow and looked up at me and said, 'This is the first time I've slept on something other than concrete in five years.'"

Somewhere on the New Jersey Turnpike, Jack was dozing also—but not for long. By midmorning, Jack had finally received *the* call from Panetta's Deputy Director of Clandestine Services—and Jack's old IOC trainee—Mike Sulick. "It was the first time in my twenty-six years that a Deputy Director of Operations ever called me," Jack said in 2016.

"Hi, Jack. I'm here to tell you that your buddy is on the swap list," Sulick said.

"Don't kid me now. This is very serious."

"I wouldn't kid about this," Sulick assured him. "I know how much he means to you."

Thinking that Gennady was still being processed in Russia, Jack knew his friend well enough to know that he'd worry that it was a ruse, another form of Sasha-style torture. "I told Sulick to assure Genya that this wasn't a trick," Jack said. " 'Have your guy tell him "Chris Llorenz" passes you his greetings.' "

Now, finally, Jack could almost confirm Michelle's hopeful message. But he still repressed the urge to rejoice out loud on the Trailways Express; he worried that Sasha, Fradkov, and the totalitarian Putin apparatus were indeed playing another cruel trick on the West, and on Gennady. He couldn't know that Kohler and others had personally escorted Gennady onto the plane. On the bus, Jack's mobile phone kept ringing with congratulations from his former CIA colleagues, confirmations that finally put Jack's concerns to rest. In Virginia, Michelle Platt was hanging by the phone, also waiting for the final validation: "Dad calls me back later that morning to say he's on the bus home, and, yes, it is indeed time to celebrate."

Sinking into his seat, Cowboy contemplated the cycles of life, trying to discern a pattern. He had just visited his sister and best friend, Polly, whom he knew he was losing. Next, he had learned that he was getting back his second best friend, Gennady. Was this how God worked, balancing things out, stealing one life and replacing it with another? No, Cowboy realized, that was just pathetic human logic trying to find a place for itself in a capricious world. Cowboy had always been more a man of values than of faith. He thought of President Kennedy's words from his inaugural address, words that had echoed through his skull as he crouched off angry Cuban waters during the missile crisis: "With a good conscience our only sure reward, with history the final judge of our deeds, let us go forth to lead the land we love, asking his blessing and his help, but knowing that here on earth God's work must truly be our own." *God's work must truly be our own.* Amen.

No, Cowboy reasoned, if God had played a role in Gennady's release, it wouldn't have been because he was seeking to even things out for this old spook. God had fallen seriously short on much bigger balancing acts in the world.

There were many poignant moments for Alan Kohler during the final few days, but the one that stood out occurred on that last Vision charter flight, about forty-five minutes from their Washington destination. "When we flew over New York and the Statue of Liberty came into view, we watched with Gennady as he looked at it through the window. He teared up."

18

END GAMES

You really get to know your friend when trouble comes.

—Russian proverb

The plane carrying the two old Russian friends, Gennady "MONO-LITE" Vasilenko and Aleksandr "AVENGER" Zaporozhsky, landed in Washington, DC, at about 5:30 p.m., Friday, July 9, 2010. Cowboy raced to meet Gennady at Dulles that afternoon, having been tipped by another insider friend as to the exact time and place of their arrival. Finally, his crazy Musketeer cohort was free—or was he? In what he would later deem "another typical CIA screw-up," Cowboy had been told by his intermediary to go to the international arrivals terminal to greet his Russian *frenemy*. Through Dulles's floor-to-ceiling terminal windows, Cowboy excitedly watched the FBI's Vision charter touch down—however, the plane just kept taxiing to the farthest end of the airport, perhaps a half a mile away, toward the Signature Fixed Base Operator Facilities, which often handled private government contracts.

At the distant terminal, the maroon-and-white Boeing 767 rolled to a stop a few feet away from a waiting cavalcade of SUVs belonging to representatives of the FBI, the State Department, and the CIA. Cowboy began speed-walking in Signature's direction as fast as his seventy-four-year-old legs would carry him, uncertain if Gennady was even on the charter as promised, and also unaware that Kohler had already handed Gennady and Aleksandr over to the CIA on the tarmac. By the time Cowboy arrived at Signature, thoroughly out of breath and nearing collapse, he saw that the motorcade was long gone. A typical IOC fast getaway, probably orchestrated by Zephyrs he had taught years earlier, Cowboy thought, cursing himself out for being such a good instructor. He turned to leave when he saw Kohler passing through the lobby.

"I told him 'Gennady's here. He's okay,'" Kohler says. "That's the last time I saw Jack."

That night, Jack had a nightmare that the wily FSB had decided to keep Gennady, and they had sent an Illegal look-alike in his place. He awoke to a call from another Agency contact that gave him the address of the safe house where his old friend was indeed waiting. Within hours, Jack and Gennady had their long-intended reunion in a nondescript suburban Maryland colonial, both laughing at yesterday's screw-up. Michelle Platt, who would also soon be reunited with the Russian, recalls, "Gennady looked like a skeleton."

"What took you so long?" said Gennady, echoing what he had said to Jack in that Guyana hotel a lifetime ago, as the two men bear-hugged.

"I went to the wrong terminal," Jack said.

"Your Agency still playing games with you?" joked Gennady.

"Fuck 'em."

"What now?" they asked each other. Jack said, "We go shooting and fishing. We'll throw a party, with Dion, Mad Dog, Bobby De Niro, Moldea, the whole gang."

"Yes, but first—I earned a good bottle of vodka," Gennady answered.

Back in Moscow that day, Russia's Ministry of Foreign Affairs confirmed the exchange of the four prisoners for ten Russian citizens, citing "humanitarian considerations and constructive partnership development." The Western news reports of the swap all noted the espionage connections of Sutyagin, Skripal, and Zaporozhsky but were confounded by the inclusion of one Gennady Vasilenko. NBC News coverage of Gennady was typical: "Reasons for his involvement weren't immediately clear."*

The great 2010 spy swap ultimately succeeded because it fell within a temporary "reset" period (2009–2014), which, as Sulick and others predicted, foundered when Russia annexed Crimea in 2014. Had the Illegals been captured before or after the reset, the US-Russian "constructive partnership" would have been nonexistent, rendering the swap not even worthy of consideration, sending Anna Chapman and the others to a supermax concrete vault and leaving Gennady to die in a Russian hellhole like Bor. "I was lucky three times," Gennady observes now. "I survived that bear that almost drowned me. I decided not to jump overboard after my Havana arrest because I decided to believe Jack, that he would never record me, and I got out of prison in 2010."

After a few days, the Agency took Gennady to Rosslyn, Virginia, and set him up with a first-class apartment. Although his living conditions had improved exponentially, Gennady's emotional health was not such an easy fix. "His cockiness and bravado were gone, and he seemed confused," recalls Michelle, who helped him set up his apartment. Although he had his freedom and Cowboy and the Platt family, Gennady had lost everything else: his wife, his girlfriend, his six children, his mother, his homeland that he loved, and his reputation as a loyal intelligence officer for the KGB; being forced to sign that deceitful confession in Lefortovo was a decision that will always haunt him. His mood greatly brightened when Michelle introduced him to Skype. "He cried because he never thought he'd see his family again," Michelle says. "We raced out immediately to buy him a laptop."

---

* On March 4, 2018 Sergei Skripal and his daughter Yulia were poisoned with the Russian-made nerve agent Novichok. Their unconscious bodies were found on a park bench in Salisbury, England.

In the weeks ahead, at the Agency's request, Michelle helped Gennady write a report about Russian prison corruption, and in future years he would visit FBI field offices to offer expertise on Russian organized crime. Over the next year, Masha and her three children with Gennady arrived in the US, and Gennady's oldest children, Julia and Ilya, his estranged wife Irina, and his mother all did the same in the summer of 2011—one big, barely functional Russian clan living in very un-Russian Virginia. At Jack's direction, HTG's Roy Jacobsen (also a real estate broker) helped Gennady find a house, picking one that was secure and had multiple exits. He also made sure the property had room for a shooting range, and he helped Gennady improve his accuracy with various firearms in case things got rough. With a push from the FBI, Gennady speedily got a concealed carry permit. With funds from the Agency, he paid $900,000 for the house. Cash.

It would be a happy ending if the story was a Hollywood movie, but it is not. The spy swap resolution was bittersweet, at best. Although this was a joyful outcome for Jack, Gennady, Dion, and Mad Dog, from the perspective of the Vasilenko children, the uprooting was traumatizing. Jack is adored by his wife and children, yet Gennady's adult children, Julia and Ilya, were forced, by no fault of their own, to abandon their careers, friends, and homeland because of their father's choices. Mike Rochford watched the transfer play out and recalls, "Gennady's kids are victims. They didn't want to come to the US—they had to." It is the rarely seen side of a life in espionage, a side the families of Zaporozhsky, Stepanov, Poteyev, the Illegals, and the others also experienced. The cumulative effect of years of spy-family exfiltrations keeps the social workers and resettlement specialists at the CIA and the FBI working overtime. In the spy universe, somebody somewhere is always paying a price.

It seems that Ilya has been the most affected by all the unsought espionage—and marital—drama, not to mention the effect of having grown up with an absentee father. After a lifetime of coping with

Gennady's happy-go-lucky unfaithfulness to Ilya's beloved mother, Irina, and the shock of meeting his father's second family—with Ilya's childhood friend, Masha!—Gennady and Ilya are now separated by a vast emotional chasm. They live near each other and attend family functions together, where they are cordial. But Ilya makes it clear to his adoring father that cordial is about all he can muster toward him and, especially, Masha, whom he blames for the fiasco as much as his father. And who could argue with him? It's obvious to all that Gennady worships his children, especially Ilya, but he also understands that the lack of reciprocation is a form of punishment for the life choices he made. In his own Gennady way, he loves all his family, Irina included.

Although neither the CIA nor the Vasilenkos can discuss it, the extended family's financial needs and permanent green cards have been taken care of by the US government, perhaps as much as a favor to Cowboy Jack for his key role in the Hanssen unmasking as to Gennady for his inadvertent contribution of signing off on Stepanov's passport application. The CIA is the only government agency that can negotiate to compensate assets for information. Another codicil to Public Law 110, part of the 1949 Central Intelligence Agency Act, states that the CIA can also handle defectors outside normal immigration procedures, hence the instant green cards. Families like the Vasilenkos typically receive housing, green cards, a monthly stipend, and free education for the entire family, even one as large as Gennady's. Sundry details fall under the jurisdiction of the CIA's National Resettlement Operations Center, or NROC. When his stipend hit, Gennady purchased his country home, spacious but not elegant.

One by one, and sometimes two by two, Gennady's Musketeer pals, Cowboy, Dion, and Mad Dog, trekked to his rural Virginia house— likely the only one with a dacha-style sauna and shooting range in the adjacent woods. Likewise, the HTG partners—Cowboy, Ben Wickham, Bob Olds, and Roy Jacobsen—often held court at the Old Brogue in Great Falls, welcoming Gennady to the US. The Shoffler Brunch gang also joined the rolling reunion fest. "On October 17, 2010," recalls Dan Moldea, "I saw Gennady at the Shoffler Brunch for the first time since his release from the Russian prison and the prisoner swap three months earlier. Vasilenko was Platt's guest at the brunch. He physically embraced me and expressed his gratitude for the roles that Fino and I had played on his behalf." For Gennady, at least, America was starting to feel like home.

Of course, "Bobby D" was never far away, and Jack and Gennady soon reunited with the actor at his New York apartment. In the fall of 2011, De Niro called Gennady with an offer. Since his Russian friend had missed out on his chance at the big time with *The Good Shepherd*, De Niro thought he might join him on an actual movie set in Philadelphia. "Bob asked if I wanted to see how a movie got made," Gennady says. On the set, the actor was once again taken with Gennady's photogenic charisma and immediately sent him to the wardrobe department in order to prep him for a walk-on role in *Silver Linings Playbook*. (Gennady is the tuxedoed man who retrieves the judges' scorecards after the climactic dance scene.)

Two years later, in August 2013, Jack and Gennady attended Bobby D's seventieth birthday bash, held at his eighty-five-acre Gardiner, New York, estate. There, the Musketeers dined on food catered by Nobu Restaurant—which De Niro co-owns—and partied with the likes of Christopher Walken, Harvey Keitel, Samuel L. Jackson, Keith Richards, Bradley Cooper, Leonardo DiCaprio, Sean Penn, Lee Daniels, Martin Scorsese, and Lenny Kravitz, who performed live.

Jack once brought HTG cofounder Roy Jacobsen and his daughter, Jen, to New York for her to sing her rendition of Carly Simon's "The Spy Who Loved Me" (lyrics altered to reflect the saga of Jack and Genya) to De Niro. At Penn Station, preparing their trip back to Washington, Jack realized he had forgotten his wallet and was worried that he might need it on the train. Roy asked Jack if he knew anybody in security at Penn Station.

"Fuck, I trained most of them," Jack said.

Jack walked up to the first security guard, who spoke up before Jack could open his mouth: "Jack, Jack Platt!" He escorted the party down to the train before the other passengers.

Shortly thereafter, Cowboy began working with the authors on this book, and it wasn't unusual for him to call for an impromptu lunch over chili (his favorite) at the Hunter's Inn in Potomac, Maryland, to impart another war story he felt should be included. In addition to the ever-present cowboy hat, he often wore some article of clothing bearing the eagle, globe, and anchor insignia of his beloved Marine corps. He particularly liked the way the Marines credo, SEMPER FIDELIS, sprung from the eagle's beak, and he never tired of pointing to it or reminding a listener that the eagle was saying "Always faithful." His voice would grow soft and vulnerable whenever he spoke about his father or the fate of the US, "this fragile experiment." Despite his enthusiasm for recounting details of his life story, Cowboy was becoming noticeably thinner.

His stance toward the Russians had gradually become more nuanced. Rather than wanting to "crush" them, he began to say things like "They can't help it. It was their system." He took a harder line on the Islamic fundamentalists who captured global attention after his retirement from the Agency. Whereas he believed that the US and Russian people never truly wanted to kill one another (as opposed to their political *systems*, which did), he thought the Islamists were a death cult that would not rest until the West lay in ruins. His sentiments toward terrorists conjured up an aging Wild West sheriff flirting with rounding up one last posse before he rode into the sunset.

Cowboy was a proponent of a vigorous US intelligence apparatus till the end. He believed that a flawed spy service was far preferable to having none at all. Unlike the news media that was forever bashing the CIA for its missteps, he recognized that failure was an inherent part of the game the same way trauma surgeons sometimes lose patients, and he resented the chin-scratching critics who had never been on the ground, in the fight, in the vortex of crosscurrents far greater than any individual. He pumped a fist in agreement with Jack Nicholson's fictional Marine colonel Nathan Jessup in *A Few Good Men* when he barked *"You want me on that wall!"* to the meddling, smart-ass young prosecutor played by Tom Cruise. Unlike Jack Nicholson, Jack Platt *really was* perched off the Cuban coast during the missile crisis, ready to storm ashore when the nukes started flying. The United States wanted him on that metaphorical wall, and he spent well over a half century astride it.

Nevertheless, having long ago replaced alcohol with philosophy, Cowboy believed in asking tough questions of the trade he loved— not to destroy it, but to make it better. He wondered if the intelligence bureaucracies hadn't become a "self-licking ice cream cone," emphasizing bureaucratic perpetuation over stopping enemies. Hell, they didn't even like using the word "enemies" anymore, preferring diluted, new age gibberish like "stakeholders." The problematic cohort were "cake eaters," overeducated but under-muscled résumé sculptors whose internationalist pretensions rendered them blind to the reality that the US did have dangerous adversaries richly in need of being spied on. He pointed to US assets like Motorin and Martynov, who lost their lives because both the Americans and the Russians were too busy chasing each other's spies rather than preventing nuclear war—a holocaust neither side ever truly wanted.

Cowboy Jack was not alone in his sober assessment of the state of modern espionage. In his book *American Spies*, former Clandestine Service Chief Michael Sulick cited the tragedy of one particular spy:

"[Aldrich] Ames proved that spies rarely change history…his espionage had no impact on the outcome of the Cold War…other overwhelming problems afflicting the Soviet empire ultimately caused its downfall." Author David Wise labeled the entire CIA "a tired bureaucracy."

Cowboy and Gennady agreed (with more than a little exasperation) that all intelligence services suffer the same paradox: they send an operative abroad to infiltrate enemy ranks and then distrust the operative the closer he gets to the enemy, for fear he has grown *too* close. *"What the fuck?"* both men said more than once. Gennady was as agitated about the state of Russia's affairs as Jack was about the United States'. Gennady said, "The old days were one hundred percent better. If someone had a gun, they'd tear up the whole country looking for it. Now there are millions of guns on the streets, and they're using them…The future of Russia is hard to tell. But we are survivors with a long, long history."

About Jack, Gennady said, "At the beginning we looked at each other through a rifle scope like an enemy. After a while we looked at each other not through a scope, but man to man, eye to eye." And this is how both men determined that while their countries' ideologies were opposed, their citizens were not inherently enemies.

After months of immersing themselves in Cold War spy history, especially Jack's and Gennady's, the authors were haunted by a central question involving failure. "All of this spying…" Eric began at one of the authors' lunches with the Boys. "It seems like both sides fail an awful lot." Indeed, the Boys failed to turn each other, the US failed to detect Ames, Hanssen, and others, the Russian Illegals failed to do much damage, and the FBI's vaunted tunnel drilled beneath the Soviet Embassy in Washington was used against it.

"So what's the point?" Gus asked.

Jack's and Gennady's answers differed. Gennady said, "Nobody wins," and he invoked the Kris Kristofferson song of the same name, which refers to the folly of placing blame on one side or the other, and that the mutual pain isn't worth it since nobody wins anyway. It was a song Roy Jacobsen used to play for retired spooks at get-togethers, which often triggered tears that flowed along with the booze. Jack said, "You pound away at each other however you can for as long as you can. You wear the other side down, and one day, one side just doesn't show up.

"Ames…" Jack snarled the name. "Ames gutted us. After he did what he did, a lot of the folks at the Agency felt like giving up. Some of them probably did." Jack said that we will never know how many CIA programs *didn't* go forward because the CIA felt so demoralized. "That's what I mean by one side just doesn't show up." Jack growled something about wanting five minutes alone in a room with Ames and Hanssen. He meant it, too.

Jack caught himself. "Then again, one day the Soviet Union didn't show up because it didn't exist."

The Boys bickered constantly about the direction of their two countries. Jack barked that the Russians were still Commies. Gennady countered that Russia was a "banditocracy." He prefers the Soviet Union pre-collapse to what the country has become. Jack said democracy prevailed, but only temporarily, as he saw totalitarianism creeping into the same American culture that championed freedom. No one enjoys America's freedoms more than Gennady: "In America, they didn't kidnap me and beat me and throw me in prison," he shouted with a rare flash of bitterness in his eyes. He had a habit of tapping Eric on the shoulder to show him the photos on his iPhone of firearms he thought Eric ought to come shoot with him. "Bobby [De Niro] likes this kind," Gennady said. What's not for Gennady to like about America? Girls. Guns. Movie stars!

A few weeks later, Jack dropped by Eric's house. He had something on his mind. It was this notion of Gennady's that "nobody wins."

"*We* won!" Jack insisted.

"Who's 'we'?" Eric asked.

"Genya and me. We won. How many people get a friend like Genya? How many men are ordered to destroy each other and end up—" Jack's voice cracked.

"I get it," Eric said, adding, "Do you think you can expand that sentiment to a friendship between America and Russia?"

"Not yet," Jack said. "Russia is still pretty Communist if you ask me, and America is headed in that direction faster than I ever imagined it would." He cited the November 1775 establishment of the United States Marines to fight for the young country's independence from Britain, and he feared the US had lost any sense of its origins, any appreciation of what freedom means. But when the trajectory of the US began to depress him, he defaulted to his admiration for Gennady and the price he had paid to get here, not to mention the price he had paid for their friendship.

Despite the danger of the Cold War with its ever-present thrum of nuclear conflict just below the surface—a danger the Boys had embraced—to see them together was to sense *their* Cold War had had a soul. It was a world of rowdy soldiers, jocks, lotharios, Machiavellis, venal cops, bitter bureaucrats wearing porno moustaches and aviator frames to look like badasses, flying fortresses, and floating Leviathans.

Today's spy game is characterized by sterile drones, faceless hackers, and treacherous nebbishes like Edward Snowden—people Jack and Gennady would have mistaken for dental floss. The Boys are dinosaurs, but the joy they exuded in each other's presence was palpable. They were on the downslope of history—the history experienced by the billions who lived through the Cold War and who still roam the planet, from the Iron Curtain to the collapse of the Berlin Wall. Both men were sentimental, but despite Gennady's assertion that "nobody wins" and Jack's fear of creeping totalitarianism in the US, one sensed that both men felt, as individuals and perhaps as the oddest couple the Cold War produced, that they were victors.

Gennady and Jack had their share of tough talks about capitalism versus communism. Neither ever wavered. Gennady still said of communism that "the idea was good" but was implemented poorly. This exasperated Cowboy because he thought the system was, as President Ronald Reagan said, "an evil empire."

When it came to reflections about his own nature, Gennady was predictably Gennady: "If I had to do it all over again, I would have done the same thing. I can't change my character. Maybe I'd make a few less mistakes, mostly with women." But the twinkle in his eye suggested he didn't feel *that* guilty, as if self-reflection was a disease that weakened one's emotional immune system. Gennady is still handsome, carefree, immature, charming, irresponsible, insouciant. He scoffs at the notion that he was ever heroic. "But Jack, that's different. He's a true American hero." He described Jack as a staunch anti-Communist, a first-rate CIA officer, and, most important, a Marine to the core. "The American eagle!"

While recklessness is an authentic aspect of Gennady's character, there are those in the spy world who believe he has a deeply serious side, that he lives by a strict moral code that isn't easily deciphered, let alone perceived in him at all. The principals associated with the Hanssen takedown insist that Gennady didn't know he was helping to nail the traitor and never betrayed the Soviet Union, which is supported by the fact that they were all operating with fragmented information about what Stepanov's cache really held. Nevertheless, there is an alternative theory to which some in the intelligence community subscribe. This theory is rooted in a spy's code of honor and the capacity of the human soul—in this case, Gennady's—for rationalization:

Imagine being deeply indoctrinated in the belief that your fellow spies in the perpetual war against very real enemies are your true family—perhaps even more than blood family. After all, Russian families may or may not disintegrate, but Russian enemies have been unrelenting for centuries.

Imagine further that there is no lower form of ghoul than a member of your spy fraternity who gets his brethren killed. A craven double agent—an *American* traitor, no less—who murders your friends from the safety of a cubicle, out of pure greed, and who wouldn't hesitate to get you killed through the bloodless act of dropping an unsigned note into an envelope and leaving it under a rock in a suburban park.

Now consider that the bureaucracy for whom you toiled for decades not only does nothing to avenge the deaths of your friends but, in fact, orchestrated their executions. Yes, they may have been traitors and deserved punishment, but not execution, especially on the word of a known dissembler like Hanssen. Hanssen lied about Gennady and Jack. What lies did he tell about Motorin and Martynov in order to gild his lily? Everybody uses double agents, but nobody trusts them. Traitors like Ames and Hanssen are to the espionage world what "rats" are to the mafia: vermin undeserving of breathing the same air you do. Indeed, gangland rats have been known to get whacked on principle by rival families without formal sanction from mafia brass. Said one US spy to the authors, "We're in the business of getting strategic intelligence, not getting each other's spies killed."

This mindset would support the following theory, which is held by more than a few sources close to the Gennady affair: after Motorin, Martynov, and other KGB assets were killed because of Hanssen's mendacity, and Hanssen made the false report that Gennady had been "turned" in the late 1980s by the CIA, which led to his first imprisonment, and the KGB rewarded such a monster, Gennady the Russian Cowboy decided to take matters into his own hands and blow up Hanssen himself.

Alas, it's just spook speculation, but it would be irresponsible to shrug off the conjecture of some spies that Gennady Vasilenko played a long shot and brought down Robert Hanssen to avenge what Hanssen, and most assuredly Sasha Zhomov, did to his friends. His brothers. Said the philosophical assassin Anton Chigurh in Cormac McCarthy's *No Country for Old Men* to a target facing his wrath: "If the rule you followed brought you to this, of what use was the rule?" If Gennady's loyalty brought him so much suffering, and Ames's and Hanssen's treachery brought them riches from the KGB, of what use has been his own fidelity?

If this hypothetical scenario is what occurred, then Gennady's code of honor as a spy was upheld, and the same man who was unfaithful to his wife and family was *faithful* to his KGB spy brothers, flawed though they be, to degrees that changed history.

To celebrate Gennady's seventy-sixth birthday, there was a Musketeers reunion—Dion, Gennady, Jack, Mad Dog—in December 2016 in Virginia. It was the last time they would all see each other, as once again, the happy ending was a tease. Another bittersweet dose of real life was waiting around the corner.

On Christmas Day 2016, Jack got food caught in his throat at dinner. The blockage was cleared, but he still

The last roundup: a final reunion of the Four Musketeers, December 12, 2016: (l. to r.) Dion Rankin, Genya Vasilenko, Jack Platt, John Denton.

complained of discomfort within his neck. A medical checkup revealed cancer, which likely explained his weight loss during the last year of his life and his difficulty swallowing. The disease moved fast. On his deathbed, Jack told Roy Jacobsen, "You take care of that son of a bitch," referring to Gennady.

The family's obituary for Cowboy read:

John Cheney Platt III ("Jack"), aged 80, died unexpectedly on January 4, 2017, of an advanced form of esophageal cancer, which had presented itself with no symptoms other than weight loss. He passed peacefully and painlessly in his sleep with loving family by his side...He led an amazing life, full of intrigue, mystery, and adventure, which he embraced and lived to the fullest...He was a hero among the Cold War Warriors and a consummate patriot for his beloved country. He was a natural leader, a mentor to many, and did not suffer fools (or bosses) lightly!

A "Celebration of Life" for Jack was held on Friday, February 3, 2017, at 2:00 p.m. at Falcon's Landing Retirement Community in Potomac Falls, Virginia. In Jack's honor, donations were made to the US Marine Corps Memorial Association. More than 450 people were in attendance, including his extended family of FBI and CIA officers, among them the operatives who ran the legendary mole hunts: Mike Rochford, Sandy Grimes, and Robert Hanssen's longtime FBI superior, David Major.

No one had ever seen a send-off for a spy like this one. ("There's no one manning the store at HQ. They're all here," one CIA official said.) The eulogies were powerful in form and content. Some called Jack "the best CIA officer ever, an icon." Pressed to elaborate, one CIA executive politely declined. But he gave a look that implied that there were many heroic Jack exploits that *no one* would ever know about.

When his turn came, Rochford read a letter from the assistant director of the FBI Counterintelligence Division:

> *[Jack's] distinguished career in [the] CIA and his lengthy service to the FBI and the US Intelligence community is cherished and will never be forgotten.*

In a thinly veiled reference to Cowboy's secret part in the Hanssen roll-up:

> *Jack played a key role in the successful resolution of several serious espionage cases and the recruitment of human sources that contributed significantly to the foreign counterintelligence mission of the FBI.*

The letter continues:

> *He was a true professional in every sense of the word and was still assisting the FBI as Christmas 2016 was approaching.*

Regarding Jack's IOC training:

> *The FBI will forever be in debt for such professional training...*
> *Jack had the nickname "Cowboy" for a reason. He was daring, aggressive, fearless, and relentless in his military service with the Marines and his intelligence and counterintelligence operations with the CIA and the FBI. He always stood up for what he believed and never wavered from the mission that became his life's work. However, Jack will always be remembered more for his humanity: his love for his family, friends, and country, and his friendly, unpretentious, and honest approach to his colleagues. Jack's stories and anecdotes are legendary and whenever his family and friends come together, I trust they will be told and retold in his memory.*

A moving slide show was played, called "Cowboy," to Jack's favorite song, "American Pie." Jen Jacobsen, daughter of HTG cofounder Roy Jacobsen, sang her appropriately customized version of "Nobody Does It Better" while looking at Gennady, the spy Jack had loved, at the front table. The Russian wept.

Robert De Niro gave a short and loving tribute. He had appeared on *The View* just two hours earlier in New York, then raced to a private plane to get to the Virginia event in time to honor his friend. Afterward, Gennady and De Niro snuck away and got lost in tequila. Four months later, a more intimate final celebration of Cowboy's life was held at the Old Brogue on Saturday, June 17, in the Snuggery Room. About seventy-five attended. Dion Rankin recalled how Jack would crush out his cigarette on his boot heel, leaving ash on the carpet of Paul Redmond's CIA office. Polly's daughters, Antonia and Sashy Bogdanovich, spoke, as did Paige, Michelle, Diana, Leigh, and grandson Cody. Gennady openly stated that his relationship with Jack had landed him in the gulag *and* had gotten him freed. Then, using a phrase he appropriated a lifetime ago from Cowboy: "Shit happens." When the party broke up, Gennady grabbed his son Ilya, who made a rare appearance, and, eyes welling up, kissed him hard. No words were spoken.

In June 2011, the Moscow District Military Court found Aleksandr Poteyev, the man who had sold out the Illegals, guilty of high treason and desertion and sentenced him to twenty-five years in prison in a trial that, like Gennady's, was closed to the public. His wife was called as a witness. One of the other witnesses who testified against Poteyev was Anna Chapman. She told the tribunal that she had become suspicious of him after an undercover FBI agent contacted her in New York using a secret code word that only Poteyev would have known. At the time, Poteyev had been stationed in Moscow overseeing the Illegals operation. In addition to treason, the military court found Poteyev guilty of desertion. He was sentenced in absentia to twenty-five years in prison and stripped of his medals, military rank, and pension. Poteyev was not present at his own trial because he had fled Russia shortly before the Illegals were arrested in June 2010, relocating in the US, where he was given a new identity. According to one unverified Russian news service, Poteyev passed away in July 2016.

Aleksandr Zaporozhsky and Anatoly Stepanov are also living with new identities somewhere in the US. Of the group of ex-KGB agents that flipped since the Ames case, only Gennady Vasilenko, who was never a traitor to his homeland, lives under his real name, not far from the Platt family home. Until Jack's sudden passing in early 2017, the duo saw each other almost every day.

Aldrich "Rick" Ames's communications are tightly monitored at the Federal Correctional Institution in Indiana, where he is serving a life sentence. Robert Hanssen negotiated a plea bargain that enabled him to escape the death penalty in exchange for cooperating with authorities. On May 10, 2002, he was sentenced to fifteen consecutive sentences of life without the possibility of parole. In his federal supermax prison in Colorado, he is in solitary confinement for twenty-three hours a day. Edward Lee Howard died on July 12, 2002, at his Russian dacha, reportedly from a broken neck after a fall. Ronald Pelton was tried and convicted of espionage in 1986 and sentenced to three concurrent life sentences and a one-hundred-dollar fine. Under sentencing rules in place at the time, Pelton was presumptively entitled to release on parole after thirty years in custody. After serving out his term at the Federal Correctional Institution, Allenwood, a medium-security facility in Pennsylvania, he was released on November 24, 2015.

In June 2016, Mikhail Fradkov, the SVR chief who negotiated Gennady's swap with the CIA's Panetta in 2010, and who ran a think tank in Moscow after leaving the SVR, suggested a cyber hack of the US election to President Vladimir Putin. According to the US intelligence community, the Russian hack was implemented, and it is being investigated as of this writing, affecting every move the nascent Trump administration makes (assuming said administration still exists when this book is published). Incredibly, Russia is dominating the US news on a scale rivaling twentieth-century Cold War coverage. If the US won the Cold War with the collapse of the Soviet Union, the Russians are displaying an impressive capacity to rise from the ashes. In the absence of "burying" the US, as Khrushchev vowed, Putin is succeeding, at the very least, in fomenting political chaos in our dysfunctional republic. As both Cowboy and Gennady often said, a country that has had nearly a millennium of war has a lot of resilience. And patience. *Softly, softly, catchee monkey.*

If Cowboy was the patriotic hero who played an unsung role in bringing down one of the deadliest traitors in modern US history, Gennady is a hero of the human spirit, a flesh-and-blood spark that somehow manages to float through the air regardless of the climate. His loved ones got burned, but perhaps the notion of a pain-free existence is a uniquely American fantasy.

As of this writing, Cowboy's ashes are with the Platt family, but Gennady is making plans to have a portion of them interred in a Northern Virginia cemetery—in the long shadow of the CIA—beneath a modest headstone paid for by the Shoffler Brunch crew. Gennady has made clear his wish to be buried beside Jack someday.

Gennady keeps Jack's cowboy hat on a shelf in his home garage in the Virginia countryside, a modest hike to the banks of the Shenandoah River. One day, the spring after Jack died, Gennady awoke to unfamiliar sounds coming from the garage. His heart skipped. One last Sasha trick? He walked in and found that a healthy-looking bird had overturned the hat and made a nest for her family inside the crown. As a chick warbled along the brim, Gennady sighed with relief and savored this dividend of freedom. The ex-KGB officer, whose temperament seesawed between casual indifference and deep Russian sentimentality, then became drawn toward the call of another creature echoing in the valley outside. When Gennady opened his garage door and stepped into the morning sun, a lone eagle glided above the gentle slope that runs westward downhill to his gun range and onto the Shenandoah.

ACKNOWLEDGMENTS

First thanks must go to the late John "Jack" Platt and his great pal, Gennady "Genya" Vasilenko. These two skilled, charismatic, and patriotic intelligence officers sat down with us numerous times over a two-year period, sharing their stories, opinions, and insight with great candor. In doing so, they gained both our admiration and our friendship. The Platt women, Paige, Michelle, Leigh, and Diana, as well as their Bogdanovich cousins, Sashy and Antonia, contributed valuable details on the Platt family history and dynamics, as well as many of the photographs that appear in this book.

We were most fortunate to get to know another outstanding civil servant, former FBI agent Dion Rankin. When we started this project, we approached it as an espionage "odd couple" tale of Jack and Genya, but as we began the interviewing, we quickly realized that for much of the time there were Three Musketeers who kept "Operation Gennady" going, the third member being Dion Rankin. Fortunately for us, Dion also made himself available countless times for interviews, or a quick fact-check, even going out of his way to verify small details with family and colleagues. Like Jack and Genya, Dion became a great friend, and entire sections of this book, photos included, would not have been possible without his gracious participation.

We are most grateful to all those additional named and unnamed interviewees who trusted us with their memories. Understandably, given the topic, some sources preferred anonymity. These did not:

Joe and Marcia Albright, Jeremy Bash, Milt Bearden, Jerry Bernstein, Antonia Bogdanovich, Sashy Bogdanovich, Robert "Bear" Bryant, Brad Byrne, Pat Byrne, General Matt Caulfield, Barry Colvert, Richard Davis, Robert De Niro, John "Mad Dog" Denton, Denis Doyle, Gregory Feifer, Ron Fino, Jeff Goldberg, Harry Gossett, Sandy Grimes, David Grossman, Burton Gerber, Linda Lee Herdering, Roy Jacobsen, Ron Kessler, Alan Kohler, Jack Lee, Amy Lovett, David Major, Phil Manuel, Keith Melton, Dan Moldea, Brian O'Connor, Michael Sellers, Tamara "Tami" Powstenko, Dion Rankin, Mike Rochford, Gary Schwinn, Phil Shimkin, Ira Silverman, Michael J. Sulick, McKim Symington, Carl Vogt, Tom Welch, Courtney "CW" West, Ben Wickham, and the International Spy Museum.

Christina Pullen was a great help as liaison to the FBI, and Tena Johnson at Dezenhall Resources provided regular—and critical—logistic assistance in a variety of ways, including transcribing, editing, photo scanning, and just plain old cheerful encouragement. Also at Dezenhall, Erica Munkwitz put the final edit under her personal electron microscope. Steve Wiltamuth, maintainance supervisor at the Gangplank Marina, helped guide us through the history of the Gangplank Restaurant, leading us eventually to photographer Linda Herdering, who supplied both her memories and her wonderful photos of the Marina and the Potomac harbor. Amy Lovett, editor of the Williams College alumni magazine, provided key assistance in connecting with Jack's classmates.

Fellow author Dan "Luca" Moldea has been a great friend and admired colleague for decades, and his support for our work has been both unselfish and encouraging. Dan's early help in navigating the Washington intel community, as well as acting as liaison to his well-connected journalistic fraternity, got the project off to a great start. Our many friends in Dan's DC Author Dinner Group were likewise always available with their expertise.

This book would not have even started without the suggestion of

Robert De Niro, who first recommended Gus to his friends and *Good Shepherd* consultants, Jack and Genya. Bob knew it was a good story, but we think he would acknowledge that even he didn't know how good it was. If there's such a thing as an Italian mensch, Bob D. is it. Bob's colleagues at Tribeca Films, Jane Rosenthal and Berry Welsh, were early supporters of Gus and Eric's involvement in developing the story. Morgan Billington and Tribeca's support staff helped with logistics. Ron Howard and Tyler Mitchell of Imagine Entertainment showed great enthusiasm for the book from its earliest proposal stages. Kris Dahl, Josie Freedman, and Caroline Eisenman of ICM have been essential touchstones and advocates throughout this project.

Publisher Sean Desmond of Twelve Books believed in this project from its initial stages, and we are indebted to him for putting his faith in us. Both Sean and Rachel Kambury provided essential editorial direction down the stretch. Copy editor Dianna Stirpe made a boatload of informed suggestions regarding the manuscript. Of course, it goes without saying that the authors had the last word on content, and thus bear responsibility for any remaining errors. Production thanks also go to Jarrod Taylor at Twelve for his wonderful art direction and to production editor Yasmin Mathew and her team for putting all the pieces together so skillfully.

Gus would like to thank:

Without the encouragement, friendship, and support of Mitzi Mabe, Jay Greer, Dale Myers, brother Bob Russo, Dr. Aga, Genius Lucas, Toudi Lechowski, Saku Ee, Jon Savitch, and furry pals Jem and Z, nothing would be possible. Jeff Silberman is much more than a gifted literary agent and entertainment attorney, "the green man" is a brother from another tribe, whose friendship, support, and guidance has been a gift to me for over twenty years. I hope he knows how much I value his presence in my life and career.

Last, but not least, I would like to thank my co-author, Eric

Dezenhall, for not only contributing his inimitable writing talents to this endeavor, but also for his great friendship, enthusiasm, and wicked sense of humor. Over the last two years, I have often thought about how the story of Jack and Genya parallels our own *odd couple* partnership: although we hail from wildly different political backgrounds, we respect each other's skill sets, fundamental decency, and good intentions. I can honestly say that I've never had a more effortless and enjoyable partnership experience.

Eric would like to thank:

My wife Donna, son and daughter-in-law Stuart and Meghan (and Brick), daughter Eliza and her alpacas, and my sister Susan Schwartz for their support during the many twists and turns this project took; Bob De Niro, who originated and believed in this story; Richard Ben-Veniste and Cary Bernstein for their encouragement; Maya Shackley and Steven Schlein and my other colleagues at Dezenhall Resources, Ltd.

I would also like to thank my co-author Gus Russo, the gold standard in investigative journalism, from whom I learned so much throughout this process and came to admire more than I did when we took on the project.

Apologies to anyone we've neglected.

BIBLIOGRAPHY

Albats, Yevgenia. *The State Within a State: The KGB and Its Hold on Russia—Past, Present, and Future.* New York: Farrar, Straus, Giroux, 1994.

Andrew, Christopher, and Vasili Mitrokhin. *The Sword and the Shield: The Mitrokhin Archive and the Secret History of the KGB.* New York: Basic Books, 1999.

Bearden, Milt, and James Risen. *The Main Enemy: The Inside Story of the CIA's Final Showdown with the KGB.* New York: Random House, 2003.

Cherkashin, Victor, and Gregory Feifer. *Spy Handler: Memoir of a KGB officer—The True Story of the Man Who Recruited Robert Hanssen and Aldrich Ames.* New York: Basic Books, 2005.

Chiao, Karen, and Mariellen O'Brien. *Spies' Wives: Stories of CIA Families Abroad.* Berkeley: Creative Arts Book Co., 2001.

DeLoach, Cartha. *Hoover's FBI: The Inside Story by Hoover's Trusted Lieutenant.* Washington, D.C.: Regnery Publishers, 1995.

Fino, Ronald, and Michael Rizzo. *The Triangle Exit.* Tel-Aviv: Contento De Semrik, 2013.

Grimes, Sandy, and Jeanne Vertefeuille. *Circle of Treason: A CIA Account of Aldrich Ames and the Men He Betrayed.* Annapolis: Naval Institute Press, 2012.

Haynes, John Earl, Klehr Harvey, and Alexander Vassiliev. *Spies: The Rise and Fall of the KGB in America.* New Haven: Yale University Press, 2009.

Helms, Richard. *A Look Over My Shoulder: A Life in the Central Intelligence Agency.* New York: Random House, 2003.

Hoffman, David. *The Billion Dollar Spy: A True Story of Cold War Espionage and Betrayal.* New York: Doubleday, 2015.

Hougan, Jim. *Spooks: The Haunting of America: The Private Use of Secret Agents.* New York: Morrow, 1978.

Javers, Eamon. *Broker, Trader, Lawyer, Spy: Inside the Secret World of Corporate Espionage.* New York: Harper, 2010.

Kalugin, Oleg, and Fen Montaigne. *The First Directorate: My 32 Years in Intelligence and Espionage Against the West.* New York: St. Martin's Press, 1994.

Kessler, Ronald. *The Bureau: The Secret History of the FBI*. New York: St. Martin's Paperbacks, 2003.

———. *Inside the CIA: Revealing the Secrets of the World's Most Powerful Spy Agency*. New York: Pocket Books, 1992.

———. *Secrets of the FBI*. New York: Broadway Paperbacks, 2012.

———. *Spy vs Spy: Stalking Soviet Spies in America*. New York: C. Scribner's Sons, 1988.

Kross, Peter. *Spies, Traitors, and Moles: An Espionage and Intelligence Quiz Book*. Lilburn: IllumiNet Press, 1998.

Levy, Shawn. *De Niro: A Life*. Waterville: Crown Archetype, 2014.

Lynch, Christopher. *The C.I. Desk: FBI and CIA Counterintelligence as Seen from My Cubicle*. Indianapolis: Dog Ear Publishing, 2009.

Mahle, Melissa. *Denial and Deception: An Insider's View of the CIA from Iran-Contra to 9/11*. New York: Nation Books, 2004.

Melton, H. Keith, and Robert Wallace. *The Official CIA Manual of Trickery and Deception*. New York: William Morrow, 2009.

Mendez, Antonio, Jonna Mendez, and Bruce Henderson. *Spy Dust: Two Masters of Disguise Reveal the Tools and Operations That Helped Win the Cold War*. New York: Atria Books, 2002.

Panetta, Leon, and Jim Newton. *Worthy Fights: A Memoir of Leadership in War and Peace*. New York: Penguin Press, 2014.

Peterson, Martha. *The Widow Spy*. Denver: Red Canary Press, 2012.

Rogers, Leigh. *Sticky Situations: Stories of Childhood Adventures Abroad*. Haverford: Infinity Publishing, 2004.

Prado, John. *The Soviet Estimate: U.S. Intelligence Analysis & Russian Military Strength*. New York: Dial Press, 1982.

Riebling, Mark. *Wedge: The Secret War Between the FBI and CIA*. New York: A.A. Knopf, 1994.

Shvets, Yuri. *Washington Station: My Life as a KGB Spy in America*. New York: Simon & Schuster, 1994.

Sulick, Michael. *American Spies: Espionage Against the United States from the Cold War to the Present*. Washington, DC: Georgetown University Press, 2013.

Theoharis, Athan. *FBI: An Annotated Bibliography and Research Guide*. New York: Garland, 1994.

Wannall, Ray. *The Real J Edgar Hoover: For the Record*. Paducah: Turner, 2000.

Weiner, Tim, Darid Johnston, and Neil Lewis. *Betrayal: The Story of Aldrich Ames, an American Spy*. New York: Random House, 1995.

Weisberger, Bernard. *Cold War, Cold Peace: The United States and Russia Since 1945*. New York: American Heritage; Boston, 1984.

Wise, David. *Nightmover: How Aldrich Ames Sold the CIA to the KGB for $4.6 Million.* New York: HarperCollins Publishers, 1995.

——. *Spy: The Inside Story of How the FBI's Robert Hanssen Betrayed America.* New York: Random House, 2002.

——. *Spy Who Got Away: The Inside Story of Edward Lee Howard, the CIA Agent Who Betrayed His Country's Secrets and Escaped to Moscow.* New York: Random House, 1988.

Unpublished

The Prison Diary of Gennady Vasilenko
The Jack Platt Journals
It Was Worth It—the memoir of Polly Platt.

Additional Sources

Interviews (see Acknowledgments)

FBI

Robert Hanssen file (obtained under FOIA)
Operation Ghost Stories file

Online Resources

SpyCast (The International Spy Museum)
C-SPAN Archives
WikiLeaks
National Law Enforcement Museum (FBI Oral History Collection)
The Vault (FBI FOIA Archives)
Crest (CIA Records Search Tool)
CIA Electronic Reading Room
Center for the Study of Intelligence (CIA)
The Black Vault
CI Centre
National Security Archives
Geneology.com
Ancestry.com
Interfax (Russia News Service)

Photos

All photos courtesy of Jack Platt and family, Gennady Vasilenko, and Dion Rankin, unless otherwise noted.

ABOUT THE AUTHORS

ERIC DEZENHALL is the CEO of Dezenhall Resources, Ltd., a nationally recognized crisis management firm that he founded in 1987. He is the author of ten books, including three nonfiction texts on scandal and crisis management, including *Damage Control: The Essential Lessons of Crisis Management* and *Glass Jaw: A Manifesto for Defending Fragile Reputations in an Age of Instant Scandal*, which explores how powerful people, organizations, and brands are brought down by the seemingly powerless through a media and internet that feed on destructive information. Eric is also the author of six novels, including *Money Wanders* and *The Devil Himself*, about the collaboration between the US Navy and organized crime during World War II to secure American ports from Nazi attack.

As an investigative journalist, Eric was the first to write about the diaries of the late mobster Meyer Lansky, which appeared in the *Los Angeles Times Syndicate*, the *Baltimore Sun*, and *The New Republic*. He is an adjunct professor at Georgetown University's McDonough School of Business, where he teaches classes about crisis management. He served in the Reagan White House Office of Communications.

Eric was the valedictorian of the bottom half of his class at Dartmouth, an achievement for which he was widely resented. His books have appeared in libraries and bookstores adjacent to those by Darwin, DeLillo, Dickens, Didion, Doctorow, and Dos Passos. In his spare time, he makes up words such as "nostralgia" (having fond memories of one's nostrils) and "handsomniac" (being so handsome you can't sleep). He lives near Washington, DC, with his family and a herd of alpacas.

GUS RUSSO is an author, musician, composer, and television documentary producer/reporter, having contributed to television specials for ABC, CBS, NBC, and PBS, in addition to networks in Germany, France, UK, Mexico, and Japan. His books include *Supermob, The Outfit, Brothers in Arms* (with Stephen Molton), and *Where Were You* (with Tom Brokaw and Harry Moses). *Best of Enemies* is his ninth book. His film scores include *Basket Case* and *Brain Damage.* He is on the Advisory Council of the International Museum of Organized Crime and Law Enforcement in Las Vegas. A former tennis instructor in Honolulu, Gus considers it his calling to improve the connotation of the word "dilettante." He currently resides in the Orion Arm of the Milky Way Galaxy (the Gould Belt, specifically).

INDEX